Compound Containment

Compound Containment

*A Reigning Power's Military-Economic
Countermeasures against a
Challenging Power*

DONG JUNG KIM

University of Michigan Press
Ann Arbor

For questions or permissions, please contact um.press.perms@umich.edu

Published in the United States of America by the
University of Michigan Press
Printed and bound by CPI Group (UK) Ltd, Croydon, CR0 4YY
First published March 2022

A CIP catalog record for this book is available from the British Library.

Library of Congress Cataloging-in-Publication data has been applied for.
ISBN 978-0-472-13298-0 (hardcover : alk. paper)
ISBN 978-0-472-03900-5 (paper : alk. paper)
ISBN 978-0-472-90280-4 (OA)

DOI: https://doi.org/10.3998/mpub.11622137

For my family

CONTENTS

Digital materials related to this title can be found on the Fulcrum platform via the following citable URL https://doi.org/10.3998/mpub.11622137

LIST OF FIGURES AND TABLES

Figures

Tables

ACKNOWLEDGMENTS

Although I am responsible for the arguments in this book, I am greatly indebted to many teachers, colleagues, and institutions. First and foremost, I am grateful to John Mearsheimer for his unflinching support. John taught me that our job as political scientists is to identify important questions and offer simple answers. In my darkest hour during graduate study, John assured me that "perseverance is genius" and enabled me to move forward. At the University of Chicago, Bob Pape also provided some of the best advice on theorizing international politics and arranged opportunities for invaluable feedbacks. I learned a great deal from these thoughtful scholars, principled academics, and inspiring teachers.

This book has also benefited from the advice and support of my colleagues. I received countless helpful comments from the participants in numerous workshops and personal meetings. I am particularly thankful for suggestions provided by David Benson, Ahsan Butt, Jon Caverley, Bonnie Chan, Adam Dean, Gene Gerzhoy, Nancy Gleason, Chin-Hao Huang, Eric Hundman, Morgan Kaplan, Kazu Kimura, Doyoung Lee, Yu-Hsiang Lei, Chad Levinson, Dan Magruder, Rohan Mukherjee, Anju Paul, M. J. Reese, Sebastian Schmidt, Yubing Sheng, Paul Staniland, John Stevenson, Risa Toha, and Kevin Weng. Kathy Anderson and Susan Lynch deserve special appreciation for their assistance. I also thank two reviewers for the University of Michigan Press for their excellent comments and suggestions.

My research was given generous support by the Korea Foundation for Advanced Studies (KFAS), the Smith Richardson Foundation, the Belfer Center for Science and International Affairs, and Yale-NUS College. I thank President In-Kook Park and the members of the KFAS for their support. The Smith Richardson Foundation's World Politics and Statecraft Fellowship enabled me to conduct archival research in Britain. The Belfer Center's International Security Program provided me with extraordinary opportunities to interact with some of the world's brightest minds and sharpen my own argument. Among many people I met at the Belfer Center, I especially thank Steven Miller, Sean Lynn-Jones, and Stephen Walt. The support I got from my first job at Yale-NUS College was essential for elaborating on both the theory and empirical analysis of the book.

I owe a debt of gratitude to those who advised me how to pursue a better academic career. Professors William Bain, John Driffill, Jane Jacobs, Jai-Kwan Jung, Sung-han Kim, Nomi Lazar, Dong Sun Lee, Geun-Wook Lee, Shin-wha Lee, Terry Nardin, Gilbert Rozman, Rahul Sagar, Naoko Shimazu, and Tan Tai Yong all helped me grow as an academic. It is my great fortune that I have met these excellent teachers and scholars as my mentors.

Several portions of this book have appeared in my previous works. Portions of Chapter 3 appeared in the 2018 paper "Realists as Free Traders: The Struggle for Power and the Case against Protectionism," which was published in *International Affairs*. Portions of Chapters 5 and 6 have appeared as "Economic Containment as a Strategy of Great Power Competition" in *International Affairs* in 2019. Portions of Chapter 7 appeared in the 2017 paper "Trading with the Enemy? The Futility of US Commercial Countermeasures against the Chinese Challenge," which was published in the *Pacific Review*. I thank Oxford University Press and Taylor & Francis for permissions to use the material here. I also thank Elizabeth Demers of the University of Michigan Press for her support and valuable editorial suggestions.

Finally, none of this book would have been possible without the support of my family. I am eternally grateful to my parents for the countless small and large sacrifices they have made. I also thank my parents-in-law, who helped me to pursue all my interests, academic and otherwise. Above all, I thank Sung Eun Kim—my wife, best friend, and greatest colleague—for her love and patience. Literally, not a single day goes by where you don't cross my mind. Last but not least, I am grateful to my son, Hajin Kim, for being the source of my happiness and hope.

CHAPTER 1

Introduction

When is a reigning great power of the international system in a position to complement military containment of a challenging power with restrictive economic measures? It has been long argued that a reigning power is inclined to militarily confront a challenging power that has the potential to undermine international stability and threaten the reigning state's privileged relative power position.[1] For many scholars, policy analysts, and practitioners of the reigning power's strategy, containment—defined as the use of internal or external military balancing measures to stop the challenging power from launching military aggression—is a particularly attractive military option in dealing with the challenging power since it is less risky and costly than other strategies such as preventive war or rollback.[2] Nonetheless, since economic capacity and military power are intimately linked to one another, containing a challenging state requires addressing both economic and military dimensions.[3] Indeed, after the United States became the reigning power, a country identified as an adversary of the United States encountered both military and economic countermeasures organized by Washington.[4] Today, the United States is in a position to decide whether it should—or can—reinforce military containment of China with economic measures.

Scholars of great power competition, nonetheless, tend to focus on examining the reigning power's military response alone.[5] This situation is unfortunate, because these scholars do not in fact assert that military force is the only consideration in containment strategy. On the contrary, most security studies scholars recognize that military measures should be supplemented by economic policies. Moreover, they agree that the reigning power's security concerns over the challenging power are fundamentally motivated by changing distribution of material capacities, which reflects the two states' differential economic growth.[6] To put the point bluntly: scholars of great power politics agree that rapid economic growth endows the challenging power with an ability or incentive to revise the status quo, and, accordingly, responding to the challenging state requires addressing both military and economic aspects.

Despite this consensus, there have been only limited efforts to theorize the reigning power's simultaneous employment of military and economic measures against the challenging power. The emphasis of the debate on economic instruments has been put on whether economic tools, as opposed to military force, can actually play an independent and effective role in advancing a state's important strategic interests.[7] Moreover, while debating the effectiveness of economic sanctions in international security affairs, many security studies scholars mistakenly dismiss altogether the roles of economic measures in great power relations.[8] Although several scholars analyze the use of economic side payments within the context of great power competition, they often focus on the independent role of economic carrots and fall short of explaining or prescribing appropriate economic complements to diverse military strategies employed by the reigning power.[9] In recent treatments of the interaction of economic relations and military outcomes, scholars offer insights to understand diverse economic aspects of great power competition.[10] Yet the analytic focus of these studies has been explaining the conditions under which a great power maintains a peaceful relationship with another great power through commercial and financial linkages.[11]

Overall, the economic aspects of containment strategy have not garnered appropriate academic attention, although scholars continue to engage with new strategies of checking a great power's military aggression in the post–Cold War context.[12] To be clear, this does not mean that scholars have not debated diverse strategic options available for a reigning power or that they lack knowledge about the economic dimension of great power competition. Yet, it still remains unclear whether and how the reigning power can complement military containment with economic measures. To be more accurate, the conceptual tools and theoretical insights that have been developed by the scholars of the intersection of security and economy deserve renewed attention to more effectively address the multilayered strategies of today's great power competition.

The Argument

This book offers a structural theory that accounts for a reigning power's decision to adopt or avoid compound containment—defined as the simultaneous adoption of economic restrictions with ongoing military containment policies against a challenging power. It focuses on a situation where the reigning power has already adopted military containment measures against the challenging power and, therefore, has strong incentives to buttress its military measures with restrictive economic measures. By imposing restrictions on major economic exchanges with the challenging state, economic measures for compound containment try to weaken the material foundation of the challenger's military power and impede translation of latent power into military power, thereby increasing the effectiveness of military containment policy. Different from economic sanctions that attempt to shape the targeted state's behavior in the bargaining process over a specific political or strategic issue, compound containment tries to weaken the challenging power's material capacity to launch military aggression in the middle to long term.[13] In line with the security studies scholarship, this book considers that economic measures play complementary, although important, roles in great power competition.[14]

This book suggests that, despite the important role of economic measures in countering the challenging power, the reigning state does not simply sever existing economic ties with the challenging state and upgrade ongoing military containment into compound containment. Economic measures for compound containment aim to inflict losses on the challenging power's material capacity. Yet restricting ongoing economic exchanges introduces losses on both the reigning and challenging powers. Therefore, economic restrictions to weaken the challenging power's material capacities—and, thus, to adopt compound containment—would be viable options when the reigning power can inflict relative economic losses on the challenging state.

I posit that this ability to impose relative losses on the challenging power is deeply affected by the availability of alternative economic partners for the two competing states.[15] Building on mainstream international economics, a state's alternative economic partners are defined as a state or group of states that can replace the majority of roles or "functions" performed by a current economic partner when ongoing bilateral economic exchanges are disrupted due to strategic competition. This book suggests that, depending on the configuration of the availability of alternative economic partners for the reigning and challenging powers, the reigning state would or would not possess an ability to inflict more losses on the challenging state through economic measures. The presence or absence of this ability, in turn, shapes the decision to employ compound containment.

In circumstances where alternative economic partners are largely available for the challenging power but not for the reigning power, the reigning state cannot impose greater harm on the challenging state, and, thus, it avoids restrictions on bilateral economic exchanges and eschews compound containment. In contrast, when alternative partners are largely available for the reigning power but not for the challenging power, the reigning state is in a position to inflict relative losses on the challenging state through economic restrictions, and, accordingly, it adopts compound containment measures.

In order to reinforce the credibility of this argument, I pit my argument against two alternative explanations. First, the reigning state—which is not a unitary actor—might avoid compound containment because of the influence of domestic interest groups that have stakes in continuing economic exchanges with the challenging state.[16] If these groups prove to be more influential than other societal groups that want to restrict economic relations with the challenging state, their preferences would be translated into the avoidance of compound containment against the challenging power. Second, for some scholars, the reigning state's important decisions reflect the convictions held by key decision-makers. In this perspective, when leaders of the reigning power have a strong belief in the peace-creating effect of international economic ties, the reigning state would avoid compound containment measures based on the conviction that continuing economic exchanges will pacify the challenging power.[17]

It needs to be noted that this book presents a theory of the reigning power's grand strategy, rather than a theory that explains outcomes of interactions between states. This theory builds on seminal works on the intersection of international security and economy that have not garnered the attention they deserve in public discourse about a reigning power's response to a challenging power. For instance, the concepts and theoretical mechanisms I advance were introduced in the works of scholars such as David Baldwin, Albert Hirschman, Jonathan Kirshner, and Michael Mastanduno.[18] Moreover, the literature on the relationship between trade and great power competition by scholars including (but certainly not limited to) Joanne Gowa, Edward Mansfield, and more recently, Dale Copeland, offers elaborate insights to understand the economic aspects of competition between reigning and challenging powers.[19] This book knits together and reinstates the conceptual and theoretical tools laid out in these works in a theory that explains a reigning power's strategy toward a challenging power.

Case Studies

This book substantiates its argument and the two alternative explanations through case studies. The empirical body of this book consists of two parts. First, it presents an exploration of major historical incidences since the late nineteenth century of a reigning power's response to a challenging power. I focus on the reigning power's decision about ongoing trade with the challenging power against which it has adopted or strengthened military containment measures. The historical cases include Britain's response to Wilhelmine Germany between 1898 and 1914 (Chapter 3), the US response to Imperial Japan between 1939 and 1941 (Chapter 4), the US response to the Soviet Union between 1947 and 1950 (Chapter 5), and two consecutive US administrations'—Carter's and Reagan's—reactions to the USSR between 1979 and 1985 (Chapter 6). In each of these relations, Britain or the United States strengthened military containment measures against the challenging powers while significant commercial ties existed between them. Accordingly, the reigning power found good strategic reason to reconsider extant trade with the challenger. Nonetheless, compound containment was not present in all the cases. While the United States countered Japan during the 1939–1941 period, the Soviet Union between 1947 and 1950, and the resurgent Soviet threat during the last year of the Carter administration with compound containment measures, compound containment was largely absent in Britain's response to Germany before World War I and the United States' countermeasures against the Soviet Union during the Reagan administration.

Second, in addition to the historical case studies, this book applies the theory to a critical contemporary great power competition: the US response to a rising China from 2009 to 2016 (Chapter 7). The Obama administration famously declared a "pivot to Asia" and strengthened the United States' military presence in the western Pacific. Nonetheless, the United States in this period did not target China's heavy dependence on foreign trade as a means to counter Beijing's growing aggressiveness. Focusing on the Obama era—and, to some extent, the Trump administration as well in the concluding chapter—this book examines whether the theory developed in this book can account for the US response to a rising China. In each of the case study chapters, I examine how well my theory and the two alternative explanations account for the reigning power's decision on compound containment against the challenging power.

In conducting the case studies, I utilize both primary and secondary sources. Secondary works, when read with care, provide good resources to verify a proposed causal relationship and mechanisms. Moreover, secondary sources are invaluable for understanding the overall context of relations between the competing states, as well as identifying key actors, ideas, and decisions. Nevertheless, many questions remain unanswered when one exclusively utilizes secondary works. Historians study a certain topic, event, or individual in a great power's foreign relations and choose not to extrapolate their observations. Scholars, moreover, might have different interpretations of the same event. Thus, there is often no substitute for examining primary records of the historical issue. I use web-based published primary sources, including the *Foreign Relations of the United States* series and *British Cabinet Records*. Based on original archival research, I also make extensive use of unpublished primary records that are publicly available at the British Library, the British National Archives, and the US National Archives. I collect and examine primary records including policy directives, government reports, communications between government agencies, minutes of cabinet meetings, and personal exchanges between leaders. Beyond these, I examine media coverage during the time periods on which I concentrate, as well as articles, speeches, memoirs, and correspondences written by key decision-makers themselves and their advisers.

Contribution of the Book

The analysis presented in this book has several theoretical implications. Contrary to realist arguments, this book suggests that relative power considerations can constrain a great power to maintain economic ties with a major security competitor.[20] The main causal mechanism is derived from the structure of international trade that is embedded within the broader international political structure. I also demonstrate that the approach taken in this book yields a more convincing explanation for a reigning power's decisions about ongoing economic exchanges with a challenging power than theories that have shown strength in explaining foreign economic policies.[21]

Moreover, this book provides a building block for a more sophisticated theorization of great power balancing behavior and grand strategy. In particular, it calls scholars' attention to the linkages between international security and economy in analyzing a reigning great power's grand strategy. In current discourse on US grand strategy, for instance, scholars have concentrated on debating appropriate use of military force in dealing with a strategic challenger.[22] Nonetheless, considering the historical developments of great power competitions, as well as the trajectory of today's most important great power relations, one cannot easily separate high politics from low politics and focus on military confrontations alone. Most scholars, in fact, would agree that an explicit focus on the military dimension of great power competition is problematic. By reinstating theoretical and conceptual tools that have been developed by prominent scholars of international politics, this book motivates more active scholarly engagement with the multifaceted aspect of great power competition and strategy. To be clear, this book does not suggest opening up an entirely new research area for the students of grand strategy and balancing behavior. Nonetheless, it does claim that the nexus of international security and economy has remained a strangely understudied research agenda.

This book also contributes to the ongoing debate in the United States on the future of its strategy toward China by shedding light on the question of what constitutes a sound economic complement to US military grand strategy. Extensive economic ties between the two countries have created a dilemma in US strategy against China, especially since Washington has strengthened its military presence in Asia and its security alignment with the countries that surround China.[23] It still remains unclear which strategic rationale Washington should adhere to in determining a multifaceted response to Beijing.

This book suggests that the United States has not been in a position to impose significant relative losses on China through compound containment measures, considering the potential availability of alternative economic partners for China and the United States. Thus, complementing military containment with extensive commercial restrictions is unlikely to be a viable option for the United States in a visible future. This book also suggests that the Trump administration's protectionist trade policies against China are far from compound containment, in which economic restrictions are employed to weaken the challenger's material capacities to launch military aggression. Indeed, it still remains unclear whether the United States would be able to effectively deny alternative economic partners to China and replace the majority of China's roles in its economy, and thereby employ compound containment against China. As long as the United States cannot assure its ability to inflict more losses on China through extensive economic restrictions, Washington might need to eschew adopting a compound containment strategy even if it decides to reinforce military containment of China.

Road Map

The rest of this book proceeds as follows. Chapter 2 lays out my theory, the alternative explanations, and research strategy. In Chapters 3, 4, 5, and 6, I test the theories against the historical record, utilizing both primary and secondary sources. Chapter 7 extends my analysis to a contemporary context, the US response to the Chinese challenge during the Obama administration. Chapter 8 summarizes my findings, discusses theoretical and policy implications, and concludes.

CHAPTER 2

A Theory of Compound Containment

This chapter explains a reigning power's decision to upgrade its military containment of a challenging power into compound containment with the adoption of restrictive economic measures. It begins by discussing the definition and key attributes of compound containment as a strategy of great power competition. Then I explain how a structural consideration—the availability of alternative economic partners for the two competing powers—constrains the reigning power's decision to adopt compound containment. Next I lay out alternative explanations so that I can pit my theory against them in the following chapters. Finally, I describe and explain the research methods that I use in this book.

What Is Compound Containment?

Compound containment refers to a state's decision to reinforce ongoing military containment efforts against a security challenger with restrictive economic policies that are designed to weaken the challenger's material capacity. It is distinguished from other strategic uses of economic measures in several ways.

From Military to Compound Containment

In this book, a reigning power refers to the state that commands the largest material capacity among the leading members of the international system and exercises leadership in the governance of major issue areas of interstate relations. A reigning power, nonetheless, is not a "global hegemon," which is altogether immune to a challenge from other states. Rather, it is a state that relentlessly tries to maintain its relative power position in the anarchic international realm.[1] A challenging power implies a potential regional hegemon in a great power region—Europe, North America, or Northeast Asia—that has grown particularly powerful compared with its immediate neighbors and is militarily contending with the reigning state. It also has the potential to achieve further material growth and displace the reigning power's position.[2]

Scholars of great power politics agree that a reigning power harbors profound strategic concerns vis-à-vis a challenging power.[3] If the two states are geographically close to each other, the challenging power's ascendance inadvertently threatens the reigning power's security. Even if the reigning power is located at a distance from the challenging power's territory, the challenging state can nonetheless become a serious military threat once it becomes capable enough to achieve regional hegemony. This is because, utilizing large resources in a major region of the world, a regional hegemon can develop a military that can be projected to distant areas and threaten the reigning state's safety or vital interests.[4]

In this theoretical formulation, the reigning power is better off checking the challenging power early on. Yet, depending on external or domestic circumstances, as well as decision-makers' worldviews, the reigning state's initial response to the challenging state take different forms.[5] The reigning power can try to shape the behavior of the challenging power through the use of economic engagement, social interactions, or international institutions. When the reigning state recognizes that the challenging state still needs to achieve significant material ascendance or does not want to predetermine the nature of the challenging power, it will be particularly inclined to take a more nuanced approach in dealing with the challenging state.[6] Nonetheless, when the challenging state continues to grow and tries to address its strategic interests in an aggressive manner, the reigning state will eventually recognize that nonaggressive strategies have been unsuccessful in pacifying the challenging power and consider containment as an effective strategy in countering the challenging power. This book focuses on a situation where the reigning power finds itself in a situation in which it determines to adopt or reinforce serious containment policy against the challenging power.

The concept of containment was first introduced by George Kennan's famous article on Soviet aggressiveness in 1947.[7] Although scholars and practitioners never fully agreed on the precise meaning of containment, it was widely understood as efforts utilizing military means to prevent territorial and political expansion of another great power.[8] One can suggest that containment strategy is implemented when the reigning state has reinforced or deployed its most capable military units against the challenging state, and it is in the process of mobilizing more domestic resources in order to increase its military ability to stop that state's military aggression. Containment is also in place when the reigning state has strengthened formal and informal military alignments with the countries that are located near the challenging state.

Moreover, the strategy of containment is closely associated with the concept of balancing. In practice, diverse military balancing measures—defined as acts of mobilizing one's own military force or pooling resources with other states against a common adversary—can be equated with containment policy against a security challenger.[9] Put simply, when internal or external balancing is translated into a grand strategy, then we have the strategy of containment. Considering that every grand strategy attempts to advance the mid- to long-term strategic interests of a great power, containment also tries to check the challenging power in the middle to long term.[10]

Given the historical and theoretical uses of the term "containment," there is no doubt that military force plays a central role in any containment strategy. Nonetheless, as long as military force rests on wealth, and amendments in relative wealth imply changes in the distribution of military power, the reigning state has incentives to adopt economic measures to make its military containment of the challenging state "compound," rather than implementing military countermeasures alone. According to Robert Art, compound containment is a strategy that "involves both military stalemate and economic denial to weaken the aggressor state."[11] It means pursuing a two-tier strategy: adopting military containment for "defense" (aiming to prevent the challenging power from launching military aggression) and, at the same time, employing economic measures for "offense" (trying to weaken the material foundation of military threat from the challenging state).

More specifically, compound containment occurs when the reigning power employs restrictive economic measures in order to weaken the challenging power's material capacity, and thereby reinforce ongoing internal or external military balancing efforts against that state. Economic restrictions for compound containment aim to block the challenging power's access to the reigning state's market, goods, services, raw materials, financial resources, technology, factors of production, firms, entrepreneurs, or production network. Specific examples of these policies include (but are not limited to) embargo, boycott, tariffs, nontariff barriers, blacklists, quotas, license denial, dumping, preclusive buying, asset freezing, expropriation, and unfavorable taxation.[12] When successful, these economic restrictions diminish the challenging power's material capacity by undermining that state's economic performance and impeding the translation of latent power into military force, in turn decreasing the challenging state's ability to start military aggression. Through economic measures, the reigning state can attain the objective of military containment more effectively and at a lesser cost. Since containment has a relatively long temporal scope, aiming to advance mid- to long-term strategic objectives vis-à-vis the challenging power, economic measures for compound containment also try to affect the challenging state's material capacity in the middle to long term.

This book explains the variations in the reigning power's employment of compound containment measures against the challenging power. As the dependent variable of my argument, whether or not the reigning power's response to the challenging power constitutes compound containment hinges on the implementation of policies designed to diminish major economic exchanges with the challenging power, since military containment measures are assumed to be already in place against the challenging power that has been clearly identified as an adversary. When the reigning power adopts restrictive economic policies that would deeply undermine major economic exchanges with the challenging power—against which it has already implemented internal and external military balancing measures—in order to weaken that state's material capacity, then compound containment is in place. In contrast, avoiding compound containment refers to complying with the current policy arrangements that regulate major economic exchanges with the challenging power, as well as sustaining the trajectory of extant policies, despite ongoing military containment efforts. More simply, the reigning state that avoids compound containment does not make any serious efforts to alter existing policy arrangements that govern major economic exchanges with the challenging power. In this case, the challenging state continues to obtain economic gains through bilateral exchanges with the reigning state, and the reigning power's internal and external military balancing measures are not reinforced by economic policies.

I consider that the complementary economic measures for compound containment address all major economic interactions with the challenging power and are not confined to military-related exchanges such as trade of dual-use goods. In distinction from Michael Mastanduno, who distinguishes strategies of economic containment into economic warfare, strategic embargo, and tactical linkage based on the content, target, and timing of economic measures, this book suggests that diverse economic measures are not clearly distinguishable in modern economic contexts.[13] I take this approach because, as long as the competition between the reigning and challenging powers is fundamentally motivated by the changing balance of material capacities, any economic exchanges that contribute to the challenging power's material capacity need to be reconsidered. For instance, exchanges such as the trade of ordinary goods facilitate resource allocation and rationalize the economy, and in turn help a state to generate more latent power that can be translated into military might. While any economic exchange can help the challenging state to advance its material capacity, there is no good reason to confine economic measures based on the type and size of exchanged items.[14] From the neoclassical economic perspective, all goods and services in international economic interactions that have significant implications for military competition can be considered "strategic."[15]

For theoretical simplicity and following the insights of mainstream economics, which suggest all goods should be considered to have strategic implications in balance-of-power competition, I consider that the dependent variable of my theory takes the value of either "adopt compound containment" or "avoid compound containment." Yet this does not mean that the policy decision to employ compound containment is completely dichotomous or that variations in the dependent variable are clear-cut. To be clear, this book recognizes that modern international economic relations are very complex, and there can be gray areas between the adoption and avoidance of compound containment. Thus, I consider the reigning power to have adopted compound containment when it implements policies that are designed to diminish major economic exchanges with the challenger— which refers to economic interactions that have the largest ramifications for the performance of the challenger's economy—while implementing military containment, even when those policies do not seamlessly cover all economic exchanges with the challenging state. Accordingly, even when I consider compound containment to have been adopted by the reigning power, there still can be ongoing, minor economic exchanges between the two powers. Similarly, even when the reigning power avoids compound containment, it can nonetheless impose restrictions on some economic exchanges with the challenging power. The book tries to explain the overall trajectory of the reigning power's decisions about ongoing major economic exchanges with the rising power, rather than account for every specific measure.

Compound Containment as a Distinct Strategy of Great Power Competition

Compound containment can be distinguished from other strategies for checking great power aggression that take economic measures seriously, as summarized in Table 2.1. To be clear, there are significant overlaps between strategic employments of economic measures in international politics. Yet these measures can be analytically distinguished from one another.[16]

Most notably, economic measures for compound containment are not identical with economic sanctions, which refer to a state's use of economic punishment to affect another state's behavior in the bargaining process over a specific political or strategic issue.[17] For compound containment, weakening the targeted state's material capacity to launch military aggression is the utmost objective. In other words, economic measures in compound containment should not be considered a component of coercive diplomacy.[18] They do not necessarily occur in the bargaining process with the targeted state over a specific issue. Instead, economic measures in compound containment aim to make the challenger less capable of launching military aggression, and they are considered complements to, rather than substitutes for, military instruments. Michael Mastanduno conceptualized these

Table 2.1. Strategies against a Challenging Power

Strategy	Attributes
Military containment	Employment of internal and external balancing measures to prevent the targeted state's territorial expansion
Compound containment	Simultaneous employment of economic restrictions with ongoing military containment to weaken the targeted state's material capacity
Economic sanctions	Use of economic punishment to shape the targeted state's behavior in the bargaining process over a specific strategic or political issue
Economic engagement	Use of positive economic inducements to shape the targeted state's short-term behavior or to alter mid- to long-term preference
Hedging	Employment of a mix of low-intensity military and economic policy measures to manage risks and assure flexibility
Soft balancing	Use of nonmilitary means to discourage the targeted state's military aggression

types of economic measures as economic containment.[19] Nonetheless, after his work in the 1990s, there has been scant theoretical and empirical attention given to the concept of economic containment, whereas economic sanctions have won extensive academic and public attention.

When the reigning power's decision-makers choose to employ compound containment, they expect to attain changes in the targeted state's material capacity for aggression, rather than seek to achieve immediate changes in the ongoing wrong behavior of the targeted state. Economic measures for compound containment might not contain clear demands addressed to the targeted state—or entail requirements that the targeted state cannot accept—because they are designed to weaken the targeted state, which is already clearly identified as an adversary. Since economic measures for compound containment aim to diminish the challenging state's material capacity, they are difficult to remove, whereas economic sanctions convey the provision of their removal in case of modifications in the targeted state's policy.

Meanwhile, compound containment is also different from what some scholars call "hedging," which in practice often comprises combining military pressures and economic inducements in order to ensure a state's flexibility in its relations with the targeted state, especially under the condition of high uncertainty.[20] Different from hedging, compound containment is adopted against a clearly identified adversary. Moreover, it is a strategy for a leading great power rather than relatively weaker states. Further, compound containment is different from soft balancing—defined as the use of nonmilitary instruments, such as diplomacy, international institutions, and economic policies, to undermine a great power's aggressive military policies—which has emerged as an attractive option in countering a powerful aggressor.[21] It refers to a mid- to long-term strategy implemented against a potential aggressor, and, in compound containment, economic tools are not substitutes for military balancing. Economic measures in compound containment attempt to diminish the challenging state's material capacity in order to reinforce military containment measures.

Explaining the Employment of Compound Containment

In what strategic situation and with what strategic considerations does a reigning power determine its response to a challenging power? This book intends to offer a theory that complements rather than refutes extant scholarship on great power competition and military containment—especially hegemonic transition theory, offensive realism, and preventive war theory. Thus, my theory builds on the theoretical core shared by these theories that have garnered attention in the discourse about a reigning power's response to a challenging power. The core theoretical mechanism articulated in this book is that the reigning power's decision to implement compound containment reflects an assessment of its ability to inflict relative losses on the challenging power through restrictive economic measures. This assessment is deeply affected by a structural factor: the availability of alternative economic partners.

Assumptions and Definitions

For theoretical simplicity, this book makes several assumptions about the reigning power's position and the setup of the interaction between the reigning power and the challenging power.[22] First, I assume that the reigning power is a roughly rational, unitary actor that pursues security as its first priority in the anarchic international realm, where no authority exists above states. I also consider that states cannot know others' intentions with certainty well into the future, and powerful states possess the ability to hurt each other.[23] These, however, do not mean that the reigning power always makes accurate assessments and comes up with optimal decisions whenever sufficient information is available.[24] As scholars suggest, a great power can act irrationally or even pathologically.[25] Thus, this book takes a cautious approach. Rather than considering the reigning power to be a perfectly rational decision-maker, it assumes that, when making important decisions, the reigning power's decision-makers tend to be capable of comparing expected gains from different choices, and try to choose the option that promises larger gains, although they might often fail to make the right choice.

Second, I consider that the reigning power is already containing the challenging power militarily, employing extensive internal and external balancing measures. It has reinforced or deployed its most capable combat units against that state, and it is in the process of mobilizing more domestic resources in order to increase its military ability to stop the challenging state's military aggression.[26] At the same time, the reigning state has strengthened formal and informal military alignments with the countries that are located near the challenging state. Thus, there is no serious disagreement within the reigning power about the nature of the challenging state. The challenging power is clearly and widely recognized as an adversary. In this context, I focus on a situation where accommodating the challenging power is not a viable option for the reigning power, and subtle strategies—such as enmeshing, binding, and engagement—are no longer attractive alternatives for the reigning state.[27] Moreover, economic measures play complementary roles rather than constituting an independent strategy because I focus on a situation where economic manipulations, such as economic engagement and sanctions, have not successfully imposed benign behavior on the challenging power, and, accordingly, the reigning power has no choice but to adopt military countermeasures to check the challenging state.

Third, I assume that ongoing economic exchanges exist between the reigning and challenging powers, which issue from economic ties that were constructed before security competition became apparent.[28] Hence, I distance myself from the "rational expectations hypothesis," which suggests that states eschew economic cooperation ex ante when they expect to face a military dispute in the future. Current security competitors might have built economic ties in the past because they were not certain whether they would be competitors in the future, or they were military allies against a third state. Also, a state may inadvertently build commercial ties with a potential adversary if there are other states that are willing to expand economic ties with the potential security competitor.[29]

Fourth, I consider that the challenging power is obtaining relative gains vis-à-vis the reigning power in terms of overall economic performance through bilateral economic exchanges. If the challenging power is experiencing relative losses, economic ties with that state are not an issue for the reigning state because economic exchanges contribute to its relative power. I consider the circumstance in which the challenging power obtains relative gains because it has a smaller and less developed economy than the reigning power. As Albert Hirschman points out, economic exchanges between an economically more developed and larger state (the reigning state) and a relatively underdeveloped and smaller state (the challenging state) are much more beneficial to the latter state's economy.[30] Through interactions at diverse levels—including informal exchanges between individuals—the challenging state not only obtains substantial material gains, but also makes intangible gains, such as economic know-how, technological innovation, and organizational skills. Given ongoing military confrontation, the reigning power's sensitivity to the challenging power's relative gains will be significantly high.[31]

In addition to these assumptions, one key concept needs clarification before laying out my argument. By gains from economic exchanges, I refer to advancements in a state's overall economic efficiency, not simple profit, such as surplus from selling goods in foreign markets. Like Joanne Gowa and Edward Mansfield, I follow the insights of mainstream international economics and do not hold the view that foreign economic exchanges contribute to national power simply by allowing a state to sell goods and services in foreign markets and accumulate more wealth.[32] In this regard, I distance myself from views that focus on the balance of payments and consider only surplus or exports as the state's gains. Putting the point simply: I do not build my theory on mercantilist or nationalist approaches to foreign economic exchanges.[33]

Instead, I consider that foreign economic exchanges encourage states to specialize in certain economic activities while purchasing other economic functions or tasks from abroad based on their comparative or competitive advantages. By doing so, states increase their industrial efficiency (by rationalizing resource allocation and reducing cost), economies of scale, and market competitiveness, and hence enhance the overall performance of their economy while obtaining larger welfare gains.[34] In this context, the challenging power's relative gains mean that it is obtaining more gains than the reigning state in terms of overall economic efficiency through bilateral economic exchanges.

The Reigning Power's Calculation

In compound containment, the goal of economic restrictions is to weaken the challenging power's material capacity. Yet, since restricting economic exchanges imposes losses on both reigning and challenging powers, the decrease in material capacities incurred by compound containment measures should be defined in relative terms. In other words, compound containment tries to inflict relative losses on the challenging power's material capacity.

In this context, as a roughly rational actor, the reigning power will adopt serious restrictions on ongoing major economic exchanges with the challenging power when it can impose relative losses on that state. It will carefully gauge how the challenging power's and its own capabilities would be altered if bilateral economic ties were restricted. Even if the reigning state is facing relative losses from ongoing economic exchanges, it will cautiously assess whether abandoning extant ties would make it better off. In short, the reigning state tries to make a relative power-maximizing choice about economic ties with the challenging state.

Thus, the reigning power makes a net assessment of (1) its current relative losses from ongoing bilateral economic exchanges with the challenging power, and (2) its expected relative losses were it to adopt compound containment measures. When reducing economic ties with the challenging state would make it even worse off—that is, when expected relative losses are larger than current relative losses—the reigning state will not consider imposing restrictions over bilateral economic ties with the challenger an attractive option. Compound containment becomes a viable option when expected relative losses are smaller than current relative losses. In other words, the reigning state assesses where it stands in relation to the challenging state in "vulnerability interdependence"—which refers to a condition where one state is likely to encounter more costs than its economic partner in the event that economic ties break—and adopts restrictive economic measures for compound containment when it is likely to encounter fewer costs than the challenger.[35]

Structural Constraints: The Presence of Alternative Economic Partners

I argue that the reigning power's ability to impose relative losses on the challenging power through economic restrictions—and, thus, the decision to adopt compound containment—is largely determined by the availability of alternative economic partners for the two competing states. Since Albert Hirschman's seminal work, scholars of the economy-security nexus have agreed that the presence of alternative partners is key to the strategic employment of economic instruments and the evolution of economic relations under security competition.[36] In the debate over relative gains of the 1990s, theorists recognized that the intervention of third states significantly complicated—or even removed—the bilateral relative gains problem that was believed to impede economic cooperation.[37] In economic sanctions, removing alternative partners is considered critical for effective employment of economic punishment.[38] In the literature on the relationship between trade and war, third states affect both the development of economic ties and the likelihood of military confrontation.³⁹ Accordingly, the role of alternative economic partners is an idea embedded in international relations literature. This book reinvigorates this idea by specifying the attributes of an alternative economic partner and advancing a mechanism through which it can affect a reigning power's grand strategy.

In this book, a state's alternative economic partners mean a state or group of states that can replace the majority of roles performed by a current economic partner when ongoing economic exchanges are disrupted due to strategic competition. In ongoing economic exchanges, the reigning and challenging powers play certain roles in each other's economic performance. In particular, when one focuses on the efficiency-enhancing aspect of foreign economic exchanges, the two states advance each other's economic efficiency as a provider of financial or technological resources, goods, services or raw materials, as a production base, as an export destination, or as a supplier of factors of production, investment, or know-how.⁴⁰ In this context, the key attribute of an effective alternative economic partner is its ability to replace a current economic partner's "function" in a state's economic activities.

These "functionally equivalent" alternative economic partners can replace the majority of roles that the reigning state plays in the challenging state's economic activities (and vice versa) when compound containment measures are adopted. By doing so, they allow the reigning power or the challenging power to achieve what Eugene Gholz and Daryl Press call the "new best" ways of doing business, after experiencing a marginal decrease in efficiency during the adjustment period.⁴¹ Put bluntly, the availability of alternative economic partners means that, after the imposition of compound containment, the challenging state can continue the majority of economic activities that previously relied on the reigning power's inputs. Similarly, the reigning power can retain the majority of its economic gains related to the exchanges with the challenging power when alternative partners can effectively replace the role of the challenging power in its economic activities.⁴² When alternative economic partners are absent, the reigning power or the challenging power loses the majority of gains that were obtained through bilateral economic exchanges.

It should be noted that I do not view these alternative economic partners as covering every element of economic exchange between the reigning and challenging powers. That is, I do not suggest that this explanatory factor is a completely dichotomous variable, and recognize that there can be significant variations between complete presence and absence of alternative partners. Similar to the variations in the dependent variable—adoption or avoidance of compound containment—alternative partners are a state or group of states that can replace the majority of the challenging (reigning) power's economic roles, rather than every economic function performed by the challenging (reigning) state. In other words, even when alternative partners are present for the reigning power or the challenging power, no state can replace every minor economic role of the strategic competitor. Similarly, even when alternative economic partners are absent, other states can still replace the competitor's role in minor economic areas.

The causal mechanism this chapter proposes, then, can be summarized as follows. From the perspective of the reigning power, the availability of alternative partners for the challenging power determines its ability to inflict losses on the challenging power. The availability of alternative partners for the reigning power decides the reigning state's own losses after imposing economic restrictions on the challenging power. The relative availability of alternative partners for the reigning and challenging powers determines the reigning state's ability to inflict relative losses on the challenging power, and the presence or absence of this ability shapes the decision to employ compound containment.

While this book advances a simple and straightforward theoretical mechanism, it does not claim that other factors—for example, domestic interest groups—are irrelevant. On the contrary, economic interest groups play an important intermediate role in my theory. Yet I suggest that, depending on the configuration of alternative economic partners for the reigning and challenging powers, interest groups within the reigning state may or may not play active roles, and, in turn, affect the reigning power's decisions regarding the challenging power. In other words, I recognize that there exists a mechanism through which domestic politics plays a role in the process leading up to the reigning power's decision on compound containment, but posit that this mechanism can be subsumed by the structural argument I propose.

In addition, I argue that the presence or absence of alternative economic partners is a structural factor that is not necessarily determined by the reigning state's actions or attributes. It refers to an economic condition that exists when the reigning power has implemented military containment policies against the challenging power. Although the reigning power commands the largest national economy in the world, it cannot persistently exercise domineering influence over other states on all economic issues. Other states might possess technology that can match the reigning state's technological development and compete with the reigning power on the market, other large markets can emerge, or several states can gather to form a monetary entity that competes with the reigning state's currency. Economically powerful states that are not threatened by the challenging state will mainly see economic benefits in their interactions with it, and refuse to incorporate the reigning state's strategic considerations in their decisions. Even for the reigning power's allies, doing business with the challenging power is an attractive option when they are not exposed to a serious and immediate military threat that requires the reigning power's support. Furthermore, the reigning state may not be able to buy-in or threaten other economic actors when they expect to obtain more profit by cooperating with the challenging power than with the reigning power. In short, there is good reason to expect that the presence or absence of alternative economic partners is not endogenously determined by the reigning power's actions.

The Decision to Adopt Compound Containment

This book suggests that the availability of alternative economic partners shapes the reigning state's assessment of its ability to inflict relative losses on the challenging state through economic restrictions, and, in turn, the decision to employ compound containment against the challenging power. For theoretical simplicity, I consider alternative partners to be either present or absent for the reigning and challenging powers. As I have discussed above, nonetheless, the dependent and explanatory variables of my theory are not completely dichotomous. The reigning power's decision to adopt compound containment covers major economic exchanges with the challenging power, and may not address all economic interactions with it. Similarly, the presence of alternative partners means that other states can substitute in the majority of economic roles—although not all functions—that are currently performed by the strategic competitor, whereas the absence of alternative partners means that others cannot easily replace the majority of roles played by the competitor. Four specific situations can be articulated, as summarized in Figure 2.1.

In one case (top left) the challenging power cannot find alternative economic partners, but the reigning power has alternative partners that can replace the role of the challenger in its economy. Under these conditions,

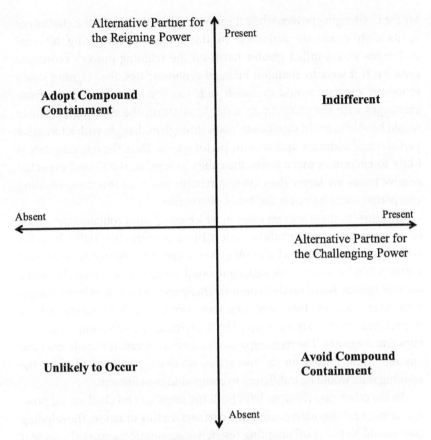

Figure 2.1. The Decision to Employ Compound Containment

the reigning power is in a position to adopt compound containment, since it can inflict relative losses on the challenging power through economic restrictions. In this case, the reigning power can keep its own economic performance largely intact through exchanges with other states. In contrast, the challenging state cannot effectively replace the reigning state in its economic performance and would face economic losses from decreased efficiency. By restricting bilateral economic exchanges, the reigning state can thus improve its own relative power position and reinforce military balancing efforts.

In contrast, under one configuration of alternative economic partners (bottom right), the reigning power is not in a position to employ compound containment. The reigning state might find that alternative partners exist for the challenging power, while it cannot replace the role of the challenger in its own economic activities. In this situation, restricting bilateral exchanges would inflict greater harm on the reigning power's economic capacity. If it were to abandon bilateral economic ties, the reigning state's economic capacity would diminish as it lost the majority of gains from exchanges with the challenging state. In contrast, the challenging power would be able to avoid significant losses through exchanges with alternative partners and maintain its economic performance. Thus, the reigning state is likely to encounter more losses than the challenging state—and expected relative losses are larger than current relative losses. In this case, avoiding compound containment is the better alternative.

Meanwhile, there are two cases in which compound containment would be an ineffective or an unrealistic option. In one scenario (top right), both the reigning power and the challenging power can find alternative economic partners. Under these conditions, compound containment is unlikely to be a relevant option. Based on the economic efficiency compensated by exchanges with other states, the two competing states would be able to minimize their respective economic losses incurred by the reigning power's compound containment measures. The reigning power's economic measures would not have any significant impact on the two states' relative capacities, and, thus, the reigning state would be indifferent to compound containment.

In the other case (bottom left), both the reigning and challenging powers cannot find alternative economic partners. In this situation, the reigning state would be better off adopting restrictive economic measures because it is encountering relative losses in ongoing economic exchanges. When bilateral economic ties are severed, both the reigning power and the challenging power lose gains from their economic exchanges. Yet the challenging power's losses are greater because it is currently gaining more than the reigning power. Since cutting off bilateral economic ties would inflict greater harm on the challenger, compound containment is a viable option for the reigning power. This case, however, is not realistic in the modern world, where multiple economic and resource centers exist around the globe.

Alternative Explanations

My argument can be contrasted with two alternative theories—one focusing on the role of domestic interest groups and the other emphasizing ideology or belief. I recognize that these factors play important intervening roles in the causal mechanism I propose. Yet, in contrast to my argument, alternative explanations posit that domestic interest or ideology is an independent variable that is not subsumed by the structural factor I articulate and has a decisive impact on the reigning power's decision on compound containment.

Economic Interest Groups

For some scholars, foreign policy decisions reflect the preference of and interaction between societal actors. They focus on systemic domestic effects that operate within the state and explore how and which domestic interests are aggregated and translated into foreign policy.[43] In this approach, individual or group interests struggle to influence political decisions so that their preferences are better represented than those of competing groups. Although a state's choice of foreign policy takes into account both its preferences and external constraints, these scholars analytically prioritize state preferences that represent certain domestic interests.[44]

In this view, economic ties with the challenging power that are sustained for a protracted period of time establish powerful interest groups within the reigning power. Even when security concerns increase, these interest groups function as a political coalition that attempts to influence the home country's economic policies regarding the challenging state. They compete with groups that want to diminish economic ties, and exert pressure on the government to continue economic exchanges.[45] If these economic interest groups prove to be more influential than other societal groups, their preferences are translated into a friendly economic policy toward the challenging state. In this approach, since the state is not a unitary actor, the reigning power can adopt competitive military and cooperative economic policies at the same time.

Still, the groups that benefit from economic ties with the challenging power might not be able to exert a dominant influence on the reigning power's decisions, again as a result of domestic political competition. For instance, in the context of intense domestic debate over the relationship with the challenging state, a security-focused group can align with economic groups that lose from current economic policy and successfully influence the reigning state's economic decisions regarding the challenging state. In this case, the reigning power would be compelled to restrict economic ties with the challenging power. Nonetheless, if this theory's causal logic is correct, domestic competition led by diverse interest groups should be the driving force behind the reigning state's adoption of compound containment against the challenger.

In sum, according to the domestic interest-based explanation, the reigning power avoids compound containment against the challenging power when commercial interest groups within the country exert sufficient influence on the government to continue economic exchanges. If those groups lose in the domestic competition, the reigning power restricts bilateral economic exchanges and employs compound containment against the challenging power.

Leaders' Belief and Ideology

For an influential group of scholars, beliefs or ideologies subscribed to by national leaders are crucial for understanding the international behavior and strategy of a great power.[46] According to this approach, a reigning state would contemplate several different options in dealing with a challenging power, but it would prefer to use some strategies rather than others because of strong convictions about what is viable or effective in international politics. The influence of ideology would be particularly pronounced in a liberal reigning state that tends to have a profound interest in pursuing "idealist" policies to recreate the world in its own image.[47] Even though one cannot claim that ideology always has a more powerful impact than material factors, it can be confidently argued that the reigning state's cultural assumptions create a pattern in its foreign policy or strategic behavior.[48]

One of the most influential ideologies in numerous great powers has been the liberal belief in the role of economic exchanges. In this liberal ideology, formalized as a policy program in Britain by the mid-nineteenth century, economic engagement is useful in shaping another state's behavior or even preferences, and thereby can help maintain peaceful great power relationships.[49] With the spread of economic globalization, manipulating economic exchanges is often viewed as an effective means to affect what others do and want. From this liberal perspective, even when the reigning power confronts a military threat from the challenging power, its leaders retain beliefs in the role of economic engagement in addressing strategic disagreements.[50]

In this account, leaders in some liberal reigning powers may have strong convictions about the pacifying effect of economic engagement.[51] Moreover, those leaders will be deeply concerned about the possibility that their assertive decisions with regard to the challenging power may unnecessarily irritate it. When the decision-makers of the reigning power believe that continuing economic engagement would be effective in dissuading the challenging power from launching military aggression, the reigning state would be inclined to avoid compound containment. In contrast, when the reigning power's leaders do not believe in the pacifying effect of economic exchanges, and instead believe that economic punishment is the more appropriate option, the reigning state will adopt compound containment, complementing military balancing with restrictive economic measures.

Summary of the Theories

As summarized in Table 2.2, my theory and the two alternative explanations present logically consistent theoretical predictions on the reigning power's

Table 2.2. Explanations for the Reigning Power's Employment of Compound Containment

Theory	Causal Logic	Predictions
Commercial interest	Certain commercial interest groups compete with other groups to influence leaders' decision on compound containment.	Compound containment is avoided if economic interest groups prevail in domestic competition and exert influence on leaders' decisions. If they lose in domestic competition, compound containment is adopted.
Ideology	Leaders of the reigning power uphold beliefs in appropriate strategy in dealing with the challenging power.	When the reigning power's leaders have strong convictions about the ability of economic engagement to pacify the challenging power, compound containment is avoided. When leaders do not have this belief and prefer economic punishment, compound containment is adopted.
Economic structure	The relative availability of alternative economic partners determines the reigning power's ability to impose more losses on the challenging power through economic restrictions, and the presence or absence of this ability shapes the decision to employ compound containment.	The reigning power does not adopt compound containment when it cannot find alternative economic partners while the challenging power can. Compound containment is adopted when the reigning power can find alternative partners while the challenging power cannot.

decision to adopt compound containment measures against the challenging power. These arguments are also based on distinct causal logics.

Research Strategy

This book utilizes the case study method in substantiating my theory and two competing explanations. To test a causal theory, one needs to confirm contemporaneous variation between the dependent and independent variables, time sequence between the dependent and explanatory variables, and nonspuriousness of the relationship between the variables.[52] The researcher utilizing case studies can confirm if the proposed theory satisfies these conditions. Further, case study has a unique advantage in tracing whether the causal mechanisms—the steps that make up the link between the independent variable and the outcome—are corroborated by historical evidence.[53] It also allows the researcher to determine how well the proposed theory explains the outcome when compared with competing theories. In short, I employ the case study method because it is the most appropriate method for examining the theories that account for a reigning power's decision to employ compound containment.

The case studies focus on the reigning power's policy on ongoing commercial exchanges with the challenging power. Thus, in the empirical analyses, the dependent variable of my theory is operationalized as leaders' policy decisions to adopt restrictive commercial measures in order to buttress ongoing military containment. Since this dependent variable refers to a political decision of the reigning power, the variations in the dependent variable may not be clear-cut. Thus, I consider that the reigning power has adopted compound containment when it implements policies that are designed to diminish the majority of commercial exchanges with the challenger, even when those policies do not cover every aspect of trade with the challenging state. When the reigning power avoids compound containment, it eschews policy measures that can significantly undermine the majority of trade with the challenging power.

The independent variable—the availability of alternative trade partners—can be considered to be present for the reigning power (challenging power) when third states are capable of providing goods and services that are equivalent to ones currently provided by the challenging power (reigning power), as well as functioning as alternative customers. In practice, alternative trade partners for the reigning power (challenging power) mean a group of states that compete with the challenging power (reigning power) on the market—because they produce similar goods and services—and states that have a strong demand for items produced by the reigning power (challenging power)—and, thus, can absorb the reigning power's (challenging power's) products that are currently being sold to the challenging power (reigning power). Moreover, these alternative trade partners refer to states that can address the majority of ongoing trade between the two powers, rather than every single trade item. Thus, even when alternative partners are available, there may be no other state that can replace the role of the strategic competitor in a certain commercial exchange.

The Universe of Cases

In this book, I analyze the entire set of cases that clearly satisfy the scope conditions of my theory. I take this approach because, when a very small number of cases are available for empirical tests, leaving one case unexamined significantly undermines the validity of the argument, since that case may be an outlier to the theory. Examining only some of the cases is also susceptible to selection bias. Thus, I pay particular attention to identifying the cases to which my theory can be applied.

The key considerations I take into account in determining the universe of cases are as follows: (1) a reigning power and a challenging power (a state that has emerged as a potential regional hegemon in a great power region of the world—Europe, North America, or Northeast Asia) indeed exist in the international system, (2) the reigning power has adopted or strengthened military countermeasures against the challenging power, and (3) there are ongoing economic exchanges between the two states. In addition, I focus on an industrialized reigning power's response to an industrialized challenging power. Thus, I look at cases of relations between a reigning power and a challenging power since the mid-nineteenth century.

In order to determine which states qualify as reigning power or challenging power, I examine several indices of national material capacity—including the Correlates of War Project's National Material Capabilities Dataset, historical economic statistics compiled by economic historians B. R. Mitchell and Angus Maddison, and the "economic dominance index" developed by the economist Arvind Subramanian—and determine whether there is agreement among them about whether a state can be identified as a reigning power or a challenging power.[54]

Identifying the reigning powers is relatively easy. There is a consensus that the United States has maintained the position of reigning power since the end of World War I. Regardless of the metric one employs, the material capacity of the United States has far exceeded that of any other major state since approximately 1918. Some might suggest that Britain was the leading great power during the interwar period (1918–1939).[55] This, however, is not convincing. After all, the British economy was far smaller than the US economy during the decades before World War II.

From the mid-nineteenth century to World War I, I consider Britain to be the power that commanded more material capacity than other great powers. There is wide agreement that Britain, after the victory in the Napoleonic Wars, maintained a preeminent relative power position throughout most of the nineteenth century. Although some sources observe that Britain's industrial capacity was surpassed by the United States at the turn of the twentieth century and by Germany in the late 1900s, others show that Britain maintained its position of a reigning power in terms of overall material capacity until World War I.[56] Moreover, the United States, under the strong influence of American exceptionalism and isolationism, was not an active participant in great power politics before the Great War. Thus, I take a cautious approach and consider Britain to be the reigning power during the several decades before World War I.

Identifying a challenging power—a potential regional hegemon—is slightly more complex. On the one hand, scholars tend to agree that a state emerges as a potential dominant power in its region by developing a material capacity surpassing that of other nearby powers. On the other hand, a state can become a potential regional hegemon by the retrenchment or precipitous decline of other powerful states. I consider the United States during the latter half of the nineteenth century, Wilhelmine Germany, Nazi Germany, and China by the early twenty-first century as potential regional hegemons that emerged through the former path. In contrast, Imperial Japan became a potential regional hegemon of Northeast Asia as the European powers that were present in Asia—Britain, France, Germany, and the Soviet Union—concentrated on European affairs and left Asia aside. Moreover, China since the late 1930s was in anomic state due to internal turmoil. Thus, even though Imperial Japan possessed considerably smaller material clout than other major states of the time, it could become a potential regional hegemon. In between these two paths, the Soviet Union emerged as a potential Eurasian hegemon in the immediate aftermath of World War II, as it achieved significant industrial development while most other major states in Asia and Europe were devastated by the war.

One might suggest that there was one more challenging power—czarist Russia in the mid-nineteenth century or by the period of the Crimean War.[57] It would be misleading, however, to identify Russia of this period as a potential regional hegemon.[58] While industrial might is the key element of a great power's relative material clout, much of Russia's material capacity represented the farm productions of its growing peasant population, which did not have significant implications for competition between industrialized great powers.[59] Moreover, the Russian economy was in a feeble state from the mid-nineteenth century until the 1920s.[60] Since Russia was not as industrialized as other European great powers and did not encounter a precipitous decline of other powers, it is difficult to consider Russia a challenging power that could bid for regional hegemony.

In a similar vein, Communist China in 1949 cannot be considered a potential regional hegemon because its economic development lagged too far behind other major states, even though Japan—the only regional power that could match China—was devastated by the Pacific War. After all, the Soviet Union was present in both Europe and Northeast Asia, and was the state that could bid for hegemony in both regions. As George Kennan observed, the Chinese Communists were viewed as a group that was willing to take part in "Soviet purposes."[61] In addition, I do not consider post–World War II Germany and Japan to be potential regional hegemons because they were "semisovereign states" that hosted a large number of US forces and depended on the United States for their security.[62]

Table 2.3. summarizes the cases that clearly meet the scope conditions and definitions discussed above. Two reigning powers in modern history—Britain and the United States—contemplated adopting compound containment against four different challenging powers—Wilhelmine Germany, Imperial Japan, the Soviet Union, and China. For the purpose of testing the theories of compound containment, I concentrate on the time periods that are characterized by a reigning power's intensifying military countermeasures against a challenging power. In other words, I address the periods during which the reigning power has good strategic reason to reinforce military containment with restrictive economic measures. In each of the cases presented in Table 2.3, Britain or the United States strengthened or deployed its major military units against a challenging power and made careful efforts to consolidate alignments with other states that were threatened by the challenging state.

In Table 2.3, I divide the US-USSR relationship into two cases because the Cold War was fought in two stages. There were significant variations in the magnitude of the reigning state's military measures against the challenging state between 1947 and 1985. The United States employed major military buildup programs during the early Cold War. From the late 1960s until the late 1970s, however, tensions were relatively low despite continuing hostility between Moscow and Washington. The period beginning in 1979—often called "the New Cold War" or "the Second Cold War"—marked a departure from such a period of détente, and the United States heavily invested in military balancing until 1985. When there is renewed attention to military containment, the reigning state will have a revived interest in implementing compound containment.

Moreover, in the case study of the early Cold War, I mainly focus on the period between 1947 and 1950 because commercial exchanges between the United States and the Soviet Union largely disappeared by 1949. Although East-West trade mattered significantly throughout the 1950s and 1960s, there was little Washington could do about its own economic relations with the USSR because its trade with the Soviet Union had already disappeared.

Table 2.3. List of Cases

Periods of Intensifying Military Response	Reigning Power's Military Measures	Reigning Power	Challenging Power
1898–1914	Naval arms race; entente with France and Russia	Britain	Wilhelmine Germany
1939–1941	Reinforcement of the US Fleet in the Pacific; fortification of the Philippines	United States	Imperial Japan
1947–1950	Truman Doctrine; National Security Act of 1947; decision to rebuild US military	United States	Soviet Union
1979–1985	Rapid Deployment Joint Task Force; massive military buildup program	United States	Soviet Union
2009–2016	Pivot to Asia; reinforcement of US forces in Asia-Pacific	United States	China

Put simply, there were no significant economic ties to restrict by the early 1950s, and, thus, the period of the 1950s and 1960s does not meet the scope condition of the theory. Similarly, I do not examine the 1970s, which was a period of détente, because my theory focuses on a period of intensifying military containment efforts against the challenging power. When military tensions diminish, it makes sense for the reigning power to consider building economic ties with the challenging power in order to affect that state's behavior. Since I view economic measures as adopted to reinforce military containment, there must be intensifying military containment efforts for my argument to apply.

In a similar vein, I exclude the United States' response to Nazi Germany because all major bilateral commerce disappeared through the US enforcement of the Neutrality Act and adoption of the "cash and carry" policy in 1939, before Washington adopted serious military countermeasures against Berlin. This case also does not satisfy the scope conditions of the theory.

One might suggest that the British relations with Germany extended for more than a decade and, thus, can be divided into several cases. Indeed, an Anglo-German détente existed between 1911 and 1914, and the two states deliberated over diverse ways to lower bilateral tensions.[63] Nonetheless, I do not divide the British response to Germany into two cases because, despite ongoing high-level exchanges between the two states, serious military balancing policies were continuously being implemented throughout the 1898–1914 period. Most notably, Britain heavily invested in naval buildup in order to meet and defeat the German naval challenge with overwhelming naval superiority. Since there were ongoing, intensifying internal balancing efforts, the 1898–1914 period is considered to be a single case.

In addition, I do not consider the British response to a rising United States in the late nineteenth century. Unlike other potential regional hegemons in Europe and Northeast Asia, the United States achieved military dominance in North America by the mid-nineteenth century, before it became a dominant industrialized power. Also, Britain did not adopt serious military balancing measures against the United States after the war of 1812.[64] Since there were no serious military counterbalancing efforts by Britain against the United States, the British-US case does not satisfy the scope condition of my theory. Thus, I exclude Britain's response to the United States in the case studies.

It needs to be noted that the US response to a rising China between 2009 and 2016—during the Obama administration—is an application of my theory to a critical contemporary development, rather than a direct empirical test of the theory. Sino-US competition is still an ongoing issue, and one cannot be certain about the trajectory of this great power rivalry. Moreover, there is only limited information available to examine the strategic calculation of US decision-makers in dealing with China. After all, almost all the direct evidence that could confirm or invalidate the causal mechanisms of my theory remains inaccessible. The main purpose of the US-China case study is to examine the applicability of my argument to today's most important great power relationship and, thus, derive lessons for practitioners and scholars.

The Conduct of the Case Studies

Taking these considerations into account, I conduct five case studies: (1) Britain's response to the German challenge between 1898 and 1914, (2) the US response to Imperial Japan between 1939 and 1941, (3) the US response to the Soviet Union between 1947 and 1950, (4) the US reaction to the Soviet Union between 1979 and 1985, and (5) the US response to China from 2009 to 2016. In each of these relations, the reigning power strengthened military balancing measures against the challenging power while significant economic ties existed between them.

The case studies focus on a reigning power's decision to restrict trade with a challenging power in order to complement ongoing military containment efforts. I concentrate on trade because it is the most prominent form of economic exchange between the competing states and is present in all cases. For instance, the United States in the early 1980s did not have any meaningful financial ties with the Soviet Union, but it maintained significant commercial relations. Thus, analyzing the decisions about existing trade ties allows this book to effectively compare reigning states' decisions in different cases.

Moreover, this book concentrates on a reigning power's actual policy measures to adopt or avoid compound containment, as well as the underlying rationale of those measures. The reigning state's decision about compound containment essentially means policies decided by the executive branch of the government, especially by the president or prime minister and his or her cabinet. Thus, I trace whether and how the availability of alternative economic partners shaped key foreign policy decision-makers' choices on compound containment against the challenging power. This book pays particular attention to whether the core causal steps I articulate—how the relative presence of alternative economic partners affects the calculation of relative losses, and how this calculation, in turn, shapes the decision-maker's choice to avoid or employ compound containment—are observed in the decision-making process of the reigning power's leaders.

CHAPTER 3

The Absence of Britain's Compound Containment against Germany, 1898–1914

Many scholars suggest that a spiral of security competition marked British-German relations in the years leading up to World War I.[1] While the balance of power shifted in Germany's favor on the European continent, the geographical proximity of the two countries meant that Germany's increasing power threatened Britain's security. More evidently, Germany's naval buildup, launched by the Naval Laws of 1898 and 1900, reinforced by a series of *Novelle*, posed a direct threat to the defense of the British Empire's maritime lifeline as well as the safety of the homeland. Britain, in response, strengthened internal and external balancing efforts against Germany.[2] It reinforced the Royal Navy's home-water fleet (including the creation of the Channel Fleet), actively engaged in a naval arms race with Germany, carefully prepared plans for a European war, and signed the Entente Cordiale with France, which eventually evolved into the Triple Entente.[3]

At the same time, Britain found the need and opportunity to reconsider its commercial relationship with Germany.[4] During the decade before the Great War, the susceptibility to foreign competition in the market and the relative ascendance of other industrialized powers had led many British to doubt the future of Britain's relative power position. For many, Britain was becoming an inefficient nation when it came to great power competition.[5] As one journalist asked in 1905, a pressing concern for contemporaries was "Will the Empire which is celebrating one centenary of Trafalgar survive for the next?"[6] This pessimism, and the need to improve Britain's relative economic, political, and military performance, was widely shared across party and factional lines, although many refused to adopt an extreme view on Britain's fate.[7] Even in debates over domestic policies, such as the Education

Bill and Land Reform, reformists emphasized their policies' instrumental value in bolstering Britain's relative position in the international system.[8]

In stark contrast to Britain's relative decline, Germany seemed to possess a young and vigorous economy. It was widely agreed that the German military threat rested upon the spectacular achievements of German industry.[9] In particular, the country's rising commercial strength was one of the main drivers of Germany's differential growth. Germany in its growth path remained highly dependent on foreign trade, with a 34 percent average trade-to-GDP ratio between 1897 and 1905, which increased to 38 percent between 1909 and 1913.[10] Britain was also running a large deficit in trade with Germany, which was about £6 million in 1895, but increased to £24 million in 1905 and to £39 million in 1913.[11] Accordingly, Britain had good reason to reassess its commercial relationship with Germany. This reassessment was part of a broader rethinking concerning the future of the British economy. Still, it was evident that Germany was the major target in Britain's economic reconsiderations, and the evolution of military containment of Germany deeply affected Britain's thinking.

Heated debates ensued as to whether Britain should maintain or abandon existing policy arrangements in its trade with Germany. For some leaders of the Unionist government (a coalition of the Conservatives and the Liberal Unionists), the key to reinvigorating Britain's relative power lay in abolishing its open trade policy and constructing a form of all-British Zollverein.[12] The proposals to abandon extant free trade policy, however, were not substantiated as an effective means of countering the German challenge. Because such a revision was expected to inflict greater harm on the British economy and result in Britain's further relative decline, maintaining current commercial policy toward Germany appeared to be the best available strategy for Britain. Accordingly, despite the strengthening of military containment against Germany, Britain avoided compound containment measures until 1914.[13]

In this chapter, I examine whether the relative availability of alternative trade partners led Britain to conclude that avoiding compound containment was the better option for Britain's relative power position. For my argument to prove convincing, British leaders should have had an understanding and assessment of the availability of alternative trade partners for Britain and Germany, and recognized the likelihood of Britain's relative losses in making the decision to avoid compound containment. I also examine if domestic politics or ideology played more prominent roles in the process leading up to Britain's decision to avoid compound containment, and whether the causal mechanisms proposed in alternative theories are corroborated by the British experience. To be clear, my theory does not claim that domestic interest groups and leaders' ideological orientation do not matter. Yet it suggests that the presence of alternative trade partners provides a simpler explanation of the reigning power's decision, and that this structural factor can subsume the alternative explanations.

Britain's Tariff Reform Debate

Throughout the 1900s, Britain considered two trade policy options—protection and preference versus open trade—in attempts to cope with the German challenge and reverse its own relative decline. All major political groups and leaders were involved in this important and salient debate about Britain's trade policy. Thus, examining the British debate on its commercial policy toward Germany during the first decade of the twentieth century gives a unique opportunity to evaluate the three theories advanced in the previous chapter.

In 1903, the Unionist government, led by Joseph Chamberlain and backed by Arthur Balfour, proposed a revision of Britain's traditional free trade policy. For these leaders, abandoning free trade was the first step to restoring Britain's relative power position.[14] In making the case for trade policy revision, Chamberlain identified "the essential thing to keep in mind—namely, that the greatness of a nation is not to be measured by a comparison with its own past, but by its relative position in the councils of the world."[15] While military competition with Germany intensified, it soon became evident that Germany was the primary target of the Unionist campaign for "Tariff Reform." Two intimately linked policies were prescribed by these Unionists: tariffs and retaliation against trade with Germany, and preference for trade with the colonies.

First, many supporters of tariff reform thought that Britain could undermine Germany's prosperity by diminishing German imports through tariffs and retaliation.[16] In their view, the absence of protectionism in Britain had contributed to the growth of German industrial strength by allowing German companies to encroach on the world's largest British market, while diminishing the market share of British firms. They asserted that protectionism was inevitable in the new international economic environment, where powerful competitors had emerged. They further argued that Britain had to adopt protectionist measures in order to punish the unfair practices of foreign governments, secure the domestic market, and encourage the growth and innovation of Britain's traditionally powerful industries. Subscribing to the obsolete doctrine of free trade would only erode Britain's industrial basis and even undermine its great power position in the long term.[17]

Second, the Unionists proposed to strengthen commercial ties within the British Empire and intended to turn much of Britain's trade into its imperial channels. For these leaders, the British Empire, producing a wide variety of goods and generating enormous wealth, was an asset that other great powers did not possess. It was thus suggested that, by "knitting our somewhat loosely connected Empire more closely together, not merely in matters political and military, but in matters commercial too," Britain would be able to compete more effectively with rapidly growing powers such as Germany.[18] Economic unification in the form of an imperial federation, or "Colonial Zollverein," would stimulate Britain's industrial growth and compensate for its deficiencies, as well as provide new resources to preserve Britain's relative power position.[19]

The Unionists advocated these protectionist policies as their solution to the challenges faced by Britain, adopting them as a major campaign agenda in the general elections of the 1900s, and as the official policy of the party in 1907.[20] Powerful political groups such as the Tariff Reform League backed the Unionist case for protectionism until World War I.[21]

Nonetheless, protectionist measures against Germany were soon rejected by free traders both within the Unionist and the Liberal Party. Among the rationales advanced by the opponents of tariff reform, one key argument is consistent with my theory: as long as alternative trade partners were largely unavailable for Britain, while Germany could effectively divert trade away from Britain, abandoning free trade could inflict more losses on Britain's economic capacity than on Germany's. Accordingly, maintaining extant trade ties with Germany was the better alternative for preserving Britain's relative material clout.

The Absence of Alternative Trade Partners for Britain

Before World War I, trade between Britain and Germany was highly specialized and complementary, with Germany supplying Britain with nearly one-quarter of its imported manufactured goods.[22] Britain's leading industries depended heavily on German economic inputs to ensure their advantage in the competitive international market, while many imports from Germany could not easily be substituted by a different foreign country. Restricting trade with Germany would have diminished those industries' productive efficiency and market competitiveness, and thus might have damaged Britain's overall material capacity.

The Structure of the British Economy

In order to understand the implications of trade with Germany for Britain's economic performance, the structure of the British economy before World War I needs to be examined. As Table 3.1 shows, by 1907 Britain's economic growth was led by manufacturing, mining, construction, trade, and transportation, which in sum generated about 65 percent of its GDP. As the first country to achieve industrialization, Britain's economic strength lay in making industrial products, with a rapidly shrinking share of "first industries." Britain also possessed strong "tertiary" sectors, including transport, trade, banking, insurance, finance, and commercial services.[23]

The composition of national income in 1907, summarized in Table 3.2, allows a closer look at Britain's economic structure. About 18 percent of its national income came from commerce, 9.5 percent from transport, and 10.1 percent from professional activities that were at least partly related to international trade, reflecting Britain's central position in global commerce. Other large sources of income were engineering and metal manufacturing, including the production of machines and vessels, and the textile and clothing industries that had been Britain's central industries since the early nineteenth century.

Table 3.1. Composition of the National Product of Britain (percentage of GDP)

	Agriculture, Forestry, Fishing	Manufactures, Mining, Construction	Trade, Transport	Government, Defense	Housing
1861	19	41	20	5	8
1871	15	42	25	4	8
1881	12	43	25	4	9
1907	6	37	28	3	7

Source: Peter Mathias, *The First Industrial Nation*, 2nd edition (London: Methuen, 1983), p. 223.

Table 3.2. Industrial Distribution of the National Income of Britain in 1907

	Value at Current Prices (£ millions)	Percentage of National Income
Agriculture, forestry, fishing	120.1	6.0
Mines and quarries	119.4	6.0
Engineering and metal manufacture	154.3	8.2
Textile and clothing	159.5	8.0
Food, drink, and tobacco	85.5	4.3
Paper and printing	32.6	1.6
Chemicals	21.0	1.1
Wood industries	20.6	1.0
Miscellaneous manufactures	29.4	1.5
Gas, electricity, water	31.0	1.6
Building and contracting	74.4	3.7
Rents of dwellings	148.4	7.4
Commerce	358.4	18.0
Transport	188.9	9.5
Government and defense	59.6	3.0
Professions, charities, and miscellaneous	202.5	10.1
Domestic service	75.8	3.8
Income from abroad	143.8	7.2

Source: Phyllis Deane and W. A. Cole, *British Economic Growth, 1688–1959*, 2nd edition (Cambridge: Cambridge University Press, 1969), p. 175.

From these data, the leading industries that drove Britain's economic growth before World War I can be pinned down. Those leading industries were concentrated in the manufacturing and commerce sectors, and included textiles, iron and steel, engineering (machinery), shipbuilding, shipping, and insurance and banking. Until 1914, trade with Germany had large ramifications for the performance of these industries. By purchasing certain goods from German firms, rather than buying them from the home market, Britain's leading industries could maintain international competitiveness, increase profit margins, and contribute to their home country's economic clout.

The Reliance of Britain's Major Industries on German Inputs

Commerce: The Shipbuilding-Shipping-Insurance/Banking Linkage

Before the war, a huge portion of Britain's national wealth was generated by the broadly defined commerce sector, which was built on an intimate linkage between shipbuilding, shipping, and insurance/banking. The backbone of Britain's global leadership in this sector was its competitiveness in ship-building, which extensively used imported German goods. If alternative trade partners did not exist, restricting trade with Germany could have adversely affected Britain's superiority in shipbuilding, and in turn could have affected its dominance in shipping and in the insurance and banking industries.

British shipbuilders had a large number of domestic and international customers and maintained superiority until World War I because the vessels they produced were cheaper than the ships of comparable quality made by builders in other countries.[24] During the transition from wooden to iron and then steel ships in the late nineteenth century, British shipbuilders kept the cost of production low and established their international competitiveness while facing challenges from other industrialized powers.[25]

The German steel that was "dumped" into the British market played an important role in maintaining this competitiveness, achieved by the turn of the century.[26] As the Treasury reported to the cabinet in 1903, by using cheap German metals, "Our ship-builders are thus enabled to build ships at a very low price, and these they sell to the Germans."[27] Even in the hearings conducted by the protectionist-backed Tariff Commission, witnesses noted the cost-saving effect of German imports.[28] British shipbuilders' reliance on German steel increased throughout the 1900s. By 1912–1913, about 43 percent of all steel castings and 10 percent of all steel plates that were consumed in Britain came from Germany, and the shipbuilding industry was one of the best customers for this steel.[29]

Moreover, the British shipbuilding industry achieved high degrees of efficiency by purchasing components, machinery, and other equipment from foreign suppliers.[30] Among these suppliers, much of the electrical equipment and parts were produced by Germany or German subsidiaries in Britain, such as Siemens.[31] British shipbuilders increasingly relied on these electrical products to operate their yards, as well as to equip their vessels. In addition, steel ships were impossible to build without reliable machine tools, and Germany remained the world's leading supplier of machine tools.[32] Accordingly, trade with Germany helped the British ship-building industry keep production costs low. Britain maintained superiority in shipbuilding in the period before the war, producing up to 60.6 percent of the world's new vessels between 1909 and 1913.[33] During the decades leading up to 1914, the annual value of new merchant vessels built in British shipyards accounted for approximately 1.25 percent of Britain's GDP.[34]

Britain's advantage in shipbuilding played another, more important role in its economy: this advantage helped Britain to dominate the lucrative shipping industry. Until World War I, the world's major shipping companies were concentrated in Britain and carried not only British goods but also transported cargo between third countries. The British mercantile marine was able to become the shipper of the world because it could buy cheaper ships in large numbers, thereby accumulating the largest fleet of commercial ships. Indeed, British shipping companies were also major owners of British shipbuilding firms. For instance, Lord Furness, the greatest individual shipowner of the world, was at the same time chairman or director of four shipbuilding and marine-engineering companies.[35] By 1890, Britain alone had more registered tonnage than the rest of the world combined, and British shippers owned 33.4 percent of the world's tonnage by 1914.[36] Income from shipping services was very large, reaching an annual average of £100 million between 1911 and 1913.[37] Minimizing the cost of ship production was important to maintaining the competitive advantage in this important industry, especially considering that challengers to the British shipping industry often emerged, such as the United States' International Mercantile Marine and Germany's Hamburg-Amerika Linie.[38]

The effects of Britain's advantage in shipbuilding extended beyond the shipping industry. Its central role in the global shipping industry ensured Britain's virtual monopoly in the insurance industry and, to some extent, the banking industry. As is the case today, the early twentieth-century maritime transportation of goods and people was insured, and British shippers signed contracts almost exclusively with British insurance companies such as Lloyd's. As Peter Mathias observes, "In a very real sense the evolution of London as the world's main centre of international banking, finance and insurancing was a function of the dominance of British shipping in world trade."[39]

Engineering and Machinery

Britain's engineering and machinery industry also relied on German industrial products to enhance productive and allocative efficiency and market competitiveness. This industry was important not only for the wealth it produced, but also for its pervasive impact on the activities of almost all industrial sectors of the modern economy. Because all major powers concentrated on developing their engineering and machinery industry, market competition in this sector had become severe.

As its defining characteristic, the engineering and machinery industry was concerned with the processing of metals, transforming them into machinery and goods for further use in the operation of other industries.[40] Starting in the late nineteenth century, Britain purchased large amounts of intermediate iron and steel products from Germany. By doing so, British engineering and machinery companies could produce final goods at a lower price and expand their sales on the international market. As the Duke of Devonshire, one of the most influential Liberal Unionists and former chairman of an iron and steel company, observed, "Nobody that I am aware of buys iron or steel [from Germany] to look at or to put in his pocket. The purchasers of iron and steel are a thousand different classes of manufacturers who convert iron and steel into hundreds of thousands of articles of general utility and advantage."[41]

Further, Britain was a major buyer of such German machinery as electricity generating plants and electrical equipment, increasingly depending on these to operate factories and make final engineering products. For technological and administrative reasons, Britain was slow to develop the newest electrical industry, with the exception of its production of electric cables.[42] Accordingly, as Francis Oppenheimer, the British consul in Frankfurt, reported in 1909, "The United Kingdom receives from Germany machines for the newer branches of manufacture, e.g., electro-technical machines, and mining machines, etc., in which the technical development of Germany strives to excel."[43]

The Iron and Steel Industry

Britain's iron and steel industry was the sector that was hardest hit by German encroachment on the market.[44] The loss of market share that occurred was mainly due to Britain's failure to adjust to technological development and reduce costs.[45] In contrast, Germany's competitive advantage in producing iron and steel allowed it to achieve further growth in investment and to adopt the latest technology.

However, even in the iron and steel industry, importing cheap German metals and materials enabled many British companies to maintain or increase their export trade. By purchasing semimanufactured German steel, British iron- and steel-producing companies could make final products at a lower price and expand their sales in rapidly expanding markets such as the United States and Britain's own dominions and colonies. In other words, many German iron and steel imports were used as raw materials to manufacture more sophisticated final steel products. In addition, foreign competition was often seen as having a modernizing, rather than destructive, impact on this industry.[46] Moreover, Germany supplied basic steel and special products such as tungsten and spiegeleisen, minerals that were used to improve the quality of steel but were not produced in Britain.[47] Thus, as Charles Ritchie, the chancellor of the exchequer, said to the cabinet, "Cheap iron and steel [from Germany] have, beyond doubt, recently enabled us to compete advantageously in the trade for finished iron and steel goods, not merely in neutral markets, but, I believe, even in the German home market, to the loudly-expressed dissatisfaction of the German manufacturers themselves."[48] In the hearings conducted by the Tariff Commission, many witnesses from the iron and steel industry also confirmed that buying cheap German products was important to maintaining competitiveness.[49]

The Textile Industry

Although the textile industry was no longer producing the largest wealth for the British economy by the late nineteenth century, it still generated a significant portion of Britain's GDP, and textiles remained a major export item until 1914. As one of the pioneers of the Industrial Revolution, however, Britain's textile industry faced severe international competition as more states achieved industrialization. By the beginning of the twentieth century, British textile producers were obsessed with reducing production costs to remain competitive on their most profitable markets.[50]

While the British textile industry wanted to keep production costs as low as possible, imposing restrictions on German imports was likely to increase the costs of key items such as machinery and raw materials.[51] Consequent increases in the price of final textile products would render British textiles less attractive on the competitive market. As long as free trade helped to keep the price of machinery and materials low, Britain could ensure that "the cost of production in Great Britain including the cost of building and equipping mills is, on the whole, lower than on the Continent, or in the U.S."[52]

For the textile industry, chemicals were another important item imported from Germany. Facing severe international competition, British textile producers concentrated on manufacturing more value-added textiles and cloths. This shift required better and cheaper dying chemicals.[53] Germany was the leader in the production and industrial application of chemicals to the extent that other industrialized powers could pose no serious challenge.[54] Hence, most of Britain's synthetic dyestuffs were purchased from Germany. In 1913 Britain imported 90 percent of this material from Germany.[55]

The Low Substitutability of German Economic Inputs

As long as imported German goods played a central role in enhancing the performance of Britain's major industries, it was evident to Britain that no unilateral loss could be inflicted on Germany by restricting trade. To the contrary, Britain would encounter significant loss in the form of decreased efficiency, market competitiveness, and real income. As the Liberal leader Asquith said of German imports, "In the first place, many of these things could be made cheaper and better abroad. In the second place, a very large proportion of these so-called manufactures were really raw material in an intermediate stage, brought here for British industry to exercise further processes upon it."[56] In this condition, as the Treasury reported to the Unionist cabinet, shutting off trade with Germany would increase the costs of production within Britain's leading and competitive industries, and place Britain in a worse position for competition on the market.[57] Britain would be less competitive not only on other great power markets, but also on the markets of its own dominions and colonies, which became very important for a number of Britain's major exports.[58] Moreover, since restricting trade ties with Germany would increase the cost of producing manufactured goods for home consumption, Britain' real income would diminish.[59] These assessments were corroborated by the experience of the British industries that used sugar as raw material and suffered from the bounties on imported sugar in the early 1900s.[60]

Economic inputs from Germany could not be easily substituted with inputs from other states since no foreign country could provide similar goods at equivalent quality and price. It was widely agreed that other industrialized European states could not match Germany in the production of high-quality and cheap intermediate and final iron and steel products, machinery, and chemicals. Even major European great powers, such as France and Russia, lagged far behind Germany in the production of these goods. Indeed, like Britain, these European powers' domestic markets were rapidly being encroached on by German products.[61] Outside of Europe, a rapidly industrializing United States emerged as a major producer of iron and steel by the turn of the twentieth century.[62] Nonetheless, its products could not replace the goods from Germany because US production was not great enough to satisfy the demand of its own rapidly expanding domestic market. While debating trade restrictions against German iron and steel products, the Treasury informed the British cabinet that "it must be borne in mind that the U.S. are still importing pig and manufactured iron for their home market."[63] The fact that Germany was the primary target of the Conservatives' campaign against dumping corroborates that Germany was the major provider of cheap industrial goods to Britain, with no potential substitute.

Thus, unimpeded access to German economic inputs was viewed as important for Britain's economic performance.[64] Alfred Marshall, the leading economist of the time and a close economic adviser to Prime Minister Arthur Balfour, elaborated on this point in his advice to the Unionist cabinet:

> It is not merely expedient–it is absolutely essential–for England's hopes of retaining a high place in the world, that she should neglect no opportunity of increasing the alertness of her industrial population in general, and her manufacturers in particular; and for this purpose there is no device to be compared in efficiency with that of keeping her markets open to the new products of other nations, and especially to those of . . . German sedulous thought and scientific training.[65]

This view was shared by the Liberal Party and a number of powerful figures in the Unionist government.

The Presence of Alternative Trade Partners for Germany

Before 1914, Britain was not in a position to effectively prevent Germany from finding alternative trade partners. Britain recognized that Germany would be able to replace its imports from the British Isles and British Empire with imports from other countries. At the same time, Germany possessed alternative markets in other industrialized powers, the Eurasian hinterland, and the American states. Also, Britain did not possess the ability to organize the collective actions that would have constrained Germany's foreign trade.

Germany's Capacity to Divert Imports from Britain

In the decade before World War I, Britain's exports to Germany mainly comprised staple goods, including coal, fish, and certain classes of textiles and yarns, and certain types of machinery and final iron and steel products.[66] These goods accounted for about two-thirds of British exports to Germany by value.[67] More importantly, the British overseas possessions supplied about 12 percent of all of Germany's raw material and food demands by 1913. Although Britain's share in Germany's imports of raw materials was steadily diminishing—from 15 percent of Germany's total raw material imports in 1890 to 8.1 percent in 1913—the empire's share continued to increase.[68] The large flow of raw materials and foodstuffs from the British Empire to Germany might suggest that, as proponents of naval blockade strategy advocated, Britain could effectively restrict exports to Germany if need be.[69]

However, there were reasons to conclude that Britain could not prevent Germany from replacing its British imports with imports from other countries. First, many of the economic inputs that Germany purchased from Britain were readily available on the international market. As early as 1903, the Balfour cabinet was informed that Britain had only limited leverage to affect the German economy by manipulating exports because "there are few of her exports which other countries need so urgently as to be willing to take them from her at largely increased cost; and because none of her rivals would permanently suffer serious injury through the partial exclusion of any products of hers with which England can afford to dispense."[70] Similarly, Percy Ashley explained to Prime Minister Balfour that "the taxation of exports is only expedient, on economic grounds, where the country imposing it has a monopoly (absolute or practical) of the commodity taxed, and where the foreign demand for that article is intense," but Britain had "practical monopoly [in exports] only in goods such as steam coal and jute."[71] Later in the decade, Llewellyn Smith, representing the Board of Trade, assessed that Germany could easily substitute British goods with ones from rival foreign suppliers. According to Smith, denying Germany's access to British goods would only cause temporary inconveniences with no broader implications for longer-term economic development.[72]

Moreover, while Germany had an enormous demand for foreign foodstuffs, the United States, Russia, and later Argentina had become its chief suppliers of food by the eve of World War I.[73] If Britain had tried to control the flow of food from its dominions into Germany—as it actually did when the war broke out—these supplying countries could have replaced the British Empire as a source. As Eyre Crowe, senior clerk at the Foreign Office, claimed based on Francis Oppenheimer's influential 1909 report, "The pressure which could be put on [Germany's] resources as regards imported food supplies and raw materials is very slight."[74]

Second, Britain's capacity to prevent Germany from substituting British economic inputs would be sharply limited due to the presence of neutral states. Regardless of their position on the effectiveness of naval blockades as a wartime strategy, British officials agreed that Germany could effectively divert its trade through neutral ports, most notably Antwerp and Rotterdam, if Britain were to impose a blockade.[75] According to Francis Oppenheimer, the Dutch and Belgian ports were "quasi-German," and could allow Germany to conduct its trade in a roundabout way, making it "doubtful whether the blockade would in the long run prove really effective."[76] Indeed, the fear of German incorporation of the Low Countries into Germany's economic and political sphere arose repeatedly in Britain. In particular, the Netherlands naturally exhibited strong Anglophobia in the aftermath of the Boer War.[77] Northern Europe was another major route through which Germany could divert its imports. Prohibiting Germany's neutral trade would have been problematic because it could have antagonized powerful neutral states such as the United States, the outcome of which might have been disastrous for Britain.[78]

When the war broke out in Europe, Britain's inability to thwart Germany's neutral country trade became clear. Food and raw materials flowed into Germany through its backdoors in Belgium, Italy, the Netherlands, and Scandinavia.[79] From August 1914, grain shipments from German companies in South America to neutral Scandinavian ports saw an unprecedented expansion.[80] The United States continued to export cotton, refined ore, oil, meat, and other foodstuffs to the neutral ports.[81] When US exports to Europe almost quadrupled with the beginning of the war, it was presumed that most of these expanded exports were heading for Germany.[82] Even after the British Expeditionary Force suffered a nearly 60 percent loss in casualties by November 1914 and public antagonism toward the Central Powers soared, Britain could not impose comprehensive restrictions against Germany's neutral trade.[83] In short, Britain's restrictions on exports against Germany were likely to be ineffective as long as alternative suppliers existed and Britain could not seize their trade.

Germany's Capacity to Divert Exports to Britain

Until 1913, Germany's major export items were manufactured goods such as chemicals, machinery, ironware, coal, cotton cloth, woolen cloth, and beet sugar, in order of export values.[84] Britain was one of Germany's most important export destinations, and this condition could have given London some leverage over Berlin in commercial matters.[85] Nonetheless, this optimistic view was unlikely to materialize. If Britain had restricted the import of German goods, Germany could have effectively diverted them to other large foreign markets.

Germany had large and rapidly growing alternative markets in Europe and America, where its products were more competitive than goods from other countries. In the early 1900s, Germany was outperforming British and other foreign firms in the manufacture and sale of diverse industrial products.[86] Its exports to Belgium and the Netherlands for their domestic consumption alone were larger than its exports to Britain. In France, German firms were encroaching on British market share, and the two states' exports to France were almost equal by 1913. In Italy and Switzerland, geographical proximity allowed Germany's advantage, and in the Scandinavian market, Germany was exporting goods worth approximately £40 million, compared to Britain's £20 million in 1912. With its ally, Austria-Hungary, Germany maintained a predominant position, exporting goods worth about £59 million, while Britain exported £10 million in 1912. Germany also maintained an advantage in the Russian market. On the eve of the war, German export trade to Russia was almost four times larger than Britain's in value.[87] With regard to German iron products, it was expected that the United States could readily absorb them if Britain had restricted importation of those products.[88]

Germany's capacity to divert its exports away from Britain was also recognized by British leaders. For instance, the Duke of Devonshire argued, "It is not easy to see that our power of competing in neutral markets would be increased by the adoption of that proposal [protective tariffs]. If . . . Germany wants to 'dump' they will 'dump' somewhere. If they cannot 'dump' here, they will be driven to 'dumping' in neutral markets."[89] The Treasury also informed the cabinet that "if a competitor can deliver here at a profit, *a fortiori*, he can do the same in a neutral market common to both."[90]

Potential Frictions with Germany's Alternative Partners

If Britain had abandoned free trade policy with Germany, it might have faced additional losses originating from frictions with other countries. In particular, Britain could have been exposed to retaliation from Germany and other industrialized powers.[91] Imposing tariffs against German goods was likely to induce a commercial war in which Britain lacked advantage, especially considering that Germany had reached several continental agreements on tariffs by the late nineteenth century. For instance, the "Caprivi treaties" and "the second European network" opened many protected markets, including Austria-Hungary, Russia, Italy, Switzerland, and Belgium, to German exports while maintaining tariffs against British goods.[92] Britain was given minimum tariffs on goods that these protectionist states considered important for their economic development.[93] In 1905, as one British journal observed, "Germany has, by the conclusion of commercial treaties with many Powers, secured for the German industries an immense outlet, almost the monopoly on the Continent of Europe to the disadvantage of our own industries, and she is now assiduously working for a Central European Customs Union of States to which Union she means to be the most favoured, and almost the sole, purveyor of manufacturing articles."[94]

Although this treaty system required adjustments, with frictions emerging frequently between the members, its basic structure was retained until World War I.[95] Even in 1911, the Board of Trade reported to the cabinet that Germany was successfully reinstating commercial treaties with the European states.[96] Based on the renewed trade agreement, Russia became one of Germany's chief suppliers of raw materials and foodstuffs, and about 45 percent of Russia's total trade was with Germany on the eve of World War I.[97] Thus, it would have been very difficult for Britain to garner support from other European powers for its economic restrictions against Germany.

In addition, restricting trade with Germany would have caused frictions in Britain's relations with its own colonies and dominions. Collaborating with the members of the British Empire against Germany's foreign trade was not a realistic option for Britain. With the exception of Canada, no colonial government was willing to adopt a discriminatory policy toward Germany in favor of products from the mother country.[98] For instance, Lord George Hamilton warned the cabinet that, for India, the free trade system, on which it [India's foreign trade] is based, has so far resulted in widening markets for its exports, and in cheap imports from abroad. . . . If, however, the principle of differential treatment of British imports, for the Benefit of the United Kingdom, and other members of the Empire, is introduced, with its concomitant risks and sacrifices, into the Indian tariff system, the change will inevitably present itself to the Native mind as implying the abandonment of principles in which it has never heartily acquiesced, and which, it conceives, has hitherto stood in the way of India's industrial advance.[99]

Outcome: Compound Containment Avoided

Under the conditions discussed above, Britain discovered that maintaining trade ties with Germany was the better option for preserving its relative material power. Compound containment was avoided in important part because it could inflict more losses on Britain's material capacity. This rationale was clearly observed in the midst of the fierce debate on tariff reform.

The Need to Maintain Extant Trade Policy toward Germany

The proponents of tariff reform argued that Britain should abandon its free trade dogma in order to more effectively compete with Germany. For many British political leaders, nonetheless, the policy option that was better than protectionism for addressing the German challenge and maximizing Britain's own relative power position was to maintain its extant free trade policy. In this view, Britain lacked effective tools for hampering Germany's growth. It was also suggested that restricting trade would harm Britain's own economic performance and "drag our country back into the dangers and errors of a discredited past."[100] As many Liberals claimed, "patriotism," defined as actions that helped Britain enhance its relative power position, was in the service of free trade.[101]

The adverse consequences of abandoning free trade policy and reducing trade ties with Germany were first recognized within the Unionist Party, where the proposals for protectionist policy originated. Indeed, disagreements over the impact of tariff reform caused a crisis within the Unionist cabinet in 1903.[102] Although Prime Minister Balfour tried to persuade his cabinet members that the free trade dogma no longer served Britain's current position in the international system, some leading cabinet figures were adamant that revising extant trade policy would only make Britain worse off.[103] The Duke of Devonshire replied to Balfour that adopting protectionism would "do more harm to ourselves than goods to our Colonial relations, or to improve treatment by our foreign rivals."[104] Charles Ritchie, the chancellor of the exchequer, agreed, arguing that Britain had much more to lose by adopting protectionism.[105] Lord Balfour of Burleigh went further, saying, "I am profoundly convinced that any departure from the policy of free trade . . . will be the first real blow to the prosperity of our British commerce."[106] The view of Unionist free traders was corroborated by leading economists and supporters of imperial unity, most notably Percy Ashley and Alfred Marshall, who warned that Britain had little to gain but much to lose by abandoning free trade.[107]

Still, the proposal to reconsider trade ties with Germany was more thoroughly refuted by the Liberal Party. The Liberals agreed with the ends of the Tariff Reform, but they disagreed with the means. Most Liberal free traders did not dismiss the fact that Britain was losing much of its market share to Germany in many of its traditional industries, and was waging a daunting struggle with that country.[108] As the Liberal leader Herbert Henry Asquith argued,

> Do not let it be supposed that because we are driven to defend the citadel of Free Trade we, therefore, think that all is for the best and are content with a policy of folded hands. That there are disquieting features in our industrial as in our social conditions no honest observer, certainly no member of the party of progress, will be found to deny. We have seen industries in which we ought to have maintained our supremacy falling behind, and in some cases entirely taken away from us by our competitors.[109]

Henry Campbell-Bannerman, the Liberal prime minister from 1906 to 1908, also acknowledged that free trade should not be regarded as a panacea, but rather as Britain's best available option.[110]

For the Liberals, protectionism was truly "unpatriotic" and would only have diminished Britain's capacity to compete with Germany.[111] Abandoning extant free trade policy would have raised the cost of production, harbored inefficiency, lowered output and employment, strangled imperial commerce, and nurtured corruption.[112] Germany, in contrast, would have been able to divert its trade away from Britain, maintaining its economic performance.[113] Moreover, while Germany relied heavily on raw materials from the British Empire, it was not certain whether Britain's colonies would have supported the mother country's imperative to diminish exports to Germany while supplying Britain at a lower price. To the contrary, restricting the British Empire's imports from Germany would have induced furor from the colonies, as they would have been forced to purchase British goods instead of cheaper and better German industrial products. Thus, protectionism and preference might have weakened the unity of the British Empire and impaired Britain's material strength.[114]

Accordingly, the Liberal Party argued that abandoning extant trade policy toward Germany would have inflicted greater harm on Britain, rather than improving its relative economic clout. A move toward restrictive measures, most notably through the adoption of retaliatory policies, would only have made Britain worse off. Leading the debate with the Unionists, Asquith made this point clear:

> Why do we—we Liberals, we Free Traders—why do we decline to assent to such a policy? Not because . . . it conflicts with some abstract proposition in some obsolete creed . . . not because we are craven . . . who are afraid to meet force with force. Nothing of the sort. If we oppose retaliation as a policy it is because we believe that experience shows—and to experience, and experience alone, we should appeal—that in practice it is fatal as a weapon of offence, and in the vast majority of cases it is infinitely more mischievous to those who use it than to those against whom it is directed.[115]

> [R]etaliation as a practice we should suffer a great deal more injury ourselves than any we should inflict on the other States concerned.[116]

> Believe me, as all experience shows, you will inflict far more and far severer wounds upon yourselves than upon the industrial rivals of your own once you begin to play with the boomerang of retaliation. Do not let us in a fit of hypochondria commit industrial suicide, for when all is said and done that is what it comes to.[117]

At a time when Britain was encountering internal and external challenges, as John Morley, a leader of the powerful Radical faction in the Liberal Party, argued, free trade was Britain's best available way of "keeping her powder dry, and of keeping her resources in steadfast charge."[118] Even the most ardent defenders of free trade, for instance the Cobden Club, did not advocate free trade on the basis of convictions alone. Instead, they argued that Britain had more to lose by restricting trade considering its main industries' linkage to foreign inputs and competition in foreign markets. According to Harold Cox, the secretary of the Cobden Club, "Protection can only diminish national wealth," and thus was detrimental to other national objectives, most importantly the unity and prosperity of the British Empire.[119] Maintaining traditional free trade policy was the best means of maximizing Britain's gains, defending its position of leadership in the international system, and cementing the British Empire.

Britain's Choice: Avoid Compound Containment

While Britain responded to the German threat through internal and external balancing, both the Unionist (1895–1905) and Liberal (1905–1915) cabinets chose not to restrict commerce with Germany and transform military containment into compound containment. The Unionists could not find enough imperatives to abandon free trade while they were in office, and the proponents of a trade policy revision continuously failed to develop a convincing rationale for protectionism or to present evidence in support their claim. As one journal observed, "No one attempted to show how, had we been a protectionist country, we should have prevented the more rapid proportionate growth of countries like the United States and Germany."[120]

In contrast, foreign policy leaders of the Liberal cabinet, recognized by their contemporaries as astute practitioners of realpolitik, were adamant that free trade was the better alternative for maintaining Britain's competitiveness vis-à-vis Germany, as well as for preserving Britain's relative power position.[121] Even the economic recessions between 1907 and 1908, the accelerating naval arms race with Germany, and the experience of near-war situations during the Moroccan Crises did not affect the British decision to maintain trade with Germany.

Consequently, Britain did not adopt either preferential policy or retaliatory tariffs on trade with Germany until 1914 and effectively avoided employing compound containment against that state. Although the British government implemented some minor economic measures in order to counter German encroachment on the British market, including the Merchandise Marks Act of 1887 and the Patent Law of 1907, these were not powerful enough to alter the trajectory of overall commerce between the two countries.[122]

Alternative Explanations

Britain's decision to avoid compound containment against Germany before the outbreak of World War I is consistent with the arguments of my theory. How well do the two alternative explanations—one focusing on domestic interest group politics and the other emphasizing the role of leaders' belief— account for the British decision? First, for the commercial interest argument to show that its causal mechanism works, the reigning power's leaders should avoid compound containment measures in response to domestic interest groups that want to sustain trade ties with the challenging state. The hallmark of this approach is a bottom-up process whereby domestic groups mobilize themselves to protect commercial interests and their interactions with other societal groups and national leaders, mainly through activities related to elections and lobbying. Second, for the ideological orientation argument to hold, British leaders would have to have chosen to maintain trade ties with Germany because they had strong convictions about the pacifying effect of commerce. The British case, however, reveals either that the causal mechanisms of these two alternative explanations do not function as expected, or that the evidence that supports their causal claims is not sufficient.[123]

The Role of Commercial Interests

Contrary to the expectations of the commercial interest argument, it is uncertain whether British commercial groups that wanted to maintain open trade with Germany played a decisive role in the decision to avoid compound containment. To be clear, there is a strong relationship between the Liberal Party's promotion of free trade and its landslide victory in the general election of 1906. In the campaign for the 1906 general election, 98 percent of the addresses delivered by Liberal candidates mentioned why Britain had to maintain free trade policy.[124] However, it is misleading to conclude that this correlation is evidence in support of the mechanism laid out by the commercial interest-based explanation. A closer look reveals that this relationship was not established through the mechanism articulated by the commercial interest theory. In other words, even though one can claim that domestic politics matters, it is difficult to argue that this alternative theory is supported by the British experience.

First, it was difficult to define who constituted the losers and winners of extant free trade with Germany. Standard trade models (the theories underlying the domestic politics-based alternative explanation) suggest that the economic groups who benefit from open trade will support free trade while those who lose will oppose it. However, in pre–World War I Britain, it was difficult to make clear distinctions among different commercial interests based on their performance under free trade. As pointed out in the hearings by the Tariff Commission, it was hard to determine which particular industries were at risk from German encroachment, since many less competitive sectors also benefited from the purchase of cheap imported German materials. Even Britain's waning industries, such as the iron and steel industry, were not completely disadvantaged by German market expansion. Thus, it remains ambiguous what specific commercial groups supported free trade with Germany and which opposed it based on their performance under current trade policy.[125] In short, it is dubious whether this alternative theory's core assumption—the distinguishability of commercial groups that gained or lost under current trade policy—is met in the British case.

Second, party position over trade policy and key supporters' interests did not match. Indeed, British domestic politics of this period, including politics over trade policy, showed signs of class-based interactions, rather than being dominated by clashing commercial interests. In the early twentieth century, the Conservatives that proposed protectionist policies were becoming the party of wealthy business and commerce that heavily engaged in and benefited the most from international commerce, while the business element declined within the Liberal Party. The Liberals, moreover, focused on social changes and actively mobilized working-class votes, while trying to consolidate their position on the center-left of British politics. Furthermore, commercial interest groups were strangely silent in lobbying for their sector-specific interests.[126]

The diverging electoral outcomes across the districts throughout the 1900s are more reflective of this class-based politics than of differentials in economic performance under free trade. In the Liberal victories in the general elections of 1906 and 1910, voters in the industries that benefited from open trade supported the Liberals alongside those in "losing" industries. For instance, of the 153 seats in England where the working class was concentrated, the Liberals won 138 seats in the election of 1906, and the Liberal free traders prevailed even in districts where competition from foreign firms was fierce.[127] Conversely, in the 1906 election, both Tariff Reform Unionists and Unionist Free Traders lost their seats.[128] In the elections of 1910, the central agenda was the Liberal Party's "People's Budget," which tried to expand social spending dramatically, and the Liberals' campaign slogan was "the peers [of the House of Lords] versus the people."[129] As the economist Alfred Marshall observed in the immediate aftermath of the 1910 election, "The division between the districts . . . does not run with the interests of the population in T.R. or F.T. [Tariff Reform or Free Trade]."[130] In this context, public support for the Liberal Party should not be conflated with the influence of commercial interests.

Third, the argument that British leaders persistently made foreign policy decisions in response to domestic interests is misleading. Put differently, many important foreign policy decisions, whether security or economic, were made through a "top-down" process.[131] Rather than serving as simple agents of their constituencies, leaders actively formulated and mobilized public support. The controversial tariff reform campaign was officially launched by Joseph Chamberlain's speech at Birmingham in May 1903, and elite and public mobilization in support of his policy was formulated only after his announcement of the new trade program, rather than shaping Chamberlain's proposal.[132] Likewise, the Unionist prime minister Arthur Balfour advocated protectionist policies through a speech at Sheffield in October 1903 only after intense discussions in the cabinet.[133] Further, evidence suggests that the Unionist Party's tariff reform program itself emerged as a last resort when the Unionist defeat in the general election of 1906 had become certain.[134] Similarly, the Liberals dashed into the fight against protectionism and endorsed free trade in the elections because it could unite the factions within the Liberal Party that disagreed on most other matters.[135] Liberal leaders such as Campbell-Bannerman and Asquith found the controversy over protectionist policy opportune because it was creating division within the Unionist Party, which in turn advanced the Liberals' electoral position.[136]

In addition to these points, if leaders had adhered to public views in deciding to adopt compound containment measures, Britain would have implemented more competitive economic and security policies toward Germany given the strong and widespread anti-German sentiment of the time.[137] British leaders, nonetheless, took care not to agitate Germanophobia and avoided mobilizing those feelings to win support. Foreign policy leaders of the Liberal cabinet between 1906 and 1914—including Herbert Henry Asquith, Edward Grey, and Richard Haldane—were Liberal imperialists who were sensitive to domestic interference in foreign affairs and tried to avoid populist policies.[138]

These points, however, do not mean that domestic politics did not matter at all in Britain's decision to avoid commercial restrictions against Germany. On the contrary, domestic political process—especially, the competition between tariff reformers and free traders—constitutes an important part of the mechanism leading up to the British decision concerning Germany. Nonetheless, structural factors—the availability of alternative partners—played a more prominent causal role in Britain's decision on compound containment against Germany, and potentially subsume the domestic politics argument.

The Role of Ideology

There is, likewise, insufficient evidence to show that Britain avoided compound containment because it retained strong convictions in trade's ability to pacify Germany. Rather than advancing a strategy based on liberal beliefs, the heart of British security policy toward Germany lay in adopting appropriate internal and external balancing measures, as well as planning for economic warfare.[139] As Secretary of State for War Richard Haldane told the German ambassador in 1912, "The theory of the balance of power forms an axiom of English foreign policy and has led to the English leaning towards France and Russia."[140] Moreover, since the importance of maintaining naval supremacy was almost unanimously agreed upon, meeting the German challenge in the naval race won wide support.[141] When the role of economic instruments was actually brought to the fore, Britain carefully prepared for economic warfare, which would be implemented hand in hand with the deployment of military forces if a war with Germany broke out.[142]

Meanwhile, there were very few influential leaders or powerful political groups in the British government that could endorse economic exchanges with Germany as a means of ameliorating security tensions. Contrary to some observations, the Radical wing of the Liberal Party—the group that sometimes embraced the idea of the pacifying effect of trade—was weakened at the cabinet level around 1908. By that year, the old and powerful leaders of the Radicals were largely absent within the cabinet: Prime Minister Campbell-Bannerman died in April 1908, James Bryce left Britain to serve as an ambassador in Washington, Lord Ripson resigned from the cabinet in October 1908, and John Morley's position was weakened by having accepted a peerage.[143] In contrast, the younger generation of Radical foreign policy leaders, most notably David Lloyd George and Winston Churchill, were not particularly "radical," as recognized by their contemporaries. For instance, as Lord Esher observed, "Lloyd George, in his heart, does not care a bit for economy, and is quite ready to face parliament with any amount of defeat, and to 'go' for a big Navy. He is plucky and an Imperialist at heart, if he is anything."[144] Lloyd George and Churchill not only chose to side with the Imperialists in important foreign policy matters, but also eventually joined the Liberal Imperialists in 1911.[145] Moreover, although the Liberal Radicals often protested the excessive investment in building new warships, their view was based on the assessment that the extent of German naval expansion was exaggerated or unclear, rather than on their disagreement with the importance of Britain's maritime superiority.[146] Furthermore, most Radicals eventually accepted foreign secretary Edward Grey's policy toward the European continent, which was based on strict realpolitik principles, because they could offer no convincing alternative.[147]

Hence, except for a few pacifists, the majority of the cabinet did not advocate for the peace-creating effects of trade. As Edward Grey pointed out, embracing the pacifist view (the one most clearly endorsed by Norman Angell, himself a Labour Party member of Parliament) was premature when one considered the nature of international politics on the Continent.[148]

Conclusion

Britain's decision to avoid compound containment in dealing with the German challenge was determined by the structural constraints imposed by the availability of alternative trade partners. Since Britain could not find other states that could substitute the role of Germany in its economy, and Germany could find alternative trade partners, diminishing trade with Germany would have inflicted greater harm on Britain than on Germany. Thus, both a number of influential Unionist leaders and the Liberal Party that was in power beginning in 1906 promoted the extant free trade policy as the best choice for Britain, and avoided complementing military balancing with restrictive commercial measures.

CHAPTER 4

US Compound Containment of Japan, 1939–1941

By 1939, the expansion of the Japanese empire, which began with China in the early 1930s, reached Southeast Asia. Japan was propagating the creation of "the New Order" in Asia (often called the Greater East Asia Co-prosperity Sphere), a political-economic entity dominated by Tokyo's military and economic preeminence that excluded foreign influence in the East Asian region.[1] This vision of a new regional order went beyond mere political propaganda. Although weaker than the European great powers, Japan achieved by the late 1930s the only significant concentration of power in Asia. As Britain and France encountered Nazi Germany's aggression in Europe, their military presence in the Asian sphere of influence diminished dramatically. The Soviet Union was also focused on the developments and opportunities on its European front, paying only scant attention to the Far East. Under these conditions, as Secretary of State Cordell Hull noted, Japan was embarking on a project to become a hegemon in Asia.[2]

The United States soon discovered that it was the only power that could meet the Japanese challenge. During this period, the eyes of the Roosevelt administration, both houses of Congress, and the American media were largely fixed on the deteriorating security environment in Europe. This, however, did not mean that Washington would acquiesce to Japan's southward advance, or to Tokyo's control of resource-rich Southeast Asia and the region's sea lines of communication. Preventing an East Asia dominated by one country became an important interest of the United States, a maritime power with important stakes in the Pacific.[3] Moreover, the United States was physically present in the western Pacific, still wielding sovereignty over the Philippines and other territories in the region. As chief of staff General George Marshall told his staff, "It was the policy of the United States to

61

defend the Philippines."[4] Thus, as the war in Europe was creating a power vacuum in Asia, it became obvious that the United States had to play a leadership role in filling that void.[5]

In response to Japan's bid for regional hegemony, the United States adopted military countermeasures.[6] On April 15, 1939, Roosevelt transferred the US Fleet from the Atlantic to the Pacific.[7] In May 1940, the Fleet was ordered to stay at Pearl Harbor instead of its regular base in Southern California.[8] The majority of the US naval forces remained there until 1941, even after the need to strengthen the Atlantic fleet rose.[9] Moreover, the Philippines defense was reinforced: five submarines were sent to Manila in November 1940, and by July 1941, General Douglas MacArthur was recalled to serve as the commander of American armed forces in the islands. In addition, the War Department announced that the Philippines Commonwealth armed forces were called into the service of the United States, and new long-range bombers were deployed in the Philippines.[10] After the fall of France, the funds to build a two-ocean navy were finally secured.[11] When this buildup was complete, the United States would obtain clear naval superiority in the Pacific, and join the remnants of the British and the Dutch forces in Asia to fend off Japan.

At the same time, the United States decided to impose trade restrictions against Japan, thereby putting into effect compound containment measures against that state. The crux of the US strategy toward Japan was to take a defensive stance in the Pacific and deter Japan's aggression until the war in Europe was settled. In the meantime, Washington intended to weaken Japan economically so that it could deal with Tokyo more easily once the European question was solved. Imposing restrictions on bilateral trade played an important role in achieving this strategic goal.

This chapter examines whether the US decision to adopt compound containment against Japan is consistent with my theory. If Washington carefully assessed the availability of alternative trade partners for Japan and the United States, and concluded that it was in a position to inflict more losses on Japan through commercial restrictions—because alternative trade partners were largely available for the United States but not for Japan—then my argument is corroborated by this historical case. Moreover, I examine whether domestic interest groups and leaders' ideological orientations played important causal roles in the making of the US decision to implement compound containment against Japan. This chapter concludes that the structural explanation I advance performs better than the alternative explanations in accounting for US compound containment against Imperial Japan between 1939 and 1941.

The Presence of Alternative Trade Partners for the United States

In the 1930s, bilateral trade between the United States and Japan was highly complementary.[12] One scholar went far enough to claim that US-Japanese trade was "almost entirely complementary and nearly a paradigm of classical economics."[13] Japan's major exports to the United States comprised textiles, raw silk, agricultural and natural specialties, fishery products, hat materials, used parts, housewares, ceramics, celluloid products, sun goggles, and toys. The United States sold Japan metal goods, raw cotton, oil and oil products, and machinery.[14] For the United States, Japan was the third largest export market, after only Britain and Canada, and its exports to Japan was much larger than imports.[15]

In this bilateral trade, the United States could easily find alternative trade partners with regard to its exports to Japan. As Table 4.1. shows, the

Table 4.1. Major US Exports to Japan (in thousands of dollars)

	1939	1940	1941
Total US exports	232,183	227,199	59,900
Ferrous metals			
Iron and steel scrap	32,526	16,971	-
Steel ingots, blooms, billets, slabs, sheet bars, tinplate bars	5,639	6,578	129
Iron and steel bars and rods	4,414	10,065	31
Petroleum products			
Crude oil	20,923	15,875	6,939
Gasoline	7,366	16,230	6,648
Lubricating oil	5,182	10,991	9,423
Raw cotton	42,498	29,608	6,566
Machinery and vehicles	35,504	30,261	2,574
Copper	27,566	24,621	5,072
Other metals (aluminum, brass and bronze, lead, molybdenum, nickel, zinc)	9,059	6,378	1,727
Wood pulp	1,948	7,133	1,689
Fertilizer materials	2,207	2,450	954

Source: Department of Commerce, *Foreign Commerce and Navigation of the United States*, 1940, 1942 (Washington, DC: Government Printing Office, 1940, 1942).

majority of US exports to Japan comprised raw materials or intermediate goods that were essential for the production of diverse industrial goods. All these products could find alternative export destinations because there was a high demand for metals, petroleum products, raw cotton, and machinery in major states in Europe that were preparing for or fighting a war with Germany. The goods the United States exported to Japan—especially, oil and oil products—were precisely the materials required for the production of weapons and military supplies, as well as to operate military units.[16] Moreover, as the European states converted their own manufacturing facilities for war-related production, importing US manufactured products for civilian use became very important. The passage of the Lend-Lease Act facilitated an enormous flow of diverse industrial products and raw materials from the United States to Europe, which could effectively absorb US exports to Japan when Washington decided to cut off trade with that state.[17] Further, the United States' own preparation for war required domestic stockpiling of a significant amount of metals, petroleum products, and machinery. In short, the demand for goods the United States exported to Japan was very high, and, thus, the United States was in a position to effectively divert exports away from Japan.

Meanwhile, the United States could find alternative partners for certain, but not all, imports from Japan. Most notably, raw silk amounted to 62 percent of all Japanese exports to the United States between 1937 and 1941 (in value terms), and Japanese silk satisfied almost all of the United States' raw silk demand.[18] In addition, silk was used for military purposes, especially when making parachutes and powderbags.[19] Many analysts expected that the United States could not fully replace Japanese silk with imports from others.

Nonetheless, the United States could minimize the impact of restricted access to Japanese raw silk, largely due to technological innovation. In the US textile industry, the introduction of nylon and the invention of rayon were fundamentally changing the landscape of the silken cloths and hosiery market. When these new materials fully replaced silk, the workers and factories in silk industry could easily switch to synthetic fibers.[20] Moreover, although raw silk from Japan was important for certain US companies, it could have affected only a small portion of the textile industry and retail business as a whole. In fact, silk was a luxury good, which remained inaccessible or unnecessary for many people. Thus, as a Navy Department report suggested, "Doubtless industry could manage without silk."[21]

Most other major imports from Japan could be substituted with imports from other states. For instance, imports of fish from Japan could be replaced through more trade with Canada. Hat materials could be obtained from the Bahamas or South America.[22] Moreover, many imports from Japan were consumer goods that were inconsequential to the activities of major US industries. American individuals and families, too, could simply sustain their living standards without consumer goods from Japan. One item that was not captured in the statistics on merchandise trade was Japanese gold purchased by the United States, but this gold did not have any serious impact on the performance of the industry or on the living standards of consumers.[23] Therefore, as the Roosevelt administration was informed, stopping imports of diverse goods from Japan "would not cause any great hardship in the United States."[24]

Overall, the United States could find alternative trade partners that could replace the majority of ongoing trade with Japan. While US exports to Japan were significantly larger than imports—that is, about 1.4 times larger in 1940—there was a high demand for US goods, which allowed the United States to swiftly divert exports away from Japan. Although the United States could not find alternative suppliers of raw silk from Japan, the impact of restricted access to Japanese raw silk would be sharply limited. Other goods from Japan could be obtained elsewhere. After all, although the United States obtained a large quantity of important economic inputs from East Asia before World War II, including rubber, tin, chrome, manganese, nickel, and tungsten, none of these came from Japan.[25] US officials made similar assessments. As the Export Control Administration reported to the Roosevelt administration in the spring of 1941, the United States could effectively ban imports from Japan without worrying about adverse economic consequences.[26]

The Absence of Alternative Trade Partners for Japan

In the 1930s, the Japanese economy depended heavily on a number of economic inputs from the United States, and Japan could not find alternative foreign suppliers. War in Europe made other industrialized powers and resource-rich areas of the world incapable of replacing the US sales to Japan. The United States was also in a position to organize joint economic restrictions against Japan and to pressure others to eschew overtaking its current sales to Japan. Further, Japan was unable to divert its exports that had been going to the United States.

Economic Inputs from the United States

Japan was a resource-poor country that needed to import large quantities and a wide variety of foreign goods for its economic growth. For Japan, the United States was a key provider of important economic inputs that were needed to run its factories and produce industrial goods. Between 1932 and 1939, Japan ranked as the third largest export market for the United States, and half of all US exports to Asia were destined to Japan.[27] A few categories of goods dominated US exports to Japan. As Table 4.1. shows, until the outbreak of the Pacific War, Japan's purchases from the United States consisted primarily of cotton, ferrous and nonferrous metals, machinery, petroleum products, and wood pulp.

Many of the goods Japan obtained from the United States were bottleneck items for an industrialized economy; their absence thus had large repercussions on the performance of the Japanese economy. As its industrialization continued, Japan faced a growing demand for iron and steel. Japan's steel production, nonetheless, was dependent on imported scrap, since it relied on the scrap-centered steel production method, which allowed it to produce a large quantity of high-quality steel at a lower cost.[28] Still, as a recent industrializer, Japan did not possess a large enough stock of scrap to produce steel itself, and the United States was a major source of scrap for the world. A similar situation emerged with regard to copper, magnesium, molybdenum, and vanadium.[29] Japan not only did not possess sufficient raw materials to produce these metals, but also did not have enough scrap within the country to satisfy industrial demands. Moreover, Japan was heavily dependent on US machine tools and machinery, products that were vital to maintain key industries. By 1938, the United States was supplying over 60 percent of Japan's machinery and machine tools demands, with Germany running a distant second.[30]

For Japan's textile industry, American raw cotton was a crucial raw material. As in many newly industrialized countries, the expansion of Japan's manufacturing was led by the textile industry. In the 1930s, Japan's cotton textile industry expanded to become the world's second largest, behind only the United States, and sold about half of its products in foreign markets. Japanese mills purchased American long-staple raw cotton to produce higher-quality cotton textiles or to blend the long-staple cotton with cheaper short-staple cotton from India.[31]

Finally, Japan relied heavily on the United States for its oil and oil products, obtaining from the United States about 80 percent of its fuel needs. For special oil products such gasoline, that figure rose as high as 90 percent. This dependence remained consistent largely because Japan lacked the technology, personnel, and know-how to refine high-grade gasoline from crude oil. Furthermore, unlike Germany, Japan did not possess the technology or resources to produce synthetic oil.[32] Indeed, Japan faced an overall shortage of trained technicians and cutting-edge technologies that could have helped it achieve technological innovation and become less dependent on foreign economic inputs.[33]

The Absence of Alternative Foreign Suppliers for Japan

Despite some earlier assessments, which suggested that Japan might be able to replace imports from the United States, by the autumn of 1939, it became evident that Washington could effectively deny Japan alternative trade partners.[34] Once war started in Europe in September of that year, only the United States had significant surplus metals, machine tools, and crude and refined petroleum that could be sold to a foreign country.[35] Britain, France, and the Netherlands, the three European states that controlled most of resource-rich Southeast Asia and could replace the United States in Japan's import trade, were saving resources for their war efforts and were willing to take parallel actions with the United States over trade with Japan. Resource-rich Latin American countries were expected to follow the lead of the United States. Meanwhile, Germany and the Soviet Union were reluctant or unable to expand trade with Japan.

Britain

Japan could not divert its import of metals, cotton, and oil from the United States to Britain or the British Commonwealth around the world. As World War II broke out, Britain erected controls around the "fortified sterling area" to secure its resources for war, while at the same time closely coordinating its export restrictions with the United States.[36] London also imposed controls on the export of raw materials from India and Malaya and restricted issuing export licenses in those areas.[37] In iron ore trade with Japan, Britain diminished exports from Malaya by about 40 percent. By 1941, Britain intended to further restrict the Malayan export of iron ore to Japan if the United States was prepared to do the same in the Philippines; Britain also proposed limiting the export of pig iron from India.[38] Tin and lead exports were controlled as well.[39] US controls on exports of nickel to Japan were to be coordinated with Canada, the world's leading producer of the metal.[40] Cotton exports from India were to be reduced to whatever level the United States decided to diminish its own exports.[41]

In general, Britain was not a reluctant follower of the US plan against Japan, but rather a provider of new ideas that would more effectively limit Japan's access to important economic inputs.[42] As early as January 1939, the British ambassador in Japan was leading studies on the effects of economic sanctions against Japan and sharing his findings with the US mission in Tokyo. The British government proposed, furthermore, that it would work closely with the United States and share its historical experiences if Washington decided to adopt economic restrictions.[43] In November 1940, the British cabinet's Interdepartmental Committee on Far Eastern Affairs suggested controlling the movement of the world's tanker fleet as a new tactic to affect Japan's oil stockpile. Since Japan did not have the capacity to transport large quantities of oil across oceans, this measure was expected to be particularly effective and easy to adopt.[44] Indeed, Japan could not find enough tankers to carry home even the limited quantities of oil that it secured in Southeast Asia.[45]

Britain also cooperated with the United States in limiting oil exports from the Persian Gulf to Japan. It controlled about half of all oil fields in that region, and showed willingness to support the United States.[46] As one US official observed, "Lord Halifax [the British foreign secretary] had said . . . that the British Government was prepared to regulate exports of Persian oil and to take the risk of trouble with the Shah of Persia in order to get adoption by the United States and Great Britain of a common policy in action which would make the said common policy effective."[47] Thus, from 1938 to 1940, oil export from the Persian Gulf area to Japan was "small in absolute amount and almost negligible in comparative amount."[48]

The Netherlands and France
The Netherlands Indies was the most likely destination from which Japan might search for oil if the United States imposed restrictions on its own exports. The Dutch authorities and oil companies in this region, however, were deeply concerned about Japan's southward advance for raw materials

and were reluctant to increase their petroleum sales to Japan. Japan's efforts to assure them of its benign intentions in Southeast Asia continuously failed. As one Japanese diplomat said to a US official, "The Dutch are not friendly to us."[49]

Hence, Japan could not easily replace its oil imports from the United States with oil from the Netherlands Indies. For instance, in Batavia on October 8, 1940, Japan asked for 1.1 million long tons of aviation grade crude oil, 1.15 million long tons of other crude oils, 400,000 long tons of aviation gasoline over 87 octane, and 500,000 long tons of other products. In response to these requests, the major oil producers—Standard Vacuum and Royal Dutch Shell—offered only 120,000 long tons of aviation grade crude oil, 640,000 long tons of other crude oil, 33,000 long tons of aviation gasoline over 87 octane, and 312,500 long tons of other products.[50] Moreover, the Netherlands East Indies was not a perfect substitute because they did not produce "the amount which the Japanese need and which they are trying to get from this country [the United States]."[51]

Meanwhile, the French authorities were willing to participate in restrictive economic measures against Japan. In fact, by early 1939, France had already "cut off all deliveries of iron from French Indo-China to Japan" and was requesting Britain to do the same in the Malaya.[52] France was also willing to coordinate its policy toward Tokyo with Britain and the United States in an effort to counter Japan's aggression and to prepare for war in Europe.[53] Even after the fall of France and the rise of the Vichy regime, French Indo-China showed a clear reluctance to sell large quantities of raw materials to Japan.[54]

Latin America

Japan could potentially obtain oil, cotton, and some classes of metal from the Latin American countries. However, the United States was able to coordinate restrictions against Japan with the governments in the Western Hemisphere. Washington could also exercise political pressure on the South American governments if they were to resist US export controls. For instance, it was suggested in the US State Department that "refusal to sell to Japan might be made a part of Pan-American cooperation, and a condition favorable for securing United States loans."[55] This pressure could be applied to the Brazilian cotton and Peruvian tungsten and vanadium that Japan was interested in purchasing.[56] Also, although surplus oil was available in Latin America, the United States could restrict the movement of tankers and pressure the companies that were operating oilfields, thereby denying Japan's access to those oil sources.

The Axis Powers and the Soviet Union

For Japan, Germany and Italy could have become alternative sources to obtain machinery, machine tools, and automobiles and parts.[57] This substitution was unlikely to be successful, however, first as a result of Japan's overall political relations with Germany and Italy and later because of the two countries' stockpiling of machinery and machine tools for their own war efforts. Until the signing of a formal alliance treaty among Germany, Italy, and Japan on September 27, 1940, Japan's relations with Germany were not particularly friendly. To the contrary, Japan was often at odds with Germany, especially after the signing of the German-Soviet Pact in August 1939. This agreement dismayed Japan because the Soviet Union was providing aid to the Chinese.[58] Hence, in early 1940, as Cordell Hull observed in a conversation with the British foreign secretary, Lord Halifax, "It seems that he has had information from trusted sources that the Japanese Government is frankly favorable to the Allied cause in the present European war and that the Japanese military had never had a more profound shock than when they received word of Hitler's agreement with Soviet Russia. They detest the Russians anyhow and now they have no longer any trust in Germany."[59] Under these circumstances, it was difficult to expect that Germany and Italy would serve as alternative trade partners for Japan.

Still, even after the treaty with Germany and Italy was signed, followed by the signing of the Neutrality Pact with the Soviet Union, it was difficult for Japan to expand trade with the Axis powers and to replace its imports from the United States. By September 1940, Washington was informed that an arrangement was being made to enable the transit of supplies from Germany to Japan via the Trans-Siberian Railroad.[60] If successful, this would have allowed Japan to replace certain US products with goods from Europe, and safely carry them home over land, thus evading British control over maritime transports. However, Germany maintained stringent controls on its exports as war in Europe intensified, without leaving sufficient surplus machinery and machine tools that could be sold to Japan. Indeed, instead of German sales to Japan, the possiblity of Japan supplying Germany with Southeast Asian raw materials through the Soviet Union won more attention.[61] The political agreement with the Soviets also did not have enough spillover effects on Japan's commerce with or through the USSR.[62] Controversies between Japan and the Soviet Union over territorial concessions—

the Soviet Union demanding the southern part of Sakhalin as well as several nearby islands—were difficult to resolve.[63] Notwithstanding these developments, Germany's invasion of the USSR rendered it impossible for Japan to obtain German goods through the Soviet Union.

Japan's Inability to Divert Exports to the United States

If the United States were to restrict exports to Japan, Tokyo could not easily replace those US products with goods from other countries. Potential alternative sources of raw materials and industrial products did not have a sufficient surplus of products to supply Japan. The largest producers of raw materials in Asia, the British Empire and the Netherlands East Indies, were ready to take parallel actions with the United States.[64] The preclusive buying of raw materials by the United States further drained those available for Japan.[65] Germany and Italy were too far away and did not possess enough surplus goods or the specific supplies for which the Japanese vied.

Moreover, Japan did not have alternative markets to which it could divert its exports to the United States. The war in Europe left the United States as the only country that could purchase large quantities of silk, since all other major states—countries that possessed large domestic markets and had significant consumer demand for luxury goods—were trying to save resources for their war efforts or were concentrating on war production. For similar reasons, Japan faced great difficulty in finding other countries to absorb its export of consumer goods, which comprised a significant portion of its sales in the United States.[66] Many countries were saving money for war.

Accordingly, as one US official concluded, "It is probable that Japan's present economy could not withstand the combined effects of an import and export embargo enforced by Group A and B [United States, Britain, France, the Netherlands, and their possessions in the Asia-Pacific region]. The tremendous shock which that economy would sustain from a simultaneous loss of export markets and sources of raw materials would probably necessitate immediate state control and operation of industry and trade."[67]

Outcome: Compound Containment Adopted

The presence of alternative trade partners for the United States and the absence of alternative partners for Japan endowed Washington with an ability to impose relative losses on Japan through commercial restrictions.[68] In response to Japanese aggression, the United States thus adopted compound containment measures, complementing its military balancing efforts with restrictions on trade.

By restricting commerce with Japan, Washington intended to weaken Japan so that Tokyo would become less capable of dominating Asia and disturbing supplies of raw materials moving from Asia to the United States.[69] Once the danger of Germany dominating Europe was contained, the United States would directly face Japan, aided by the British if possible. In the meantime, as one report to the State Department suggested, it was expected that "a joint embargo by the United States, British Empire countries, and the Dutch East Indies would limit the life of Japan's war efforts to the size of her stockpiles."[70] Also, while Japan needed the dollar to purchase raw materials from the world, if the United States stopped buying from Japan, Tokyo's foreign currency reserve would dry up.[71]

Table 4.2. summarizes major US decisions restricting trade with Japan. A prelude to the upcoming comprehensive economic restrictions was the "Moral Embargo" of 1938, which informally forbade selling arms, munitions, or instruments of war to Japan and China. After Japan's bombing of Chinese civilians, the Department of State announced that it would not "issue any licenses authorizing exportation, direct or indirect, of any aircraft, aircraft armament, aircraft engines, aircraft parts, aircraft accessories, aerial bombs or torpedoes to countries the armed forces of which are making use of airplanes for attack upon civilian populations."[72] The State Department also requested major oil and engineering companies stop sales or delivery of "plans, plants, manufacturing rights or technical information, or of related patents, processes, or engineering assistance" to Japan.[73] Although these "requests" were informal and asked for voluntary participation, US businesses responded favorably and followed the instructions from the State Department. For instance, the United Oil Products Company decided not to fulfill its contract with the Japan Gasoline Company for the production of high-grade fuel.[74] Many other companies took similar actions. Consequently, Japan protested that Washington was implementing a "discriminatory export embargo."[75]

The second major US action regarding trade with Japan was the abrogation, in July 1939, of the Treaty of Commerce and Navigation between the United States and Japan (signed in 1911). Abrogating this treaty had powerful consequences because it removed legal barriers for more far-reaching actions. As some in the US media observed, the abrogation was "clearing the decks for action."[76] Following the declaration of abrogation, by December 1939, the State Department introduced plans for deliberate restrictive measures against Japan.[77]

While these two measures did not induce a precipitous decrease in bilateral trade, Roosevelt's proclamation on July 2, 1940, marked the beginning of comprehensive restrictions on trade with Japan.[78] The fall of France gave the Roosevelt administration strong incentives to respond to the rapidly changing global security environment. The United States was now willing to exploit its position as the major supplier of Japan's industries.[79] Thus, as the National Defense Act gave the president authority to subject US exports to a licensing system, Roosevelt set up a powerful scheme to control many goods that were being sold to Japan. Within a year, 259 items, including petroleum products, tetraethyl lead, iron and steel scrap, machinery and machine tools, and nonferrous metals (copper, brass and bronze, zinc, nickel, potash, and articles using them) were put under license.[80] The export of most of these goods was limited to friendly nations. Further, multiagency task forces were established in early 1941 and produced evaluations of the impact of embargoing US goods on Japan's economic performance.[81] Accordingly, the United States developed a policy arrangement that could be used to wage economic warfare against Japan.[82] Japan called these policy measures a "virtual embargo" imposed against it.[83]

By July 1941, the export control system was in effect, resulting in a sharp decrease in US trade with Japan.[84] Applications for the export of wood pulp,

Table 4.2. Major US Economic Actions against Japan

1938	June 11	"Moral embargo" on export of aircraft, armaments, engine parts, accessories, aerial bombs, and torpedoes
1939	July 26	Washington announces termination of the 1911 US-Japan Treaty of Commerce and Navigation, effective January 26, 1940
	December 15	Moral embargo expanded to include molybdenum and aluminum
	December 20	Equipment and information relating to the production of high-quality aviation gasoline added to the embargo list
1940	January 26	US-Japan Treaty of Commerce and Navigation abrogated
	July 2	Adoption of National Defense Act. Congress gives the president authority to subject US exports to a licensing system
	July 26	Restrictions placed on the issuance of export licenses for aviation motor fuel and lubricating oil, tetraethyl lead, and heavy melting scrap
	October 16	All exports of iron and steel scrap to Japan restricted
	December 10	Restrictions on export of iron and steel products
1941	January 10	Export of copper, brass and bronze, zinc, nickel, potash, and semimanufactured products made from these materials put under export license
	July 26	President freezes Japanese assets in United States

Source: Mira Wilkins, "The Role of U.S. Business," in Dorothy Borg and Shumpei Okamoto, eds., *Pearl Harbor as History: Japanese-American Relations, 1931–1941* (New York: Columbia University Press, 1973),p. 372.

metals and manufactures, machinery and vehicles, rubber and manufactures, and chemicals and related products (except certain pharmaceuticals) were denied. Although raw cotton was not included on the control list, its monthly export to Japan diminished to about $600,000 during the first six months of 1941, from the $4 million monthly average of 1938.[85]

In petroleum products, although a significant amount of oil continued to be sold to Japan, the US government issued directives and revoked a number of specific and general licenses in order to limit its export to Japan. On April 8, 1941, the Division of Control withheld processing export licenses for crude oil, lubricating oil, and gasoline.[86] The State Department also recommended placing containers for petroleum products, in particular steel drums, under license, so that Japan would be unable to carry home US-produced oil.[87] A Petroleum Coordinator for National Defense was designated to facilitate interdepartmental cooperation on oil exports to Japan.[88] Thus, total Japanese procurement of American petroleum and petroleum products declined from 33.2 million barrels in 1938 to 29.9 million barrels in 1939, 24.9 million barrels in 1940, and 12.6 million barrels in the first seven months of 1941. Japan's total stockpile of oil also declined from 51.4 million barrels in April 1939 to 49.6 million barrels in April 1940 and to 48.9 million barrels in April 1941.[89] By August 1941, all licenses for the export of petroleum products were revoked, except for those governing sales in the Western Hemisphere, to the British Empire, Egypt, Netherlands Indies, unoccupied China, and the Belgian Congo.[90] During the summer of 1941, a powerful and comprehensive control agency, the Economic Defense Board, was established, chaired by Vice President Henry Wallace.[91]

US restrictions on trade with Japan climaxed with the freezing of Japanese assets in July 1941. By this measure, Japan lost its ability to buy from the United States, and could no longer sell goods on the US market.[92] By mid-September 1941, a de facto, full-scale embargo against Japan was in place. Together with ongoing military balancing efforts, these commercial restrictions constituted comprehensive compound containment measures against Japan.

Alternative Explanations

In addition to my argument, this chapter also examines the two alternative theories that focus on domestic interest group politics and leaders' convictions, respectively. For the domestic interest theory to demonstrate that its causal mechanism is at work, the commercial groups that benefited from trade with Japan would have to be shown to have tried to protect their interest in the decision-making process of the US government. Although they might have failed to affect the national decision to employ compound containment, those interest groups, according the domestic interest theory, would have actively protested the adoption of more stringent economic measures or at least tried to protect their vested interests. In order for the ideological orientation argument to be supported, the United States would have to be shown to have adopted restrictive economic measures against Japan because US leaders did not uphold beliefs in the pacifying effect of trade, and instead had convictions about economic punishment. The evidence that lends support to these claims, however, is insufficient.

Commercial Interests as "Patriots"

Contrary to the expectations of the domestic interest-based explanation, commercial interest groups were invisible or largely irrelevant in the making of the Roosevelt administration's decision to adopt compound containment against Japan. First, when the US government considered imposing restrictions on trade with Japan to complement military measures, business groups that traded with Japan did not actively defend their economic stakes. Instead, as many historians agree, those who might suffer economic losses actively supported restrictive US policies rather than being vocal about their interests.[93] Of note, when the relationship with Japan deteriorated in 1939, American businessmen who benefited from flourishing trade with Japan in the 1930s "not only became champions of preparedness, but . . . argued that their leadership was indispensable in preparing America for war."[94]

Second, the relationship between the US government and American economic interests was close to a two-way interaction, rather than reflecting a bottom-up process. In implementing restrictive commercial policy, State Department officials contacted and dissuaded American firms from doing more business with Japan. In turn, US business leaders consulted with the government on whether they should proceed with ongoing contracts with Japan. For instance, when Japan attempted to purchase steel worth $11 million from the United States Steel Company for construction in Manchukuo, J. P. Morgan and Company on its behalf contacted State

Department officials to inquire about the opinion of the US government.[95] Similarly, the Mesta Machine Company, producing steel works equipment, consulted the State Department to find out whether the US government was imposing or considering embargoes.[96]

These developments suggest that the business groups were not simply moved by economic interests alone. Instead, the position of commercial interest groups was in important part determined by security considerations. In other words, American business groups acted as if they were "patriots," rather than seekers of profit.

The Impact of Leaders' Belief

According to the alternative explanation, which focuses on leaders' convictions, a decision to adopt compound containment reflects key decision-makers' beliefs about the role of economic instruments in great power competition. In the US-Japan case, however, evidence suggests that US leaders did not have any serious convictions about the ability of economic tools to shape the targeted state's behavior.

First, there are reasons to doubt whether the United States believed that economic restrictions were useful tools in changing Japan's behavior. Instead, historical records suggest that the embargoes were aimed at weakening Japan rather than coercing it. In January 1939, in the aftermath of the "moral embargoes" against the Japanese aggression in China, one official suggested, "It is believed that nothing short of defeat in war would, within the foreseeable future, 'get Japan out of China.' But the objective of the measures contemplated is not to 'get Japan out of China,' as desirable an accomplishment as that would be. The objective is to prevent Japan from consolidating her position in China and drawing sufficient strength therefrom to allow for further aggressive action in other fields which would seriously menace our interests and probably lead us to war."[97] Ambassador Grew also denied that "anything short of force can lead to substantial moderation of Japanese policy in China," and he could not "therefore . . . conscientiously recommend to his Government recourse to economic sanctions."[98] In the summer of 1941, the prevailing view among decision-makers was that tougher sanctions could weaken Japan and give the United States a military advantage, rather than being effective in changing Japan's thinking.[99]

Second, Washington did not tell Tokyo that economic restrictions were imposed because of Japan's bad behavior. If US leaders believed that economic restrictions would be useful in shaping Japan's behavior, Washington would have conveyed to the Japanese government the idea that trade restrictions were being adopted to punish certain behavior. It would have lucidly communicated with Japan what it wanted. This was not the case when the United States imposed embargoes on iron and steel scrap, machine tools, and oil, the three most important items Japan obtained from the United States for its industrial performance. The United States did not clearly convey its demand to Japan or Japanese diplomats and businessmen directly or indirectly.

In fact, throughout 1940, when Japan protested unfair treatment by the United States, the State Department answered that the new controls did not aim to punish Japan's behavior in Asia.[100] For instance, when the United States imposed controls on all kinds of iron and steel scrap exports in September 1940, Japan protested by stating "the Japanese government finds it difficult to concede that this measure was motivated solely by the interest of national defense of the United States. . . . In view of the fact that Japan has been for some years the principal buyer of American iron and steel scrap, the announcement of the administrative policy, as well as the regulations establishing license system in iron and steel scrap cannot fail to be regarded as directed against Japan, and, as such, to be an unfriendly act."[101] To this, the Department of State responded, "It having been found by the appropriate agencies and authorities of this Government that the restrictions on exportation to be effected by the regulations under reference are necessary in the interest of national defense, the Government of the United States perceives no warrantable basis for a raising of question by any other government, in the circumstances—not of this Government's making—which prevail today in international relations, with regard to the considerations which necessitate the adoption by the Government these measures of conservation."[102] Secretary of State Cordell Hull also told the Japanese ambassador that "it was only at the height of our national defense preparations that we were imposing a few embargoes on important commodities."[103] Similarly, with regard to machine tools, the US government told the Japanese representatives that restrictions on those items were imposed for national defense.[104] When the United States imposed comprehensive restrictions on oil, Japan was told that "the additional restrictions on exports of petroleum products are being put into effect because of the defense needs of the United States."[105] An oil shortage on the East Coast was another explanation that the United States offered to Japan in imposing a tighter embargo on oil.

These points suggest that US leaders not only lacked convictions about the pacifying effect of trade, but in general dismissed the overall idea of using economic tools to shape another state's behavior. For US leaders, commercial restrictions were imposed to reinforce military containment policy. They were largely designed to weaken Japan's ability to launch military aggression.

Conclusion

The United States adopted compound containment measures against Japan, combining military counterbalancing policies and restrictive commercial measures. Through these measures, the United States intended to create a military stalemate and, at the same time, weaken Japan's capacity to dominate East Asia. As my theory suggests, the presence of alternative trade partners for the United States and the absence of alternative partners for Japan allowed the United States to inflict relative losses on Japan through diverse restrictive measures on bilateral trade.

CHAPTER 5

US Compound Containment of the Soviet Union, 1947–1950

The Soviet Union emerged from World War II as the single significant concentration of power in the international system aside from the United States.[1] Despite some expectations of a cooperative postwar relationship, the two powers soon found themselves on a collision course. Expansion of the Soviet sphere of influence in Eastern Europe, communist encroachment in the Middle East, Greece, and Turkey, and the growing assertiveness of the Kremlin provoked a response from the United States to draw a clear line that the USSR should not cross.[2] Joseph Stalin also recognized that the Soviet Union was confronting animosities of what he referred to as the "Anglo-American bloc."[3]

By 1947, a strategy of containment was being formulated in Washington, although the United States was still reluctant to be directly involved in Eurasian affairs.[4] The Truman Doctrine and the National Security Act of 1947 began to lay the institutional foundation for an all-out Cold War confrontation. Moreover, the Truman administration decided to expand the army from its existing 542,000 personnel to 790,000 by June 1948, and purchase 1,165 new aircraft. The number of active navy combat ships was to be increased to reach 280 by June 1947.[5]

Emerging military containment policy soon had repercussions in bilateral commerce. During World War II, significant commercial ties emerged between the United States and the USSR, mainly based on the Lend-Lease agreements. By September 1945, the Lend-Lease aid reached $11 billion. The Soviets also benefited from US credits for trade, and expected that further aid and loans would follow after the war.[6] In the immediate aftermath of World War II, moreover, the USSR needed considerable imports from the United States in order to rebuild or further develop its iron and steel, coal, chemicals, and transport industries and power plant installations.[7] The Soviet Union was also obsessed about "catching up" to the advanced economies' technological superiority, which required continued exchanges with the leading US companies and technicians.[8] Further, the USSR had demands for industrial goods that would help to build a strong industrial foundation for the military.[9] As George Kennan observed in 1946, the Soviet leaders "view international trade for themselves a means of increasing Soviet strategic economic strength and of achieving economic independence."[10] Although its ultimate goal was to create an autarchic economic bloc, the Soviet Union needed US economic inputs for a protracted period of time.[11]

Between 1947 and 1950, the United States effectively employed compound containment measures by severing major trade with the Soviet Union. Diminishing commercial exchanges served as the economic equivalent of military balancing, and the strategy was expected to help curtail the Soviet Union's economic gains and to delay further growth of its military power.[12] This chapter examines whether the configuration of alternative trade partners for the United States and the Soviet Union convinced the United States that it could impose relative losses on the USSR by abandoning bilateral trade and, in turn, led Washington to adopt compound containment. It finds evidence in support of my theoretical claims. This chapter also examines whether domestic interest groups and leaders' beliefs played prominent roles in US decisions concerning compound containment.

With regard to the economic policies that complemented military containment during the early Cold War period, many have focused on the European Recovery Program (the Marshall Plan).[13] Instead, this chapter explores Washington's decisions on trade ties with the Soviet Union, adopted to complement military endeavors against the USSR. If the Marshall Plan aimed to strengthen Europe's position as a counterweight against Soviet expansion, severing major trade was expected to weaken the Soviet Union's economic basis of military power. While the USSR refused to join the Marshall Plan, it nonetheless wanted to retain trade ties with the United States to facilitate its industrial development. Abandoning trade ties with the Soviet Union started as a US initiative.

One might argue that, considering its unmatched power in the immediate aftermath of World War II, the United States did not care much about its own losses in imposing trade restrictions to complement military balancing. Contrary to this perspective, this chapter shows that Washington thoroughly assessed its ability to impose relative losses on the USSR through restrictions on trade before adopting compound containment measures.

The Presence of Alternative Trade Partners for the United States

During the early Cold War period, the United States could easily find alternative trade partners for both its export and import trade with the Soviet Union. By the end of World War II, the majority of trade between the United States and the Soviet Union comprised the United States exporting diverse industrial products to the Soviet Union. Although the Soviet Union's imports from the United States were small in quantity, reaching only $150 million in 1947, over two-thirds of this trade consisted of machinery and vehicles—goods that were important for the USSR's postwar reconstruction and further industrial development.[14] In the immediate aftermath of World War II, US goods were in high demand by all major countries around the world. Thus, the United States could easily divert its exports away from the Soviet Union to other foreign markets, and, accordingly, export-related losses were not an issue of concern for Washington in considering commercial restrictions against the USSR.

In contrast, several economic inputs imported from the Soviet Union and its satellites had significant ramifications for the US economy. Major US imports from the USSR included chrome, fur, manganese, and platinum group metals.[15] Among these, a change in the trade of nonferrous metals could have had significant implications for the US economy because they were used for steel production. Especially, while manganese was the essential material in turning iron into steel, the United States purchased most of its manganese from the Soviet Union. Since steel was the sinew of a modern economy, being an essential product for heavy industries, manufacturing, and construction sectors, disturbances in steel production would have generated significant spillover effect and might have weakened the economy as a whole. The import of fur had a negligible impact on the US economy, except for the business of certain firms.[16]

The United States, however, could find alternative foreign suppliers of diverse metals that could replace those from the USSR. It also established ad hoc committees to investigate and facilitate the substitution of metal imports from the Soviet Union with imports from other states. For manganese, India became the primary target for diverting the Soviet imports. The

Union of South Africa, Cuba, the Gold Coast, and Mexico were other sources where the United States could purchase diverse nonferrous metals. Major US steel producers, such as United States Steel and Bethlehem Steel, also increased investment in Brazil to replace the import of manganese ore from the Soviet bloc.[17] In 1949, the Interdepartmental Manganese Coordination Committee reported that, during 1949, while shipments from the USSR had become negligible, the United States could obtain 1.4 million tons of manganese against an industrial requirement of about 1.6 million tons.[18] For chrome, the Philippines replaced the Soviet Union as the largest supplier to the United States.[19] Since economic inputs imported from the USSR could be obtained through trade with other states, the United States would not encounter any significant losses if Washington restricted trade with Moscow. In short, because alternative trade partners were widely available, the United States could effectively minimize its own losses from restricted trade with the USSR.

The Absence of Alternative Trade Partners for the USSR

In 1947, US officials determined that trade partners capable of replacing the United States as a provider of diverse industrial products were largely unavailable to the USSR. Since most other industrialized states were recovering from the war, it was expected that no country could expand production and replace the United States as a supplier of machinery, vehicles, and other industrial products for the Soviet Union. The United States, moreover, was in a position to establish a coordinated control scheme with the potential alternative suppliers of industrial goods.

Limited Supply of Equivalent Goods in the Postwar Environment

During the first few years after the end of World War II, there was simply no state that could replace the United States as the supplier of important industrial products, if Washington were to stop exporting its machinery and industrial equipment to the Soviet Union.

First, while they were recovering from the war, other industrialized states did not possess sufficient surplus products to take up US sales to the Soviet Union. In Britain, France, West Germany, and Japan, domestic demand for machinery and industrial products was enormous. Those goods were needed to rehabilitate their own factories and rebuild the infrastructures and cities, and no country but the United States had large amounts of surplus goods for export. For instance, US officials determined that the Soviet Union wanted to purchase diesel and electric locomotives, precision instruments, cranes, machine tools, electricity-generating equipment, blast furnaces, machinery for mines, and refineries from the West.[20] However, as the Ad Hoc Subcommittee of the Advisory Committee of the Secretary of Commerce reported, "It is probable that at the present time much of this equipment cannot be obtained elsewhere in the desired qualities and quantities, if at all."[21] Although Western Europe was selling a small quantity of industrial products to the Eastern bloc, it was expected that the industrialized economies would not be able to expand their sales and replace the United States because "Western Europe is already selling all that it can produce currently. It cannot increase exports of complex equipment rapidly."[22] In short, at least in the near term, the Western bloc countries were unable to increase the production of machinery and equipment equivalent to those made by the United States. As a result, other countries could not serve as a replacement provider of goods to the USSR.

Second, the USSR had difficulty exploiting its newly acquired sphere of influence in Eastern Europe to obtain goods for industrial development. Before World War II, compared with the relatively backward Russia, Eastern European countries achieved significant industrial development. East Germany before division was also part of the most advanced economy in Europe. If these countries had their industrial centers well preserved, they could have become major suppliers of machinery and equipment to the Soviet Union.[23] Yet, ravaged by the war, the industrial capability of Eastern European countries to supply for the USSR was significantly limited.[24] Moreover, by 1947, the USSR had already stripped Romania, Hungary, Bulgaria, and Finland, as well as East Germany, by forcing them to pay reparations.[25] Meanwhile, the Soviet Union could not simply continue exploiting the East European countries. As a leading international banker noted in late 1947, the Soviet Union was having trouble "trying to hold" Eastern Europe together economically because it could not meet the economic needs of the region.[26] Since Europe was being divided into two camps, the USSR had to organize its own economic bloc rather than simply extracting resources from the states under its control.[27]

Moreover, Germany's industrial core was the Ruhr-Rhine area, located in the western part of Germany and administered by the United States and

Britain. It would not serve as a source of supplies for the USSR. When the Soviets demanded plants and equipment from the western zone, the United States denied shipment of industrial reparations from that area. As Secretary of State James Byrnes made clear, the United States was determined to adopt a "First Charge Principle," which prioritized German productivity increases to pay for Western imports, rather than replying to Soviet reparation demands.[28]

Third, with regard to some bottleneck items for industrial development, the USSR could not replace its US imports because the United States possessed a technological and managerial advantage unmatched by other industrialized countries. Soviet leaders, including Stalin, recognized that the machinery made by the United States was qualitatively superior, though expensive, and they wanted to maintain access to US machinery, which began under the Lend-Lease arrangements.[29] Furthermore, as long as building highly mechanized mass-production factories was a central goal of the Soviet Union's economic development programs, access to US machinery, technology, and entrepreneurial skill was needed. The United States was where the "Fordist" modern manufacturing system, a model that the Soviets wanted to mimic in their factories, originated.[30] Thus, as a representative of AMTORG, the Soviet state trading company in the United States, stated in 1947, the Soviet Union was eager to sustain friendly relationships with major US firms.[31] Leading US companies such as General Electric reported to the Department of State that the USSR wanted to sign contracts even when they imposed stiffer terms, as instructed by the Department, because the Soviets wanted the most advanced products, which were only available from the United States.[32]

The Establishment of a Coordinated Control Scheme

The United States, at the same time, was in a position to derive cooperation and support from other industrialized states in denying the USSR's access to machinery and industrial equipment. A number of states in Western Europe had the potential to reemerge as suppliers of advanced industrial products once they recovered; if these states regained industrial vigor, they could become alternative partners for the USSR in certain products. Furthermore, while the United States was helping the recovery of many states, the possibility of transshipment and resale of the US European Recovery Program aid to the Eastern bloc became an important issue of concern.[33] Thus, the United States needed to persuade Western Europe to employ similar restrictive measures against the Eastern bloc. As the Policy Planning Staff suggested, "We must face the bitter fact that in present circumstances any increase in the economic strength of the Soviet Union and the satellite countries will be used to oppose, rather than to promote, the interests of real European recovery, unless some compulsion operates in the other direction."[34]

The United States started negotiations with the Western European countries, which eventually resulted in the formation of the Coordinating Committee for Multilateral Export Controls (COCOM) and the adoption of a common control list. Talks with the European states about the need for export controls began based on a bilateral framework, starting from the meetings with the British and expanding to negotiations with France, the Benelux countries, Denmark, Austria, and Norway. States such as Italy, Greece, Turkey, Ireland, Iceland, and Portugal were not taken seriously because they were not capable of replacing US exports to the USSR.[35] After a series of bilateral exchanges, the negotiations began to take a multilateral form, led by tripartite meetings between the United States, Britain, and France.[36] In these meetings, a common control list gradually emerged, although Britain and France presented the "Anglo-French list," which was less restrictive than the US list and hence induced frictions with Washington.[37] Nonetheless, by late 1949, the United States, Britain, France, Italy, the Benelux countries, and Denmark agreed on a tentative common control list, establishing an informal regime to monitor East-West trade. The consultative groups were also created for joint policy making and execution. In late 1950, the member countries agreed to adopt the control list proposed by the United States.[38]

Two developments helped the United States to attain a formalized multilateral arrangement and substantiate the denial of the Soviet Union's access to important industrial goods. First, observing the USSR's growing aggressiveness, a general consensus emerged among the West European states that agreeing on a common export control scheme was needed to enhance their security.[39] Intensifying Cold War tensions throughout 1948 and 1949 pressed the Europeans to follow the US lead. As British diplomats asserted at a meeting of the Organization for European Economic Cooperation in January 1949, it was seen as imperative for Western Europe to take a similar course of action with Washington and to delay the Soviet Union's building up its military power.[40] Outbreak of war on

the Korean peninsula in June 1950 and materializing fear of Soviet military aggression in Europe consolidated Western European thinking about
the need for trade controls.[41]

Second, based on its unique leadership position after World War II,
the United States set directions for common control policy at important
junctures.[42] In the meetings with British and French delegates, US representatives continuously persuaded the European states to adopt a list as
extensive as that of the United States, moving the negotiation forward
when it might otherwise have faced an impasse.[43] Once the Economic
Cooperation Administration established offices in the European countries to implement the Marshall Plan, its officials regularly asked the governments of participating countries to abide by the US embargo lists.
They also made requests to immediately terminate existing contracts with
Eastern Europe for commodities that were directly related to the Soviet
Union's military buildup.[44] Moreover, when neutral states' trade with the
Soviet bloc was creating disharmony among the Western countries,
inducing strong French protest in particular, the United States actively
negotiated with the neutrals to join the West.[45] Further, while West Germany's legal status for multilateral negotiations was not fully established,
the United States observed its own control list and imposed strict restrictions on West German exports to the Eastern bloc.[46]

In this process, domestic pressures in the United States pushed the
Truman administration and Western Europe to develop a common control scheme on trade with the Eastern bloc.[47] In particular, the US Congress exerted strong pressures on the White House to disallow any European recipient of the Marshall Plan aid from exporting goods to a
nonparticipating country of the Marshall Plan. Through legislations such
as the Mundt Amendment, the Foreign Assistance Act of 1948, the Export
Control Act of 1949, the Kem Amendment of 1951, and the Battle Act of
1951, both the House and the Senate forced the Truman administration to
pressure the European allies to adopt control measures as stringent as
those of the United States.[48] The US government might have mediated
these overt pressures on Western Europe, but the European countries
nonetheless acknowledged the seriousness of the US concern, sometimes
expressing resentment at the breaching of their sovereignty by the political leaders in Washington.[49]

In sum, in the immediate aftermath of World War II, the Soviet Union
was not in a position to replace its US imports with goods from other coun-

tries. Other industrialized countries were incapable of or unwilling to capitalize on US restrictions of its own exports, and the United States and its allies came up with a common control scheme. Even though Western Europe's trade with the Eastern bloc continued, the size of trade eventually diminished during the 1947–1950 period.[50]

Outcome: Compound Containment Adopted

The availability of alternative trade partners for the United States and the absence of alternative partners for the USSR enabled the United States to implement compound containment measures by restricting ongoing commercial exchanges. Such restrictive policies were expected to inflict relative losses on the Soviet Union's economic strength, and at the same time to complement the developing military containment strategy. As Adler-Karlsson observes, the main purpose of US restrictions on trade with the Soviet Union was to improve US power superiority vis-à-vis the Soviet Union.[51]

Until 1947, the United States was committed by treaties and trade agreements to treat the Soviet bloc countries as most-favored nations and not to engage in discriminatory practices.[52] Those arrangements included the Treaty of Friendship, Commerce and Navigation with Poland signed in 1931, the Treaty of Friendship, Commerce and Consular Rights with Finland of 1934, a Reciprocal Trade Agreement with Finland of 1936, the Treaty of Friendship, Commerce, and Consular Rights with Hungary of 1925, the Treaty of Commerce with Serbia of 1881 (currently in effect with Yugoslavia), the General Agreement on Tariffs and Trade currently in force with Czechoslovakia, the Provisional Commercial Agreement with Romania of 1930, reinstated in March 1948, and Commercial Agreement with the USSR of 1937.[53] Of note, the 1937 agreement with the Soviet Union was still in effect and contained the provision that exports from the United States to the USSR would "in no case be subject to any rules or formalities other than or more burdensome than those to which the like products may be subject when consigned to the territory of any third state."[54] Other policy arrangements over trade such as the Lend-Lease program were not extended because their terms were applicable only during wartime.

The United States started to reconsider its trade relations with the USSR by 1946. In January 1946, when the Soviet Union showed interests in purchasing surplus US properties, the US ambassador in Moscow, Averell Harriman, warned Washington that "our Government should not make any more isolated economic arrangements with the Soviets until we have an over-all understanding with them about outstanding economic matters."[55] The United States also refused to provide loans to the Soviet Union to purchase American goods, while it provided similar credit to the British.[56] In the spring of 1947, the Truman administration announced that it would retain the comprehensive system of export controls that was adopted during World War II, in order to concentrate on assisting the Western European countries.[57] In July 1947, President Truman signed the Second Decontrol Act that gave to the executive the authority to maintain controls on materials that could be utilized for US foreign policy purposes.[58] This legislation allowed for a very flexible interpretation, permitting "virtually unlimited control over all shipments we may decide to place under license."[59]

Later in 1947, the United States made important decisions that eventually resulted in the severance of trade ties with the Soviet Union. In autumn 1947, Secretary of Commerce Averell Harriman started reviewing trade policy toward the Soviet Union and Eastern Europe. This review led Harriman to advocate the virtual cessation of trade with the Soviet bloc, and make a proposal to the National Security Council to take all necessary measures to prohibit export of important commodities to that region.[60] Harriman's advocacy for trade restrictions was reinforced by the USSR's refusal to join the European Recovery Program, and by the suspicion that grew following the formation of the Cominform by the Soviet Union.[61] By November 1947, as the Policy Planning Staff observed, "There is general agreement that it is not desirable for U.S. merchandise or technology to go forward, directly or indirectly, to the Soviet Union or its satellites, where these shipments would increase Soviet military potential or operate to the detriment of the European recovery program."[62]

In November 1947, Harriman submitted a paper to the NSC that became the framework of the US approach on trade with the Soviet bloc:

> The National Security Council therefore considers that U.S. national security requires the immediate termination, for an indefinite period, of shipments from the United States to the USSR and its satellites of all commodities which are critically short in the United States or which would contribute to the Soviet military potential. This result, however, should be achieved if possible without any overt act of arbitrary discrimination against the USSR and its satellites.

The National Security Council therefore recommends, in the interests of economic recovery, world peace, and, in turn, U.S. national security, that Europe, including the USSR, and such affiliated areas as the Secretary of State may designate, should be declared a recovery zone to which all exports should be controlled. Exports to any country in this zone should be permitted only when (a) the country furnishes adequate justification for its requirements, (b) European recovery and world peace are served thereby, and (c) the position of the United States is not adversely affected.[63]

In this statement, it was evident that US trade controls targeted the USSR and its sphere of influence. US officials were well aware that the Soviet Union would not satisfy the three conditions. Still, Washington wanted to legitimize its decisions and deny any propaganda advantage to Moscow, while also avoiding blame that it was responsible for the division of Europe. Hence, by designating all of Europe as a "recovery zone" and obliging all European countries to provide detailed economic data if they were to import from the United States, Washington intended to mask overt discrimination against the USSR. At the same time, these conditions were expected to contribute to removing potential legal and practical loopholes in the control scheme.[64] Moreover, since the goods that the United States sold to the USSR mainly comprised industrial products that were at least partly related to the industrial basis of military power, controlling commodities "which would contribute to the Soviet military potential" meant that the United States would restrict most, if not all, of its sales to the USSR.

In December 1947, President Truman approved Harriman's proposal to the NSC with only minor revisions.[65] He ordered the Commerce Department to implement what was to be called the "R" procedure, which intended "to provide for export license control of all shipments to Europe and dependent territories, which are regarded as a recovery area."[66] As the NSC director Sidney Souers observed, the "R" procedure theoretically achieved "total control of shipments to Eastern Europe without apparent discrimination."[67]

The decision by the NSC was soon translated into powerful regulations. In mid-January 1948, the Department of Commerce announced that, starting in March, all US exports to Europe were required to obtain individually validated licenses.[68] The controls were to be imposed expediently and extensively. On March 9, 1948, the Department of Commerce reported that, with regard to the goods that were under its authority, "all shipments to the USSR and satellite countries, regardless of whether or not the goods concerned are in scarce supply in the United States, have been subject to individual licensing since March 1."[69] The export control scheme proved to be very effective, as confirmed by US chiefs of missions in the Eastern bloc countries.[70] In April 1948, the licenses issued for Eastern European destinations amounted to $1,435,200 worth of goods, of which $1,323,000 was for shipments by relief agencies, while licenses for commercial exports amounted to only $116,574. This was a dramatic decrease in commercial exchanges, since in the previous year average monthly exports to the same destination were $27,115,000 and nearly all of them were commercial in character.[71] Hence, a number of officials concluded by April 1948 that the United States was effectively imposing a virtual embargo on exports to the Eastern bloc.[72]

The United States also strengthened institutional frameworks to support export control. In 1947, an ad hoc subcommittee, chaired by the Commerce Department, was established to assist restrictions on exports to the Soviet bloc, under the interdepartmental Advisory Committee on Exports (renamed Advisory Committee on Requirements in 1948). On March 10, 1948, the Truman administration assigned the ad hoc subcommittee the task of making recommendations for the establishment of an organization that would orchestrate peacetime economic measures against the Soviets.[73] The Technical Steering Committee, comprising officials from the Departments of Defense, State, Commerce, and Agriculture and the Central Intelligence Agency, was also ordered to present a comprehensive list of items that were to be controlled.[74] Further, legal basis for export control was strengthened by 1949. While the Truman administration's decision in December 1947 relied on the Second Decontrol Act, the Export Control Act of 1949 gave the Department of Commerce greater authority to control goods "that were likely to make a significant contribution to the military potential of the Communist country for which it was destined."[75] By 1950, as the Department of State noted, the US export control system that was in effect was comprehensive and restrictive.[76]

The US objective in severing extant trade ties with the Soviet Union was to "inflict the greatest economic injury to the USSR and its satellites," so that commercial restrictions could effectively complement military balancing.[77] It was expected that Washington could effectively "minimize the damage to the United States and the Western Powers."[78] Thus, starting in 1947, the United States imposed restrictions on most exports to the Eastern bloc. Also, as Michael Mastanduno points out, US officials believed that Soviet industrial potential could not be separated from its military potential, and they consequently refused to distinguish between the two. In their view, export controls "must be broad and deep enough to affect the entire production complex of the Soviet state."[79] This implied that the United States was determined to deny Soviet access to American goods even when those goods were only marginally related with the military.[80] By 1950, US compound containment measures were fully in place against the Soviet Union.

Alternative Explanations

Considering the rich historical literature on early Cold War period, the US-USSR case allows a thorough examination of the two alternative explanations. First, if the commercial interest group argument were correct, there should be evidence of extensive debates and clashes between different societal groups, and the groups and individuals who had stakes in continuing trade with the Soviet Union should have tried to defend their interests when the US government contemplated commercial restrictions against the USSR. Those interest groups would have failed to influence governmental decisions to adopt compound containment because they were less influential than other groups that wanted to sever trade ties. Even if these economic interests were small in number, they would have competed with the more powerful groups, at least to have their voices heard. Second, for the ideological orientation argument to prove that its causal mechanism was at work, US leaders should be shown to have dismissed the pacifying effect of trade, and believed that economic punishment was the better economic option. Neither of these two claims, however, is well substantiated by the evidence of the early Cold War. No significant domestic interest group that benefited from trade with the Soviet Union endorsed trade with the USSR and pressured Washington to eschew compound containment. US leaders also did not advocate beliefs about US ability to affect the Soviet Union's course of action through economic means.

The Absence of Domestic Pressure to Preserve Trade Ties

During, and in the immediate aftermath of ,World War II, there were powerful advocates for trade with the Soviet Union. For many US officials and entrepreneurs, including Secretary of Commerce Henry Wallace and the president of the United States Chamber of Commerce, Eric Johnston, the USSR was the perfect destination for American industrial and consumer goods, and it was expected that the two countries would easily construct a complementary economic relationship. Furthermore, as the Russian Economic Institute of New York noted in December 1944, "The Soviet Union represents potentially the largest market the world ever saw." Russia's potential as a market was viewed as so great that it might be able to mitigate the economic downturn that was expected to follow the postwar demobilization.[81] Leading US companies such as Chase National Bank, Dupont, General Electric, International Telephone and Telegraph, Radio Corporation of America, Warner Brothers, and Westinghouse were actively engaged in trade with the Soviet Union. They continued to receive orders from the USSR in 1946, and by the end of that year approximately fifty US companies held technical assistance agreements with the Soviet Union.[82]

However, when the Truman administration began to reconsider trade ties with the Soviet Union, these economic groups did not try to advance their interests or pressure the government. Instead, many commercial interests publicly opposed trading important items with the Eastern bloc or openly supported export controls that were being adopted by the administration.[83] For instance, representing about two thousand firms that were engaged in international trade, Joseph Sinclair, secretary of the Commerce and Industry Association of New York, testified that "most foreign traders recognized the necessity for a continuation of export controls under present international economic and political conditions, although, with the exception of a few who have actually profited as a result of such controls, American exporters believe that export licensing should be instituted and maintained only when absolutely necessary to carry out our international commitments and for the political and economic security of the country."[84] Major companies that traded heavily with the Soviet Union also chose not to oppose the embargo, in order to avoid the risk of being charged with "trading with the enemy."[85] As Dresser Industries stated in 1947, the prevalent position of the business community was that "if accepting further business from those people is inimical to the over-all interest of the United States, then we do not want any part of such business."[86]

Further, while Congress bombarded the administration with pleas to impose more stringent measures against trade with the Soviet Union, no noticeable voice representing economic interests in East-West trade was heard.[87] Indeed, bipartisan support emerged for the Truman administration's restrictions on exports.[88] Under these circumstances, business groups had to be sensitive to the rising public anticommunist sentiments, and they refrained from challenging export controls that were being considered by the administration. In short, there is little evidence that supports the causal mechanism of the domestic interest argument, because the process of interest groups competing with one another was absent in the first place.

The Limited Impact of Liberal Convictions in Trade

During the last days of World War II, influential figures in the United States expressed strong convictions about the ability of economic exchanges to shape the Soviet Union's future behavior. For some US officials, trade with the USSR would establish peaceful relations between the two countries while also establishing "a model for the other countries in the world."[89] For instance, Alexander Gerschenkron emphasized that the United States should incorporate the Soviet Union into the world economy to avoid political friction and to reconstruct world trade.[90] Further, between 1945 and 1946, building more economic ties was often viewed as a useful way of weakening the Soviet Union's control of Eastern Europe.[91]

In this context, one might argue that the belief in the role of economic exchanges led the United States to employ two forms of economic statecraft to shape the Soviet Union's behavior during the early stage of the Cold War: (1) positive economic inducements by proposing the USSR to join the Marshall Plan, and (2) negative sanctions by imposing restrictions on exports. These two propositions, however, are not well supported empirically. US policies over trade with the USSR did not in fact build on the convictions in the ability of economic exchanges to induce pacifist behavior from the Kremlin.

First, the sincerity of inviting the USSR to the European Recovery Program was dubious. Before George Marshall's famous speech in June 1947, the United States was stipulating a European economic federation without assuming the participation of Eastern Europe, and it expected that incorporating the USSR might paralyze US efforts to stabilize Europe.[92] Later, US officials feared that potential Soviet participation would be for more "destructive than constructive purposes."[93] Indeed, the proposal to the Soviets to join the Marshall Plan in part aimed to avoid the blame that the United States was responsible for the division of Europe.[94] In the unlikely event of the Kremlin joining the European Recovery Program, the United

States would be able to weaken the USSR's control over its European satellites.[95] In short, offering the European Recovery Program was not an economic "carrot" to affect Moscow's behavior. Thus, it is difficult to conclude that US leaders reached out to the Soviet Union because of their belief in the pacifying effect of economic exchanges.

Second, the United States did not expect that restricting exports would be effective in shaping the behavior of the Soviet Union. In fact, the United States did not say what Soviet actions it intended to punish, and recognized that economic sanctions would not be able to coerce the Soviet Union.[96] As the Office of International Trade Policy of the State Department reported, economic tools would not change the behavior of the Soviet Union because "Its population has long been accustomed to a low standard of living. It also has an autocratic government that can see to it that low living standards are maintained and human, as well as natural, resources are utilized in the interests of state planning objectives."[97] Instead, the aim of US export control was to make the Soviet Union weaker, as was suggested in the same report: "It is true, however, that by a system of controls the western world can retard the rate at which the Soviet Union continues industrial development and thereby augments its aggressive war potential. This is precisely the policy that is now being followed by the United States."[98]

Conclusion

The Truman administration decided to employ compound containment measures against the Soviet Union by severing bilateral trade ties because the United States could impose relative losses on the USSR through commercial restrictions. The United States' ability to divert trade away from the USSR and the Soviet Union's inability to replace its American imports created the condition for such a decision. By imposing almost complete restrictions on exports, the United States intended to delay the USSR's economic growth as well as its military buildup.

CHAPTER 6

Fluctuations in US Response to the Soviet Union, 1979–1985

This chapter presents a comparative examination of two successive US administrations' decisions on compound containment against the Soviet Union. The previous chapters demonstrated how the presence or absence of alternative trade partners constrained a reigning state's compound containment decision regarding a challenging state. However, one can still suggest that my analysis does not effectively take into account important factors that need to be addressed to demonstrate the robustness of my arguments. For instance, one can argue that, although Chapters 4 and 5, respectively, examined the US responses to Japan and the Soviet Union, these chapters do not account for the different attributes of the two challenging powers that might have affected the reigning state's decision. To tackle this issue, I examine how variations in the availability of alternative trade partners for the reigning and challenging powers during a short period of time have resulted in the reigning state's different decisions with regard to the same challenging state.

By the end of 1979, the United States encountered a resurgent threat from the Soviet Union, which marked the beginning of the "New Cold War." The Carter and Reagan administrations responded to the Soviet challenge by strengthening military countermeasures, both internally and externally. At the same time, each of the two presidents found the need to reconsider the commercial ties with the Soviet Union that had been established during the détente of the 1970s. However, the two administrations differed in the employment of compound containment measures.

During this period, US-USSR trade was dominated by US export of grains, which mostly comprised feed grains for livestock herds.[1] Grains were bottleneck items in the Soviet economy, and Brezhnev and Andropov intended to utilize imported US grains for their ambitious program of increasing Soviet meat consumption and labor productivity.[2] For this program, ensuring a stable supply of foreign grains was essential. Moreover, grain trade was seen to have security implications as well. As Deputy Secretary of Defense W. Graham Claytor observed, "The Soviets are making special demands on their economy to support their forces. . . . Poor agricultural production is a particularly heavy burden for the Soviet leadership."[3] The United States also exported industrial products to the Soviet Union, including machinery and equipment, chemicals, and crude materials. Nonetheless, these goods together constituted about 21 percent of US exports to the Soviet Union in 1981, and their share continuously decreased until 1985.[4] Meanwhile, Soviet exports to the United States, which mainly comprised raw materials, were very small in quantity.

Thus, in assessing the availability of alternative trade partners and the decision to employ compound containment, this chapter mainly focuses on grain trade, although it does not dismiss US exports of diverse industrial products—including high-technology products—and imports from the USSR. I analyze whether the two US administrations' assessment of the US ability to inflict relative economic losses on the USSR diverged because they had different views about the availability of alternative trade partners for the United States and the USSR. I also examine whether the alternative explanations that focus on domestic interest group politics and leaders' belief better account for the US decisions regarding the Soviet Union.

One potential criticism must be addressed from the outset. As is widely acknowledged today, the Soviet economy started to stumble beginning at least as early as the latter half of the 1970s.[5] This might suggest that the Soviet Union by the late 1970s was indeed a declining power rather than a potential regional hegemon, which would imply that this case does not satisfy the scope condition of my theory. In retrospect, however, the USSR remained a formidable security challenger for the United States until the mid-1980s. Thus, the US response to the USSR during the latter stages of the Cold War can be taken as a case in point to investigate a reigning power's use of compound containment strategy against a challenging power.

Carter's Decision to Adopt Compound Containment, 1979–1980

In December 1979, the détente between the United States and the Soviet Union was decisively undermined by the military intervention of the USSR in Afghanistan. Having suffered criticism for its lack of response to Soviet military assistance in Angola, Ethiopia, and South Yemen, as well as in Central America, and having watched the Soviet deployment of SS-20 intermediate range missiles in Europe, the Carter administration finally implemented a major revision of its strategy toward the Soviet Union.[6] The United States intended to utilize both military and economic measures in confronting Soviet aggression. On the military side, Washington formally recognized the Middle East–Persian Gulf area as a region of crucial security interest, and declared that "the Persian Gulf shall have highest priority for improvement of strategic lift and general purpose forces in the Five Year Defense Program."[7] Consequently, the Rapid Deployment Joint Task Force was established in March 1980, and the United States strengthened local capabilities to counter Soviet advancement.

At the same time, commercial links with the USSR that were established throughout the 1970s became a target of revision for the Carter administration. The United States expected that bilateral trade contributed to the Soviet Union's economic vitality and, by extension, its military capability. Imposing restrictions on bilateral trade could thus transform military balancing into compound containment.

The Presence of Alternative Trade Partners for the United States

The Carter administration concluded that the United States could easily find alternative trade partners that could replace the Soviet Union both in imports and in exports. By the mid-1970s, major US imports from the Soviet Union included petroleum and petroleum products, nonferrous metals, and metalliferous ores and metal scrap.[8] From January to November of 1979, in nonagricultural imports from the Soviet Union, gold bullion accounted for $442 million, palladium for $56 million, ammonia for $50 million, nickel for $16 million, platinum for $14 million, titanium for $13 million, and chrome ore for $12 million.[9]

The Carter administration determined that alternative trade partners for imports from the Soviet Union were readily available. As the Secretary of Commerce Philip Klutznick observed with regard to importation from the USSR, "It is very small, and it has been comprised of things like metals which can generally be found elsewhere."[10] Moreover, the United States did not rely on manufactured products from the Soviet bloc—mainly clothing, textiles, and shoes—and could easily replace these imports from the USSR with goods from other states. As one US official observed, "American consumers have expressed little demand for Eastern manufactured goods that are usually inferior to Western quality."[11]

At the same time, Washington anticipated that the United States could effectively divert its exports—especially, grain exports—away from the Soviet Union. While most of the US grains exported to the Soviet Union were feed grains for livestock, it was expected that the world's growing meat demand would easily consume surplus feed grains from the United States. Moreover, there was a strong belief in the United States that, as one of the world's largest producers of diverse grains, the United States could exercise substantive influence over the flow of grains around the world. Some went far enough to suggest that the United States was an "OPEC of grain," with "potentially more control over world food supplies than Saudi Arabia has over oil."[12] Thus, it was argued that the United States could easily manipulate international trade of grains, most notably by resetting the price, and thereby minimize the losses of American farm industry.[13] For the United States, redirecting international movement of grains was expected to absorb most US grain exports to the USSR, although Washington needed to invest some resources to build warehouses that could temporarily stockpile the grains that were originally destined to the Soviet Union.

The Absence of Alternative Trade Partners for the Soviet Union

The Carter administration also assessed the availability of alternative trade partners for the USSR. Considering the nature and broader economic implications of extant US-Soviet trade, this implied that the US government carefully examined whether Moscow could replace its imports of grains and high-technology products from the United States once Washington decided to impose restrictions. The United States expected that no foreign country would be able to replace its position in the Soviet Union's procurement of foreign supplies.

First, the Carter administration concluded that the Soviet Union would be unable to find alternative sources to replace US grains. By 1979, the United States was supplying approximately 83 percent of Soviet imports of coarse grain and 65 percent of its imports of wheat. After a poor harvest in 1979, Moscow was expected to import about 35 million tons of grain, and 25 million tons were to be purchased from the United States.[14] Washington expected that it could restrict the Soviet Union's access to foreign grains because no country was considered capable of replacing the United States' exports. In the process leading up to Carter's imposition of grain embargoes, the Agriculture Department reported to the president that no other country had the productive capacity to replace US grain exports to the Soviet Union.[15] Secretary of Commerce Philip Klutznick also confirmed that "grain exports to the Soviet Union are an area in which the United States possesses considerable leverage. It would be difficult for any other nation to effectively supply the Soviet's near term grain needs, even if we did not have the cooperation which most other supplier nations have now promised us."[16]

At the same time, other grain-exporting countries assured Washington that they would not capitalize on US restrictions on its grain exports. After a conference with the representatives of Australia, Canada, the European Community, and Argentina on January 12, 1980, the United States stated that "there is general agreement among the export representatives here that their Governments would not directly or indirectly replace the grain that would have been shipped to the Soviet Union prior to the actions announced by President Carter."[17] This agreement was interpreted as implying that all major grain exporters agreed to cooperate in order to achieve "our common purpose."[18] Consequently, according to Under Secretary of the Department of Agriculture Dale Hathaway, "Under the most extreme conditions, the USSR will be able to import no more than 26 million of the 35 million they apparently had hoped to import from all sources. And our best estimate is that even with the minimum operation, they will get no more than 22 million metric tons."[19] From the US perspective, no other measure was as costly to the Soviet Union as the imposition of grain embargoes.[20]

Second, the Carter administration concluded that other advanced economies would not take advantage of the United States in supplying high-technology exports. Indeed, in response to Carter's plan to deny the Soviet Union access to important industrial products, US allies committed themselves not to capitalize on US actions or to increase sales of the items that the United States intended to ban. British and Canadian governments promised to adopt tighter restrictions on high-technology exports to the USSR. Japan supported US measures by promising not to agree on new joint development projects with the Soviet Union. President Giscard d'Estaing of France assured Carter that French firms would not supply the high-technology goods the United States cut off. West German chancellor Helmut Schmidt also articulated the need for solidarity in the West and agreed not to replace US exports to the Soviet Union.[21] Accordingly, at the inception of Carter's imposition of trade restrictions against the USSR, it was expected that the United States could effectively deny alternative partners to the Soviet Union in important trade domains.[22]

Outcome: Compound Containment Attempted

As it was expected that the Soviet Union would suffer relative losses, the Carter administration employed compound containment measures by imposing restrictions on most important dimensions of commerce with the USSR. In the 1970s, US administrations since Nixon had continuously relaxed controls on exports, although trade arrangements between the United States and the Soviet Union were often challenged by Congress.[23] The new economic measures by the Carter administration were thus reversing the trajectory of increasing economic exchanges between the two countries that had begun in 1972.

In grains trade, the United States decided to withhold delivery of 17 million tons from the 25 million tons contracted for 1979 and 1980, shirking its commitment to the 1975 grain agreement.[24] By extension of the grain embargoes, phosphate—used as fertilizer—exports were also banned. These measures directly targeted Brezhnev's and Andropov's programs to enlarge Soviet meat consumption and labor productivity, since restrictions on grain exports were expected to cause a "distress slaughter" of Soviet livestock herds.[25] In high-technology trade, the Commerce Department first froze all existing licenses for export to the Soviet Union and stopped processing new license or renewal requests in January 1980, which was soon followed by more stringent export guidelines in March 1980. Under the new control policies, the United States adopted a "no exceptions" approach, which implied that the United States would no longer allow exceptions for US firms to evade the Coordinating Committee (COCOM) control list. By September 1980, only 281 of the 476 suspended licenses had been reinstated, and the extent of control expanded to "process know-how to militarily relevant industrial sectors" in the Soviet Union.[26]

Overall, trade between the two powers, which reached $4.5 billion in 1979, plummeted to $2 billion in 1980.[27] US economic measures against the USSR, adopted side by side with a military balancing policy, were intended to inflict significant damage on the Soviet economy, and complement ongoing military counterbalancing efforts. The main objective of the grain embargo was to deprive the Soviet Union of the goods that were needed for its livestock herds, as well as to damage its food industry and the diet of the population.[28] Stringent controls in high-technology exports aimed to constrain Moscow's access to the Western technology that was believed to help the Soviets save resources for technology development. These technology controls were planned to remain effective even if the Soviet Union changed its short-term behavior.[29] In the 1979–1980 period, the Carter administration responded the resurgent Soviet challenge with compound containment measures.

Reagan's Decision to Avoid Compound Containment, 1981–1985

The Reagan administration came to office committed to rebuilding US military superiority and containing and reversing the expansion of the Soviet Union.[30] After becoming president, Reagan acknowledged that the Soviet economy "was a basket case, partly because of massive spending on armaments," and suggested, "I wondered how we as a nation could use these cracks in the Soviet system to accelerate the process of collapse."[31] Reagan's first directive on national strategy explicitly stated that the United States would make serious efforts to force "the USSR to bear the brunt of its economic shortcomings, and to encourage long-term liberalizing and nationalist tendencies within the Soviet Union and allied countries."[32] Thus, against the resurgent threat of Soviet aggression, the Reagan administration not only accelerated a military buildup, but also envisioned cutting off economic ties with the Soviet Union. By doing so, it intended to push the USSR to the breaking point.[33]

Despite this pledge to implement both military and economic countermeasures against the Soviet Union, the Reagan administration shirked from adopting restrictive measures over the most important aspect of US trade with the Soviet Union. With the lifting of the grain embargo in April 1981, US grain exports to the USSR were restored to pre-Afghan sanctions levels, while in high-technology products the size of trade remained miniscule and the Carter administration's control measures remained effective.[34] Reagan refused to reimpose the embargoes on grain that comprised the majority of US trade with the Soviet Union, contradicting his own security policy toward the USSR.

In contrast to the Carter era, the Reagan administration believed that the United States could not effectively divert trade away from the Soviet

Union, while the USSR could find alternative trade partners. The United States was not in a position to inflict relative losses on the Soviet Union through trade restrictions.[35]

The Absence of Alternative Trade Partners for the United States

For the United States in the 1981–1985 period, alternative trade partners meant states that could absorb its current exports of grain and high-technology products and minimize its own losses if Washington decided to impose trade restrictions. In 1981, the Carter administration's grain embargoes against the Soviet Union's invasion of Afghanistan provided a good baseline against which the Reagan administration could evaluate the United States' position with regard to the availability of alternative export destinations.

Through the experience of post-Afghanistan sanctions, the Reagan administration concluded that the United States could not effectively divert its grain exports away from the Soviet Union. In the process leading up to Carter's grain embargo, optimism about the United States' ability to manipulate international grain trade was widespread. This confidence, nonetheless, soon proved to be misguided. The US farm industry could not easily find alternative export destinations, and grains destined to the USSR had to be stored in warehouses. These developments exerted a significant financial burden on US agriculture industry, and, as Reagan stated, American farmers were "made to bear alone the burdens of this policy [grain embargoes] toward the Soviet Union."[36] In 1981, the Reagan administration recognized that the United States did not possess as much influence over international grain trade as it wished, and calculated that imposing a new grain embargo against the Soviet Union would cost the Treasury at least $3 billion in payments to farmers in compensation.[37]

Although high-technology exports were significantly smaller than grain exports, the situation was similar. As noted in a series of hearings in Congress, international competition in high-technology industries was fierce. By 1981, there were a number of developed economies around the world—especially, Western Europe and Japan—and these states produced many high-technology goods that were equivalent to goods made by US firms. Thus, for US high-technology products to be diverted away from the Soviet market, US companies had to prevail in a competition with foreign firms on an increasingly competitive global market. This competitive advantage, however, was difficult to attain, and the United States was likely to lose its high-technology exports to the Soviet Union and the Eastern bloc when Washington decided to impose export restrictions.[38]

Thus, the Reagan administration was aware that economic measures complementing military balancing entailed costs for the US economy, in forms of additional federal spending and loss of an export market.

The Presence of Alternative Trade Partners for the USSR

At the same time, the United States in 1981 recognized that alternative trade partners existed for the Soviet Union. Reagan officials believed that Carter's post-Afghanistan sanctions of 1980 were a failure, mainly due to the presence of alternative trade partners for the Soviet Union. As Table 6.1 shows, between 1979 and 1980, exports from Britain, West Germany, France, Japan, and Italy to the Soviet Union increased, while those of the United States decreased precipitously. The Soviet Union could easily find alternative trade partners, and even US allies were willing to take up the slack.

In particular, the Reagan administration believed that the United States could not effectively control the flow of grains into the Soviet Union from other states. During the sanctions of 1980, the Soviet Union took steps to reduce reliance on US grain and diversify its grain imports. In the 1979–1980 crop year, for example, Argentina exported 7.6 million tons of grain to the Soviet Union, and in July 1980 the two countries concluded an agreement to trade 4.5 million tons of corn, sorghum, and soybeans annually for the next five years. Brazil also increased grain sales to the Soviet Union, signing a five-year agreement to provide soybeans, soya oil, and corn. Not only the South American countries, but also Australia, Canada, and the

Table 6.1. Western Exports to the Soviet Union, 1979–1982 (millions of dollars)

Country	1979	1980	1981	1982
Britain	891	1,058	871	620
West Germany	3,619	4,373	3,394	3,870
France	2,005	2,465	1,865	1,559
Japan	2,443	2,796	3,253	3,893
Italy	1,222	1,267	1,285	1,499
US	3,616	1,513	2,431	2,613

Source: IMF, Directions of Trade Yearbook, 1983, in Michael Mastanduno, Economic Containment: CoCom and the Politics of East-West Trade (Ithaca, NY: Cornell University Press, 1992), p. 233.

European Community countries, withdrew or reconsidered their support of the grain embargo by late 1980.[39] In May 1981, Ottawa went further and concluded an agreement with Moscow to sell a minimum of 25 million tons of grain over the next five years.[40] Overall, according to one US estimate, the Soviet Union was able to import a total of 31 million tons of grain from alternative partners, which was only 2.5 million tons less than it had planned to import prior to the Carter administration's embargo.[41]

The United States found out that, as long as alternative partners existed for the Soviet Union, grain embargoes would not only be ineffective but would also hurt the United States more than the Soviet Union. Indeed, it was reported that Soviet diversification efforts resulted in the US loss of the Soviet market. During the eight years before the embargo of 1980, the United States supplied between 55 and 75 percent of Soviet grain imports, but after 1980 one-third or less was provided by the United States.[42] As Reagan stated in early 1981, the grain embargo "was not having the desired effect of seriously penalizing the USSR for its brutal invasion and occupation of Afghanistan. Instead, alternative suppliers of this widely available commodity stepped in to make up for the grain which would have been normally supplied by U.S. farmers."[43]

In addition, the Reagan administration also recognized that the USSR had alternative partners in high-technology trade.[44] Since coming to office, the new administration considered technology control an essential measure to weaken the Soviet Union. Officials believed that denying Soviet access to advanced technologies would affect its military capability directly by blocking it from achieving technological breakthroughs, and indirectly by rendering it costlier to invest in the military. Given that multiple advanced economies emerged in the 1970s, US measures to limit technology transfer to the Soviet Union had to be reciprocated by others, especially Western Europe and Japan.[45]

However, cooperation from allies was difficult to attain, and US companies were losing due to unilateral controls. For instance, James Giffen, president of Armco International, testified that Armco and the Nippon Steel Corporation lost a contract worth $353 million to build a specialty steel mill in the USSR to a French competitor after the Carter administration's Afghanistan sanctions. Caterpillar Tractor Company also lost a contract worth $90 million to a foreign firm.[46] As was pointed out in the Senate, many high-technology products were "readily and competitively available from other places in the world," and by restricting export of those goods, "we were depriving American manufacturers from having access to those markets."[47] Different views on the geopolitical competition with the Soviet Union, disagreements about the security implications of East-West trade, and the increasing economic power of Western Europe as a unit were suggested as causes of disagreement between the United States and its allies.[48]

The problem of alternative partners in high-technology trade was compounded by Western Europe's decision to participate in the pipeline project to purchase Soviet natural gas. While the United States was against exporting pipeline equipment that could have spillover effects on the Soviet Union's military production, the Western European states were determined to proceed with the project as planned. The United States had only limited leverage in affecting the development of the project because, as the Office of Technology Assessment pointed out, "with few exceptions, adequate quantities of the energy equipment sought by the USSR are produced and available outside the United States, and the quality of these foreign goods is generally comparable to that of their U.S. counterparts."[49] Pressuring its allies with negative incentives was not an attractive option, since that policy could induce more losses for the United States by introducing frictions among the NATO countries. Indeed, when the United States imposed extraterritorial pipeline sanctions on the affiliates of US firms in Western Europe, British, French, and German leaders were infuriated and the EC formally protested the US decision as "unacceptable interference in its sovereign affairs."[50]

Outcome: Compound Containment Avoided

Despite its promulgation of competitive military policies against the Soviet Union, the Reagan administration did not adopt serious compound containment measures. Considering the composition of bilateral trade and the implication of this trade for the USSR's overall economic performance, the most important goods were grains, which accounted for about 80 percent of all US sales to the Soviet Union between 1981 and 1985. In fact, corn and wheat alone constituted two-thirds of all US exports to the USSR, and they were to be used for the Soviet Union's economic reform program.[51] Thus, in evaluating whether compound containment was adopted or not, one should focus on the decision on grain trade with the Soviet Union.[52]

In this important trade, the Reagan administration refused to reimpose embargoes and decided to continue existing export policy. On July 30, 1982, the United States extended the 1975 grain agreement with the Soviet Union for one year, and in October 1982, Reagan announced that the Soviets would be allowed to purchase up to 23 million tons of grain.[53] Even though limiting food supplies could be the most effective economic tool that the United States could wield to weaken the Soviet Union, the presence of alternative grain suppliers for the USSR and the absence of alternative trade partners for the United States constrained Washington's ability to inflict relative losses on Moscow.

In high-technology trade, the United States contemplated strengthening domestic and international control schemes. Nonetheless, while the United States successfully strengthened domestic controls over high-technology trade, it soon encountered difficulties because of strong resistance from other advanced economies. Even though the United States first expected that it could force allies to stop supplying important equipment and know-how to the Soviet Union, especially those for the ongoing pipeline project, it soon turned out that the Western European countries would choose to blame the United States rather than conceding to Washington's demand. Those countries also criticized the United States for refusing to pay its own price by continuing grain trade.[54] Consequently, as Martin Feldstein, chairman of the Council of Economic Advisors, pointed out, by pressuring other advanced economies to adopt more stringent control measures, "We were hurting the allies and ourselves."[55] Observing that embargoes on high-technology pipeline equipment resulted in US losses and controversies within NATO, on November 13, 1982, President Reagan lifted the sanctions against US allies. Even though the Reagan administration took technology control very seriously, the United States had no choice but to maintain extant policy arrangements when it lacked an ability to inflict relative losses on the Soviet Union.

Since the United States did not cut off the majority of trade with the USSR, it can be safely concluded that compound containment was avoided during the Reagan era. The massive military buildup program launched by the administration and the president's open animosity toward the USSR were not complemented by policies designed to diminish major trade with the Soviet Union.

Alternative Explanations

Comparing two US administrations' responses to the resurgent Soviet threat gives us an opportunity to evaluate the validity of two alternative explanations as well. One alternative explanation suggests that commercial interest groups that benefited from trade with the Soviet Union would try to defend their economic interests by pressuring the government to eschew compound containment. In this approach, the adoption or avoidance of compound containment of the Soviet Union should reflect the success or failure of those commercial interests in influencing governmental decisions, as well as their competition with other societal groups. For the other alternative explanation that focuses on leaders' beliefs, compound containment measures against the Soviet Union should be outcomes of decision-makers' convictions in economic instruments. The evidence that supports these alternative explanations, however, is limited.

Domestic Interest Group Politics

For the Carter administration, domestic economic interests did not have a significant impact on the decision to impose commercial restrictions against the USSR.[56] In particular, commercial groups that traded heavily with the Soviet Union did not actively defend their interests. During his campaign for a second term, Carter was prepared to accept losing some electoral support from farm states by adopting grain embargoes. Still, a rising patriotic tide made farm lobby groups endorse rather than protest the president's economic measures.[57] For instance, major farmers' organizations, including the Farmers Union and the Farm Bureau Federation, announced their tentative support of the embargo.[58] Also, as one congressman from a farm state suggested, the loss of profit from foreign sales was expected to be compensated by setting the price more realistically at home. In this view, the grain embargo and the profit of farm states were not necessarily mutually exclusive.[59]

In lifting the grain embargo, the Reagan administration justified the decision by arguing that only American farmers were losing, without penalizing the USSR.[60] In fact, Reagan promised to remove the grain embargo during the presidential campaign in order to garner support from farm states, and this promise constrained Reagan's decision when he came to office. Thus, the Reagan case might buttress the domestic interest theory, which treats the activities of interest groups as decisive. Still, it needs to be noted that Reagan was at first reluctant to lift the grain embargo in March 1981. He was well aware that such a decision would disappoint large political groups and supporters who wanted the United States to become more

assertive against the Soviets, especially after the brutal suppression of pro-
testers in Poland.[61] Further, relaxing export controls directly contradicted
Reagan's own agenda in the security realm. Hence, Reagan officials sometimes appealed to an ostensible logic that selling grains would drain the
Soviet Union's hard-currency reserve.

The presence of alternative trade partners for the Soviet Union was a
crucial fact that enabled the Reagan administration to solve the conflict
between its military and economic policies toward the USSR. At the same
time, the claim that only US farmers were losing from grain embargoes—
due to the presence of alternative grain producers—allowed Reagan to
avoid the criticism that he was captured by parochial domestic interests. In
other words, even though the farm interests played an important role in
Reagan's decision to maintain grain exports, the logic I set forth was
embraced by the Reagan administration when it actually made decisions on
commerce with the USSR. Thus, the theory I advance can subsume the
domestic interest explanation in this particular case.

Leaders' Belief

The other alternative explanation, which emphasizes leaders' convictions in
economic engagement or punishment, is not convincing. Regarding post-
Afghanistan sanctions, the Carter administration did not uphold beliefs in
the ability of economic measures to shape the USSR's behavior. Indeed,
leaders in the Carter administration did not expect that the United States
could coerce the Soviets to leave Afghanistan through economic measures.[62] Instead, economic restrictions were adopted to weaken the Soviet
Union's material capacity, however marginally. Thus, it is difficult to view
the post-Afghanistan sanctions as policies reflecting beliefs of key decision-
makers in the Carter administration.

Reagan officials also did not embrace the idea of pacifying effect of continuing trade when they lifted restrictions on grain trade with the Soviet
Union. If there were an idea that powerfully affected US strategic behavior
during the Reagan era, it was the firm belief in the difficulty of shaping the
Kremlin's behavior through peaceful means. Indeed, the idea of unstoppa-
ble Soviet aggressiveness was the rationale underlying Reagan's military
buildup against the USSR.

Conclusion

This chapter compared US responses to the reemerging Soviet threat during the Carter and Reagan administrations. This period offers an opportunity to observe how US compound containment measures with regard to the USSR changed during a short period of time, while controlling for the effect of diverse confounding factors. Consistent with my theory, variations in the availability of alternative trade partners for the United States and the Soviet Union constrained Washington's decision on compound containment.

CHAPTER 7

The Absence of US Compound Containment against China, 2009–2016

During the Obama administration, with the declaration of "pivot to Asia," many of the most capable US military units concentrated in the Middle East or mobilized for the war on terror were redeployed to East Asia.[1] The United States also increased investments in its ability to project forces across the Pacific.[2] Moreover, Washington made careful efforts to revamp its alliance system in Asia, while building foundations for closer security cooperation even with its former adversaries such as Vietnam.[3] These developments could be interpreted as an incipient form of military containment of China, although it was still unclear whether Washington would take more dramatic military countermeasures against Beijing.[4]

Meanwhile, the United States continued to be China's major trade partner and actively supported China's participation in the global economy. After the United States backed China's accession to the World Trade Organization in 2001, trade in goods between the two countries skyrocketed from $121 billion in 2001 to $365 billion in 2009 and $578 billion in 2016.[5] The United States also actively endorsed China's ascendance to the center of international processing trade. Indeed, China became one of the most trade-dependent powers in the world, whose trade-to-GDP ratio reached as high as 53.2 percent (on average) between 2010 and 2012.[6] Moreover, China retained its position as the world's largest exporter and second largest importer of merchandise.[7] Analysts suggested that expanding exports directly contributed to China's growth by increasing income and rationalizing production and, indirectly, by stimulating domestic consumption, investment, and government spending. The central role occupied by Chinese firms in the global processing trade and imports from advanced economies also aided China by enhancing productivity and advancing technology development.[8]

Focusing on the period of the Obama administration, this chapter examines whether my theory of compound containment can account for this coexistence of military balancing and cooperative economic policies in the United States' response to a rising China. I concentrate on the US response to the Chinese challenge since the late 2000s because only during this period did China become the world's second largest economy and the United States actively reinforce its major combat units against China. Simply put, I view that the United States' relations with China before 2009 do not meet the scope conditions of my theory because the Chinese economy was still smaller than the Japanese economy and the United States was militarily bogged down in the Middle East.

It needs to be noted that an assessment of the US ability to employ compound containment measures against China is bound to be truncated or even flawed. Almost all quantitative data and primary sources that allow a direct test of my argument against the US experience vis-à-vis China are classified or proprietary information of private companies.[9] A more certain evaluation might also require sophisticated simulations in order to accurately calculate the expected loss to the United States from restricting trade with China, but a reliable simulation model is not publicly available yet.[10] Most importantly, documents that reveal US leaders' actual belief, debate, and decision-making processes in dealing with China will remain inaccessible for the next several decades.[11]

Accordingly, this chapter has modest goals. It examines government reports, academic writings, and data and indices that are widely used by economic analysts in order to assess whether the United States and China could find alternative trade partners when Washington imposed restrictions on bilateral trade during the 2009–2016 period. Then I explore how the relative availability of alternative trade partners could be linked to the Obama administration's refusal to impose serious restrictions on trade with China despite its evolving military counterbalancing efforts.

One might suggest that this chapter should examine the Trump administration's "trade war" with China. For some observers, Trump's commercial pressures against China can be interpreted as an incipient form of compound containment measures. Nonetheless, I do not focus on this commercial conflict mainly because it is unclear whether Trump's restrictive economic measures against China constitute compound containment where economic restrictions aim to weaken the targeted state's material capacity to launch military aggression. Instead, they entail elements of economic diplomacy that attempts to change the targeted state's economic policy, rather than military and strategic behaviors. Moreover, despite Trump's emphasis on strengthening the US military, it is dubious whether the United States indeed reinforced internal and external balancing measures against China. In addition, while there is no publicly available direct evidence to substantiate or disprove my theory and the two alternative explanations, the unique attributes of the Trump presidency make it difficult to rely on secondary sources. Since President Trump deliberately distanced himself from US foreign policy establishments, experts, and the media, it is difficult to suggest that observations offered by foreign policy analysts or even former officials accurately represent the administration's strategic thinking. This book does visit the Trump administration's relations with China in the concluding chapter, where policy lessons for the United States are offered.

The Likely Absence of Alternative Trade Partners for the United States

In interindustry trade (trade between states that have different industrial compositions, such as the trade between China and the United States), a large portion of bilateral commerce in effect entails exchange of factors of production or tasks.[12] From the mainstream trade economists' perspective, when US manufacturers trade intermediate or final goods with their Chinese subsidiaries or subcontractors, that transaction entails importing Chinese labor or tasks.[13] Similarly, when the United States obtains Chinese final consumer goods for wholesale and retail, the United States in effect is purchasing Chinese factors of production or tasks.[14] Considering major US manufacturing and retail/wholesale industries' massive purchase of Chinese economic inputs—and their productivity and competitiveness gains vis-à-vis powerful foreign competitors—there is good reason to conclude that, during the 2009–2016 period, the United States could not effectively replace the role of China in its economy through trade with others. Accordingly, the United States was likely to encounter a large loss in terms of overall economic performance were it to restrict trade with China abruptly.

Inputs from China: Chinese Labor/Tasks and Their Implications for the United States

US Manufacturing Industries' Use of Chinese Economic Inputs

Since the entry of China's massive labor force into the global economy, the US manufacturing sector has heavily purchased Chinese economic inputs in the forms of labor and tasks performed by China's large industrial clusters. Between 1990 and 2011, while the proportion of US manufactured imports from the Pacific Rim countries in its overall manufactured imports changed only slightly from 47.1 percent to 46.1 percent, China's share in this trade increased from 3.6 percent to 25.3 percent.[15] A large portion of these increased imports from China entailed the US manufacturing industries obtaining labor and tasks from China. Analysts pointed out that the United States' purchase of Chinese inputs started with low-value-added consumer goods such as apparel, cloths, and other miscellaneous manufactured commodities, but these were soon overtaken by advanced technology products, most notably communication equipment, computers, and other electronics.[16] By concentrating final or intermediate assembly in China, which is rich with low- and semiskilled labor, the US manufacturing industry could elaborate its competitive advantage and contribute to the overall economic efficiency of its home country.[17]

An assessment of available quantitative and qualitative data reinforces the view that the US manufacturing industries' massive purchase of Chinese labor and tasks was a central feature of bilateral commerce during the 2009–2016 period. Table 7.1 summarizes major goods imported from China, the percentage share of those goods in all US imports from China, and what portion of those items were produced by US firms' partners or subsidiaries in China.[18] An important pattern is observed in this data: advanced technology products comprised the largest portion of US imports from China, but many of those products were goods made by US firms in China. Indeed, the more technologically advanced the imported products were, the more likely it was that they were produced by US firms' initiatives in China. Moreover, on average, more than 90 percent of US manufacturing industries that imported from China produced goods through their subsidiaries or partners in China between 2008 and 2016.[19] In short, US firms in the manufacturing sector extensively utilized Chinese economic inputs by 2009.[20]

Table 7.2 compiles specific examples of major US manufacturing indus-

Table 7.1. Related Party Share of Major US Imports from China

	2009		2011		2013		2015	
	% of Imports	Related Party	% of Imports	Related Party	% of Imports	Related Party	% of Imports	Related Party
Computer equipment	14.6%	64.0%	16.5%	58.2%	14.2%	53.2%	11.9%	56.3%
Communication equipment	7.8%	48.6%	9.5%	44.5%	12.9%	46.6%	13.4%	35.7%
Women's apparel	5.3%	2.3%	4.6%	3.7%	4.5 %	5.2%	4.0%	4.9%
Semiconductors / electric components	4.2%	44.4%	5.0%	46.1%	3.6%	51.4%	4.1%	55.2%
Footwear	4.5%	2.1%	4.1%	2.2%	3.8%	2.2%	3.5%	2.6%
Toys	6.2%	48.1%	4.1%	29.8%	3.4%	29.5%	3.5%	26.3%
Audio and video equipment	6.1%	40.4%	4.0%	41.2%	3.1%	40.7%	3.1%	40.8%
Furniture	3.1%	7.0%	2.8%	8.6%	2.9%	10.6%	3.2%	10.7%
Plastic products	1.9%	6.8%	1.9%	7.1%	1.9%	6.6%	2.0%	7.2%
Small electrical appliances	2.0%	15.7%	1.9%	16.5%	1.9%	10.7%	1.9%	13.4%
Leather products	1.8%	3.2%	1.8%	3.8%	1.6%	3.3%	1.5%	4.5%
Other manufactured commodities	1.8%	7.2%	1.7%	8.0%	1.6%	9.8%	1.7%	9.8%
Men's apparel	1.9%	3.5%	1.8%	4.6%	1.6%	4.1%	1.5%	4.1%
Lighting fixtures	1.1%	5.8%	1.2%	6.8%	1.4%	11.4%	1.7%	13.7%
General purpose machinery	1.3%	35.1%	1.3%	37.2%	1.1%	32.9 %	1.2%	38.2%
Navigational, measuring, medical, control instruments	1.2%	41.1%	1.2%	48.8%	1.5%	46.2%	1.7%	41.8%
Basic organic chemicals	1.0%	28.6%	1.2%	24.8%	1.3%	26.9%	1.2%	22.6%
Curtains and linens	1.4%	3.6%	1.3%	3.8%	1.4%	5.6%	1.4%	6.9%
Fabricated metal products	1.1%	9.3%	1.2%	12.8%	1.0%	12.1%	1.0%	13.4%
Motor vehicle parts	0.7%	15.7%	1.0%	16.6%	1.1%	22.8%	1.3%	23.8%
Electrical equipment	0.9%	31.2%	1.0%	33.7%	1.2%	38.3%	1.2%	38.6%
Major appliances	0.9%	15.5%	0.8%	13.5%	1.1%	31.4%	1.2%	34.0%
Sporting and athletic goods	1.2%	8.6%	1.1%	8.2%	1.1%	8.2%	1.1%	9.1%
Electrical equipment and components	0.8%	20.8%	1.0%	22.1%	1.0%	25.2%	1.2%	26.4%

Source: US Census.

tries' purchase of Chinese economic inputs in the 2010s and the contributions of those inputs to their overall performance. Usually, a supply chain or production relationship was involved in those industries' trade with China: US firms purchased supplies ranging from nuts and bolts to semiconductors and computers in order to make final goods at lower costs. On many other occasions, China functioned as a production base for American com-

Table 7.2. Examples of Major US Industries' Gains by Purchasing from China

Industry	China's Role in the Supply Chain (supply industries)	Chinese Contributions to the Performance of the Industry
Aerospace	Circuit boards and electronic components; computers; engines and turbines; semiconductors and circuits	Cost reduction
Agriculture, construction, and mining machinery manufacturing	Engines and turbines; power tools and other general purpose machinery; wind turbines; tires; ferrous metal foundry products	Stable supplier; cost reduction
Computer and peripheral equipment manufacturing	Semiconductors and circuits; wires and cables; semiconductor machinery	Cost reduction; major production base
Semiconductor and other electronic component manufacturing	Aluminum manufacturing	Cost reduction; major production base
Communications equipment manufacturing	Circuit boards and electronic components; computers; computer peripherals; semiconductors and circuits; telecommunication networking equipment	Cost reduction; major production base
Motor vehicle manufacturing	Automobile brakes; automobile electronics; automobile interiors	Cost reduction; stable supplier
Motor vehicle parts manufacturing	Aluminum; nuts and bolts; textile mills; circuit boards and electronic components; lighting and bulbs; power conversion equipment; semiconductors and circuits; wires and cables; leather goods and luggage; synthetic fiber; ball bearings	Cost reduction; stable supplier
Navigational, measuring, electromedical, and control instruments manufacturing	Electric equipment; glass products; hoses and belts	Stable supplier
Engine, turbine, and power transmission equipment manufacturing	Ball bearings; metalworking machinery; screws, nuts and bolts	Reduce cost; avoid environmental regulations

Source: IBIS World; Orbis.

panies, an activity often called offshoring of production. In this trade with China, US firms, in effect, imported Chinese labor or tasks in order to reduce costs and enhance competitiveness.[21]

Meanwhile, a number of the United States' major industries imported Chinese labor and tasks not only to consolidate their position in the home market, but also to enhance their performance in the global market. Many

Table 7.3. Goods Supplied by Majority-Owned US Affiliates in China (in millions of dollars)

	2009	2010	2011	2012
To affiliated persons	29,051	36,304	47,464	48,192
To unaffiliated persons	88,821	101,690	125,584	143,415
To US parents	8,397	9,047	13,295	12,266
To unaffiliated US persons	1,686	1,672	2,150	2,282
To other foreign affiliates	13,688	19,229	20,291	20,466
To unaffiliated foreign persons	8,990	10,852	13,672	14,186
To other local foreign affiliates	6,966	8,027	13,878	15,460
To unaffiliated local persons	78,145	89,166	109,763	126,947

Source: Bureau of Economic Analysis.

US firms created majority-owned affiliates around the world in order to more effectively utilize local economic inputs and expand sales in certain foreign markets.[22] Those affiliates not only produced goods that could be sent to their mother companies, but also sold their products in local and foreign markets. In other words, to more effectively purchase labor and tasks from China, US firms set up affiliates in that country and exported to the world through those local subsidiaries. Table 7.3 shows that exports by US multinational corporations (MNCs) to unaffiliated foreign and local destinations were far larger than their exports to the home market or other affiliated parties. It also illustrates that a significant part of major US industries' commercial performance was dependent on sales through affiliates in China.

It needs to be noted that major US industries also purchased Chinese labor and tasks through exchanges with non-majority-owned suppliers and subcontractors in China. However, while the data in Table 7.3 only capture business activities conducted by US affiliates in China, US MNCs' activities through nonaffiliated companies in China are not known. When non-majority-owned suppliers and subcontractors in China are taken into account, the extent to which major US industries purchase from China increases significantly. Moreover, their gains from the exchanges with China dramatically expand.

Why Chinese Inputs Matter: Severe International Competition

For major US manufacturing industries, Chinese economic inputs were important because these industries were exposed to severe international competition. Considering the fact that powerful foreign competitors existed in almost all manufacturing industries, even a small decrease in competitiveness was likely to result in a decrease in the US manufacturing firms' overall performance and revenue. Table 7.4 presents examples of foreign competitors in major manufacturing industries. In this table, "US MNCs" are major American firms that lead US manufacturing industries, and obtain important economic inputs from China within the context of supply chains or through production activities in China. Table 7.4 shows that, while US manufacturing industries (and manufacturing MNCs) were concentrated in areas where technology and economies of scale are important, there were foreign firms that possess equivalent technology and size. These US and foreign firms competed with each other over market share, and tried to utilize diverse resources from around the world in order to achieve greater competitiveness. Indeed, the presence of severe international competition was one of the most important reasons why major US industries established relationships with China.[23] In this situation, it was evident that the loss of access to Chinese economic inputs would only weaken US firms' position vis-à-vis their foreign competitors.

In sum, during the 2009–2016 period, US manufacturing industries successfully reduced the cost of production through trade with China. By doing so, they could more effectively compete with other foreign companies, in particular those from other advanced economies. Moreover, China also functioned as a "stable" supplier to US industries. With the rising importance of the global supply chain, establishing relationships with foreign suppliers that could provide diverse items at needed quantity and standardized quality became very important for manufacturing industries around the world.[24] Supply chain relationships with China proved to be particularly advantageous in reducing risks related to the globalization of production.

Retail/Wholesale Industry

Another sector of the US economy that purchased large quantities of Chinese economic inputs—in the forms of labor and tasks—was retail/wholesale industries. As economic theories suggest, importing final consumer goods from a foreign state entails the purchase of that country's labor or tasks.[25] In this regard, when the United States purchases final consumer goods from China, it is in effect purchasing cheap Chinese labor and tasks.

As is often noted disparagingly by US nongovernmental organizations, US retail/wholesale industries, led by giant firms such as Walmart, pur-

Table 7.4. Foreign Competitors of Major US MNCs

Industry	US MNCs	Foreign Competitors
Aerospace	Boeing, United Technologies, Lockheed Martin, Textron, Spirit Aerosystems	EADS, Bombardier, BAE Systems, Embraer, Rolls-Royce, Turbomecanica, Mitsubishi, Kawasaki, GKN, Dassault
Agriculture, construction, and mining machinery manufacturing	Caterpillar, Deere & Co, Baker Hughes, AGCO, Cameron International, FMC Technologies, Joy Global	Komatsu, Kubota, AB Volvo, Doosan Infracore, MAN SE, Atlas Copco, Siemens, Aker Solutions, Mitsubishi, Hitachi, CNH Global
Computer and peripheral equipment manufacturing	Apple, Hewlett-Packard, Dell, EMC, Western Digital, Seagate Technology, SCI Systems, Netapp, Sandisc	Acer, Lenovo, Toshiba, Canon, Fujitsu, Samsung, Hitachi, Sony
Semiconductor and other electronic component manufacturing	Intel, Jabil Circuit, Texas Instruments, Micron Technology, Tyco Electronics, Corning, Broadcom, Sanmina, Advanced Micro Devices	Samsung, Renesas, STMicroelectronics, NXP, Infineon, Denso, Sumitomo, Asahi Glass, Shin-Etsu, Heraeus, Prysmian, OC Oerlikon
Communications equipment manufacturing	Cisco, Qualcomm, L-3 Communications, Ratheon, Motorola, Harris	VIA Technologies, Ericsson, Fujitsu, Mediatek, Renesas, Samsung, Spreadtrum, Panasonic, Alcatel Lucent, Datalogic, Sepura, EADS, Thales
Motor vehicle manufacturing	General Motors, Ford, Chrysler, Paccar, Navistar	Daimler, Toyota, Honda, Volkswagen, Mitsubishi, Hyundai
Motor vehicle parts manufacturing	Johnson Controls, Lear Corp, Autoliv, Tenneco, Dana, Borgwarner, Visteon, Federal-Mogul, Delphi	Daikin, GS Yuasa, Siemens, Robert Bosch, Schneider Electronic, Faurecia, Toyota Boshoku, Magna, Leoni,
Navigational, measuring, electromedical, and control instruments manufacturing	Honeywell, General Dynamics, Northrop Grumman, Emerson Electric, Raytheon, Danaher, Medtronic, Thermo Fisher Scientific, Boston Scientific, Agilent, Rockwell, Exelis, St. Jude Medical	Mitsui & Co, IHI, Daikin, Teijin, Tosoh, Yokogawa, Akebono, Siemens, Basf, Olympus, Terumo, Koninklijke Philips, Getinge, Bruker, Shimadzu, Anritsu
Engine, turbine, and power transmission equipment manufacturing	General Electric, Cummins, United Technologies	Siemens, Hitachi, Toshiba, Mitsubishi, Denso, Hino, AB Volvo, Robert Bosch, Weichai, MAN, Gutenberg Group

Source: Orbis.

chased a large amount of tasks performed by Chinese labor in the form of final consumer goods.[26] For instance, by 2004, Walmart had established supply relationships with more than five thousand Chinese companies; and about 70 percent of the goods it sold in the United States were made in China.[27] Moreover, Walmart alone accounted for about 9.2 percent of all US imports of merchandise from China in 2006.[28] Although specific data on US retail/wholesale companies' purchases from China remain proprietary information, it can be reasonably expected that the quantity and extent of those purchases are still very large.

By purchasing a large quantity and variety of consumer goods from China, all else being equal, US retail/wholesale businesses could expand their sales and profit. Moreover, the purchase of cheap Chinese final goods increased the real income of the United States because American consumers could buy more goods with less money. Furthermore, by purchasing the labor and tasks entailed in Chinese final goods, the United States could reallocate its resources to more productive areas, further rationalizing its economy.

Low Substitutability of Chinese Economic Inputs

During the 2009–2016 period, while major US industries in the manufacturing and retail/wholesale sectors extensively purchased Chinese labor and tasks, other states were unlikely to be able to effectively replace China as the supplier of those inputs. Some might claim that the rising cost of Chinese labor and the emergence of other labor-rich countries in the global economy weakened China's position as the provider of labor and tasks for the United States.[29] Nonetheless, there are reasons to doubt the US ability to replace Chinese economic inputs with inputs from others.

During the Obama administration, many economic analysts agreed that other potential production bases around the world were still incapable of replacing China as the provider of labor and important tasks. Although other labor-rich countries such as India, Indonesia, Malaysia, Thailand, and Vietnam existed, there were entry barriers to the tasks that were performed by China. Simply put, other labor-abundant countries were not ready to do much of what China did for major US industries.[30] Such barriers would not exist at the low end of the global production chain.[31] However, the ability to create scale economies and the presence of sufficient technological backgrounds, as well as reliability as the supplier, were very important as a state moved up the value chain (and started to do the job China performs). Other labor-rich countries did not possess that ability and reliability.

Further, over one hundred industrial clusters endowed China with a unique advantage in the global processing trade compared with other potential manufacturing centers. Each of these clusters specialized in producing certain goods and provided foreign firms with governmental support, sophisticated supply chains, knowledge of the production process, and the flexibility to rapidly adjust to changing product specifications.[32] Indeed, low wages were not the sole reason for US producers to locate their production bases in China starting in the 1990s.[33] China was a "strong first-tier supplier" for manufacturing industries that focused on more advanced technologies, while other developing countries were not.[34] In fact, it would be more accurate to suggest that the tasks Southeast and South Asian countries performed were different from what China did for the United States.[35]

Moreover, business analysts suggested that China offered unique profit advantages to major US MNCs.[36] Although rising labor costs in China led many firms to consider the "China plus one strategy"—adding a production base in a Southeast Asian state in addition to a base in coastal China—utilizing Chinese economic inputs had at least four advantages that were not available in other countries: access to the booming Chinese domestic market, increasing Chinese labor productivity that offset increasing Chinese wages, a pool of labor that was large and flexible enough to accommodate rapidly changing market demands, and a reliable and flexible supply chain that could minimize risks.[37] Others suggested that the undervalued renminbi made it profitable to purchase Chinese labor and tasks and sell goods in the world market through China.[38] These attributes of Chinese economic inputs helped US industries obtain more profit, and were not available in other countries. Accordingly, although a number of US firms decided to "reshore" some portion of their manufacturing activities from China to the United States, they were limited to certain types of high-value-added and automated production. Those companies continued to rely on Chinese inputs to remain competitive.[39]

In sum, between 2009 and 2016, the risk of "not being in China" was likely to be larger than the risk of "being in China."[40] All else being equal, if the United States restricted trade with China, major US manufacturing industries (and to some extent, the wholesale/retail industry) were likely to become less competitive, lose revenues to foreign firms, and obtain significantly less profit, thus generating less material clout for the United States as a whole.

The Potential Availability of Alternative Trade Partners for China

During the 2009–2016 period, China had the potential to find alternative trade partners in important aspects of its trade with the United States. While the most important economic inputs China obtained from the United States comprised advanced technology products, food, and services, there were other advanced economies and food producers around the world that would be willing to take over US sales to China. Moreover, under certain circumstances, China could divert a significant portion of its exports away from the United States. Washington was also likely to experience frictions with China's alternative partners were it to impose extensive compound containment measures.

Alternative Partners with Regard to Imports from the United States

China purchased a wide array of goods from the United States. As Table 7.5 shows, between 2009 and 2015, for instance, the single largest Chinese import item from the United States was oil seeds, oil nuts, and oil kernels. China also imported a large quantity of raw materials from the United States, including metal scraps, cotton, hides and skins, coal, coke, and briquettes. Still, the majority of China's imports from the United States comprised manufactured industrial products, especially electronic products, machinery, transportation equipment, chemicals, and equipment for diverse industrial purposes.

While Beijing pursued "indigenous innovation" as an important national objective and tried to transform itself into an "innovation society," these economic inputs from the United States had important ramifications for China.[41] In particular, as many US officials argued, the US export of diverse advanced technology products helped China nurture its own advanced technology sector.[42] Thus, when the United States cut off bilateral trade, China could encounter significant economic loss if it could not find alternative suppliers of its current imports from the United States.

China, nonetheless, was likely to be able to find alternative trade partners to obtain important industrial goods and raw materials. Most notably, there were several advanced economies around the world that produced goods similar to the United States and competed with American manufacturers on the market. For the firms in those advanced economies, US restrictions on its own exports to China would be a wonderful opportunity to expand their market share and advance their competitive advantage. The

Table 7.5. Major US Merchandise Exports to China (in millions of dollars)

	2009	2011	2013	2015
Total	69,571	103,715	121,440	115,993
Oil seeds, oil nuts, and oil kernels	9,230.4	10,485.6	13,326.5	10,559.3
Electrical machinery and apparatus	6,452.7	6,705.0	7,498.5	8,171.9
Special transactions not classified according to kind	5,918.1	7,268.0	13,569.9	16,394.7
Regenerated plastic materials, cellulose and resins	4,019.7	4,598.0	4,243.5	4,323.7
Machinery and appliances nonelectrical parts	3,965.4	6,474.8	6,409.8	7,108.9
Nonferrous metal scrap	2,661.1	6,320.2	5,147.9	3,027.4
Scientific, medical, optical, measurement, control instruments	2,583.9	3,549.5	4,062.8	4,731.7
Pulp and waste paper	2,497.6	3,998.0	3,610.4	3414.0
Iron and steel scrap	2,478.0	2,290.5	1,172.3	651.9
Organic chemicals	2,363.4	3,475.5	2,877.8	2,555.2
Office machines	2,032.8	2,044.7	1,928.9	2,158.5
Road motor vehicles	1,842.0	6,612.2	10,201.2	10,769.0
Telecommunications apparatus	1,495.2	1,771.6	2,647.7	2,818.3
Electric power machinery and switchgear	1,455.2	1,896.3	2,228.7	2,188.1
Chemical materials and products	1,161.3	1,759.1	2,276.2	2,173.8
Machines for special industries	957.5	1,288.4	1,125.4	933.3
Power generating machinery, other than electric	899.7	1,583.5	1,709.6	1,153.2
Cotton	867.9	2,634.4	2,202.0	860.3
Inorganic chemicals elements, oxides, halogen salts	727.2	1,022.9	584.8	550.5
Ores and concentrates of nonferrous base metals	721.2	1,149.8	940.1	825.0
Electronic apparatus for medical purposes, radiological appliances	646.3	988.4	1,261.9	1,340.1
Petroleum products	416.0	1,157.6	1,663.0	1,232.1
Wood in the rough or roughly squared	244.1	1,092.2	1,153.7	857.7
Medicinal and pharmaceutical products	532.8	1,057.0	1,361.0	2,038.3
Hides and skins	576.3	1,049.4	1,470.7	1,143.8
Maize (corn), unmilled	52.5	850.0	1,255.2	186.8
Coal, coke, and briquettes	121.9	835.1	906.8	22.8

Source: UN Comtrade.

advanced economies that were not threatened by China in security relations would be particularly eager to take over US exports to China.[43] During the Obama presidency, the EU states were such countries.

Table 7.6 suggests that the EU states could be alternative suppliers of important commodities for China. Except for certain raw materials, the EU exported to China the same categories of goods as the United States. The

Table 7.6. EU-28's Major Merchandise Exports to China (in millions of dollars)

	2009	2011	2013	2015
Total	112,794	171,215	195,728	176,936
Machinery and appliances non electrical parts	17,338.4	25,725.4	24,676.1	21,125.4
Road motor vehicles	11,372.3	30,196.7	37,714.5	30,813.3
Electric power machinery and switchgear	7,276.5	8,769.2	9,112.9	8,727.0
Other electrical machinery and apparatus	5,158.2	6,554.1	7,992.6	7,658.1
Power generating machinery, other than electric	5,142.5	6,332.3	7,148.8	5,410.1
Aircraft	4,640.1	6,833.0	8,371.8	9,872.4
Regenerated plastic materials, cellulose and resins	3,856.1	4,077.6	4,608.3	4,443.3
Scientific medical, optical, measurement, control instruments	3,807.7	5,930.5	7,692.9	7,646.3
Machines for special industries	3,562.2	4,820.7	3,856.4	2,563.5
Metalworking machinery	3,506.8	4,381.7	4,342.0	3,166.5
Special transactions not classd.accord.to kind	3,479.0	4,075.4	4,642.9	3,447.2
Organic chemicals	3,049.1	3,347.7	3,374.4	3,365.3
Medicinal and pharmaceutical products	3,018.6	4,761.1	7,057.7	8,325.7
Nonferrous metal scrap	2,916.7	4,315.3	3,656.9	2,570.5
Copper	2,139.4	2,769.7	2,880.9	1,697.7
Telecommunications apparatus	1,897.2	2,193.7	2,661.9	2,805.7
Pulp and waste paper	1,504.5	2,557.4	2,423.0	2,264.3
Office machines	1,470.1	1,382.2	1,340.2	1,172.7
Chemical materials and products	1,332.0	2,119.0	2,539.9	2,361.7
Textile and leather machinery	1,298.2	2,325.7	1,990.1	1,509.7
Tubes, pipes and fittings of iron or steel	1,166.8	764.3	952.9	628.9
Manufactures of metal	1,023.3	1,437.8	1,736.9	1,579.9
Universals plates and sheets of iron or steel	1,019.0	1,398.9	1,311.9	1,082.3
Petroleum products	491.4	1,416.3	1,904.9	916.6
Electronic apparatus for medical purpose, radioactive appliances	785.2	1,259.1	1,716.2	1,533.4

Source: UN Comtrade.

similarity of the EU and the United States' exports to China was notable in advanced technology products, including electronics, machinery, and equipment. This similarity suggests that the EU and the United States were competitors in the Chinese market; and it was likely that European companies would readily expand their sales to China if American firms cut off their exports for political reasons.

Indeed, according to the Chinese Ministry of Commerce, the EU became China's principal source of technology imports by 2009, accounting for about 30 percent of all technology imports.[44] Moreover, during the 2000s, on average 65 percent of the EU's exports to China were machinery, equipment, transport, and electronics, in which the Europeans transferred technology to meet the requirements of the Chinese government.[45] Although the Western European states sometimes could not fully compete with cutting-edge US technology, the EU possessed many advanced technologies that were nearly equivalent to those of the United States.[46]

China's ability to find alternative trade partners—in particular the ability to obtain diverse advanced technology products from the EU—had been recognized by US practitioners as well. As former national security adviser Brent Scowcroft observes, "The United States has competition in most areas of advanced research and development, including military-related science and technology. The number of access points to advanced science and technology has grown considerably and perhaps more to the point, outside the control of the United States . . . the alliance has lost its Cold War consensus."[47]

Meanwhile, if the United States were to restrict its export of raw materials and agricultural products, China could find alternative suppliers. As shown in Table 7.5, oil seeds, oil nuts, and oil kernels were some of the largest US exports to China in value. A large portion of these grains were soybeans that were used as animal feed or processed into cooking oil for human consumption.[48] Moreover, the United States sold a large quantity of natural resources and materials to China that were further processed by Chinese factories to make diverse merchandise.

Nonetheless, there were several grain-producing states and raw material rich countries that would willingly take up US sales to China.[49] As shown in Table 7.7, with regard to oil seeds, oil nuts, and oil kernels, Argentina, Brazil, and Canada already exported a significant quantity to China. Especially, Brazil was already the largest exporter of those grains to China. In this situ-

Table 7.7. Alternative Suppliers of Certain Raw Materials for China (in millions of dollars)

Year	Oil Seeds, Oil Nuts, and Oil Kernels			Coal, Coke, and Briquettes			
	Argentina	Brazil	Canada	Australia	Canada	Indonesia	Russia
2009	1,203.6	6,343.0	1,371.1	4,434.9	576.3	2,079.5	649.6
2011	4,393.7	10,957.3	925.4	4,693.8	829.2	7,570.2	933.9
2013	3,220.9	17,145.7	2,259.6	8,779.6	1,406.3	6,894.0	2,272.3
2015	3,562.8	15,787.7	2,236.2	4,746.7	439.5	2,718.5	1,017.9

Source: UN Comtrade.

ation, if the United States restricted its export of these grains to China, just as it did against the USSR during the Carter administration, Brazil could repeat its history of becoming an alternative supplier for the United States' adversary. In addition to the three non-US grain exporters in Table 7.7, European states had the potential to expand their grain production and sales to China, although their current agricultural exports to that country were dwarfed by sales of manufactured goods. Australia was another source from which China could obtain diverse grains.

With regard to the US export of coal, coke, and briquettes—materials used as fuels for industrial purposes or in households—Australia, Canada, Indonesia, and Russia could be effective alternative trade partners.[50] As shown in Table 7.7, these countries were already competing with the United States in the market. In the export of hides and skins to China, Australia and Canada could be alternative suppliers, and Australia, Canada, and Russia would be able to replace the United States as the source of wood.[51]

Different from the historical adversaries of the United States, China was a very large market that was actively engaged in foreign trade, and, at the same time, had immense foreign currency reserves. Simply put, China had large purchasing power and could pay cash for foreign goods. This meant that other countries would seek opportunities to expand their business with China if the United States were to impose extensive restrictions on its own trade.[52]

Alternative Partners with Regard to Exports to the United States

Throughout the 2009–2016 period, the United States was one of the largest export destinations for China. In 2013, for instance, China's exports to the United States exceeded $369 billion, accounting for 16.7 percent of all Chinese merchandise exports to the world.[53] The enormity of Chinese goods sold in the United States might suggest that, if Washington decided to restrict trade with China, Beijing would not be able to divert exports away from the United States and would lose the related economic benefits. Thus, one might argue that the position as the world's second largest market (and the largest national market) endowed the United States with a unique advantage in dealing with its strategic contenders.

Nonetheless, there were reasons to expect that China could minimize the loss caused by restricted exports to the United States, and might even be able to find countries to absorb its current exports to the United States.

First, the contribution of exports—specifically, exports destined for the United States—to China's GDP was considerably smaller when processing trade was taken into account.[54] Functioning as the production base of many MNCs, China was situated at the very end of the international production network. Much of China's manufacturing was organized around purchasing parts, technologies, and raw materials from other countries, assembling them in its industrial clusters, and selling the final manufactured goods on the world market. In this process, what China actually gained through exports was the compensation for assembly. Although China sold an enormous quantity of goods to foreign buyers, a large portion of payments from buyers was eventually transferred to countries from which China purchased parts, materials, or technology. Accordingly, after exporting to the United States, what was left as value added to China's GDP—or China's GDP gains—was small.

This implied that, if the United States stopped importing from China, China would lose much less than was anticipated by arguments that built on reported (ordinary) trade statistics. One estimate suggested that, in 2007, 62.5 percent of China's exports to the United States comprised processing exports.[55] According to the US International Trade Commission, the United States' bilateral trade deficit with China in 2004 was about 40 percent smaller when value-added trade measures were used instead of conventional statistics. A different value-added trade measure suggested that the US deficit was 53 percent smaller in 2005 and 42 percent smaller in 2008.[56] These estimates showed that China's gains from exports to the United States were significantly smaller than what appeared in reported statistics. Thus, China had much less to lose from restricted access to the US market.

Second, there were other major markets in which China could potentially expand the sales of its goods and maintain its economic activities linked to exports to the United States. During the 2009–2016 period, the EU, not the United States, was the largest market in the world and the largest export destination for China.[57] Although economic crises in several member states constrained the growth of the EU's commerce with China, the EU still remained China's largest trade partner. The enormous size of exports to the EU suggested that China might be able to attain benefits related with the economies of scale even if the United States cut off imports from China. Moreover, considering its size as a market, the EU had a good potential to expand its purchase of Chinese products.

More importantly, mainstream international economics suggests that there is a subtler mechanism through which China might be able to divert its exports away from the United States. If the United States restricted imports from China, the EU states could advance their competitive advantage vis-à-vis the United States and, consequently, absorb China's exports. Specifically, as discussed above, several major US manufacturing industries obtained economic inputs from China such as labor and tasks in order to ensure their competitiveness in the market. Moreover, it was shown that the American MNCs that led those manufacturing industries competed with foreign companies based in Europe or other advanced economies. Meanwhile, similar to the US-China trade, commerce between the EU and China was built on comparative advantages.[58]

While the United States and the EU were competitors in many manufacturing industries and both heavily utilized Chinese economic inputs, US restrictions on American companies' trade with China could provide an opportunity for rival European firms to enhance their advantage and expand market share. In this case, as American firms lost access to Chinese economic inputs that were entailed in imports from China, they would become less competitive in the market. In contrast, by continuing to do business with China, European firms would be able to maintain their current level of competitiveness. Accordingly, European companies would achieve significant competitiveness gains vis-à-vis US firms, and, all else being equal, European firms would effectively increase their market share and also encroach on the US market.

As European advanced economies triumphed over the United States, China's current exports to the United States could be potentially absorbed by the European economies. Those countries would purchase more economic inputs from China in order to expand the production of goods for which they would now have a competitive advantage (vis-à-vis the United States). Thus, China's current export of labor and tasks to the United States could be diverted to Europe. Moreover, the European states would also purchase more Chinese final products in order to concentrate on making certain goods for which they enjoyed a competitive advantage and that allowed them to obtain the largest profit, while importing others from China. As European countries expanded their specialized commercial relationship with China, China's current exports to the United States might be diverted to Europe.

Third, China had the potential to diversify its export destinations to countries other than the EU and the United States. As Figure 7.1 illustrates,

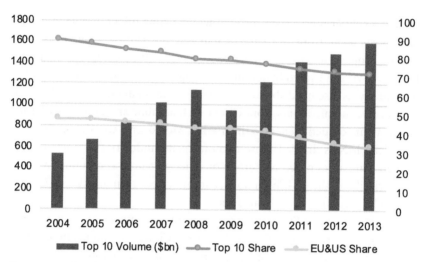

Figure 7.1. China's Major Export Destinations
Source: UN Comtrade

China's exports were concentrated in about ten states between 2004 and 2013.[59] Moreover, the quantity of China's exports to those ten destinations increased dramatically, from about $532 billion in 2004 to $1,594 billion in 2014. Nonetheless, as the "EU&US Share" in Figure 7.1 shows, the portion of China's exports to the EU and the United States in its overall exports continuously decreased. In 2004, about 48 percent of China's exports headed to the twenty-eight EU states or the United States. In 2013, this portion diminished to 33.5 percent, revealing that China's dependence on the world's two largest markets decreased significantly. Furthermore, the proportion of China's exports to its top ten export destinations decreased, from 89.7 percent of total exports in 2004 to 72.2 percent in 2013. These developments suggested that, while China's export concentration to certain markets decreased over time, China expanded its market presence in more diverse parts of the world. Thus, since China nurtured significant potential to sell its goods to markets outside of the United States, Washington's restrictions against Chinese imports might have limited impact on China.[60]

Fourth, once the United States imposed restrictions on imports from China, a significant portion of Chinese final consumer or industrial goods might enter the US market in roundabout ways. China's growing industrial clout and the global spread of bilateral/regional trade agreements would give China opportunities to relocate its production facilities to places that were not affected by US restrictions but had good access to the US market. Goods made in those new production sites would at least partly use Chinese materials, parts, and technologies, yet the final product would be considered non-Chinese. For instance, when the United States imposed duties on Chinese solar cells in 2012, China revealed the ability to relocate its manufacturing facilities to Canada.[61] The Chinese solar panels assembled in Canada would enter the US market free of duties and be sold as Canadian products in the United States. In this case, China might have circumvented US import barriers by exploiting the commercial network of the North American Free Trade Agreement. Considering that there were numerous preferential trade agreements in place and more extensive open trade arrangements were under discussion, it could be expected that China would be able to sell a wide variety of its goods in the United States through third countries.

These assessments do not mean that China could divert all of its exports away from the United States. I also do not suggest that the Chinese economy was unlikely to be affected by restricted access to the US market. Nonetheless, there were reasons to expect that China could find alternative export destinations and ways to sell its goods in the United States if Washington were to impose extensive trade restrictions on Beijing. China's losses accruing from restricted access to the US market might not have been as large as some observers anticipated.

Potential US Losses from Frictions with Other States

While China could potentially find alternative trade partners for many aspects of its foreign trade, the United States needed to be concerned about the losses that might arise from interactions with third countries. US policies designed to diminish imports from and exports to China could disrupt the overall flow of goods, services, and economic factors around the globe, and thereby affect the economic performance of all major economies. Considering the spread of the globalization of production and China's position at the end of the global production network, US restrictions on trade with China would almost automatically lead to the economic losses of other major states. For instance, the United States might sell China certain advanced technology products to be further processed in China and sold to the EU. Similarly, the EU states might export goods to China to be further processed and sold to the United States. Then, US trade restrictions against

China in effect mean denying the EU access to important Chinese goods that entail US technology, or the United States imposing barriers against European goods. Thus, US trade measures against China could introduce tensions between Washington and third countries. The losses accruing from such tensions are the United States' relative loss vis-à-vis China.

Indeed, the EU demonstrated some possibility of standing at odds with the United States in defense of its own economic interest.[62] Although it was not fully substantiated, the Sino-EU "strategic partnership" signed in 2003 suggested that China and the EU could be natural partners in both economic and political realms.[63] The controversy between the United States and the Europeans over the lifting of the arms embargo on China between 2004 and 2005 revealed that it would be very difficult for the United States to persuade the EU states to forgo their economic interests in China in support of US security interests.[64] If an issue concerning arms exports induced such severe disagreements, US efforts to control an inflow of goods and technologies that have indirect military application to China would spur even more controversies. Further, not only the EU but also other countries that maintain close trade ties with China would collide with US restrictions on trade.

Outcome: Whither Compound Containment against China?

An assessment of available data, reports, and government documents shows that, during the 2009–2016 period, many of the United States' major industries could not find alternative trade partners that could replace the role of China, and China could find alternative trade partners in important dimensions of its trade with the United States. It can be cautiously suggested that the United States under these conditions could not effectively employ compound containment against China. Adopting policies designed to cut off major trade with China would not only be ineffective but also could inflict greater harm on the United States.

US behavior over trade with China during the Obama administration was consistent with this argument. Although there were strong voices within the United States favoring restrictive trade policies, the tensions over trade with China did not translate into actual policies.[65] Specifically, four serious restrictive measures against China were avoided. The danger of potentially larger US losses was an important rationale that was advanced in each of these cases.[66]

First, repeated efforts to designate China as a "currency manipulator" were refuted by Washington, which was concerned about negative repercussions to the US economy. Since Senators Charles Schumer and Lindsey Graham's request for a formal declaration of China as a currency manipulator in 2005, many in the US Congress and leading political figures such as Mitt Romney advocated punishing China's deliberate undervaluing of its currency.[67] They pointed out that fixing China's exchange rate would restore the bilateral trade balance to be in favor of the United States, and, to some extent, reverse the increasing American reliance on Chinese manufactured goods.

Nonetheless, there were what several observers called "deeper structural reasons" preventing serious actions against China's foreign trade, including the designation of that country as a currency manipulator. On many occasions, US firms utilizing Chinese economic inputs were actually benefitting (in terms of profit) from the undervalued renminbi.[68] Moreover, designating China as a currency manipulator could lead to an increase in the price of Chinese goods in the United States, which in turn would diminish the real income of American citizens.[69] Although large imbalances in the balance of payments existed, it was unclear whether adjusting the exchange rate would really help the US economy.

Second, the protectionist pressures during an economic recession were effectively subdued. A state is likely to have strong incentives to adopt restrictive trade measures during economic downturns. In the US case, the Great Recession of 2007 might have led Washington to pass laws and legal procedures seeking to diminish imports from China.[70] Nonetheless, in the midst of the recession, the Obama administration intended to boost the US economy and reduce its deficit by bolstering exports rather than restricting imports. In January 2010, President Obama proposed the National Export Initiative, which aspired to double US exports in the next five years, and created the Export Promotion Cabinet and the President's Export Council to support that plan.[71] In the administration's overall trade policy, it was repeatedly stated that US economic interests and prosperity could be best served by remaining committed to existing rules, while more aggressively seeking access to foreign markets.[72] Protectionist policies were adopted over a few less important items such as tires and solar panels, but their effectiveness was doubted.[73] Moreover, criticisms of the increasing trade deficit and pressures from Congress to adopt new and more stringent policy measures were often countered by evidence that they failed to recognize processing trade that was conducted through China.[74] Maintaining trade ties with China was viewed as the better option for US economic performance even during a recession.

Third, despite the strategic importance of denying China's access to cutting-edge technologies, the United States did not strengthen its export restrictions.[75] Even on goods with significant military relevance, the United States did not strengthen existing control regimes.[76] Despite the Obama administration's pledge to revamp its export control system, the dual-use nature of important modern technologies, the need to rely on Chinese production facilities for competitive advantage, and the existence of alternative foreign suppliers together restricted the effectiveness of existing control schemes and delayed the development of a new framework.[77] Through the debate in Congress and the administration, it was revealed that unilateral controls would not be effective since China could simply obtain the technology from other countries. In many cases, stringent controls on US firms would only harm the US economy.[78] Moreover, while US dominance over cutting-edge technology could no longer be assumed, multilateral control regimes such as the Wassenaar Arrangement, the descendent of the Coordinating Committee for Multilateral Export Controls (COCOM), had become ineffective in the post–Cold War context.[79] Consequently, instead of strengthening the existing export control system, the US government adopted or considered policy measures that could facilitate US high-technology exports to China.[80]

Fourth, the ambitious goal of creating a trade bloc exclusive of China did not make progress. A number of US leaders suggested that the Trans Pacific Partnership (TPP) would help restore Washington's commercial leadership in the Asia-Pacific, as well as creating enormous wealth for the United States.[81] It was also suggested that, through this agreement, the United States' economic dependence on China would diminish and Washington would be able to exercise more pressure on Beijing. Moreover, several practitioners and scholars in and outside of the United States suggested that the TPP had the potential to become an instrument for "economic containment" of China.[82]

However, it was illustrated that a trade agreement excluding China would not make a significant contribution to the United States' relative economic performance. Even if the TPP were in place, China could establish its own free trade agreements with the East Asian states in order to weaken the cohesiveness of the US-led economic bloc, as well as collaborating with the EU states.[83] Thus, it would be very difficult for the United States to advance its economic position vis-à-vis China through a series of exclusive trade agreements.

The developments in these four important and popularized agendas during the 2009–2016 period suggest that Washington recognized that it was not in a position to adopt compound containment against China. The United States was aware that extensive economic restrictions against China could harm its own economy. This assessment, of course, does not mean that clear causal relationships can be established between the conditions I examine and the US decision to avoid compound containment against China. In order to confirm if the causal mechanism I propose is working, more detailed and direct data, as well as extensive analyses of primary sources, are necessary. Such evidence, however, is currently unavailable. Thus, this chapter tentatively suggests that US behaviors over trade with China during the Obama presidency are consistent with the overall proposition of my argument, rather than claiming that the causal relationships I propose are confirmed by the US experiences between 2009 and 2016.

Alternative Explanations

The difficulties of evaluating a contemporary case are also pervasive when examining the two alternative explanations that, respectively, focus on the role of domestic interest group politics and leaders' belief. It is still difficult to trace whether and to what extent the Obama administration's decisions regarding China were affected by the influence of interest groups or leaders' convictions. Moreover, documents that directly reveal leaders' thinking, interests, and interactions are not publicly available. Yet an assessment of US relations with China during the 2009–2016 period suggests tentatively that leaders' belief could have played a prominent role, while the impact of domestic interest group politics was unclear.

Domestic Interest Groups

According to the argument that focuses on the role of domestic interest groups, continuing US commercial engagement with China reflects the interest of powerful commercial groups that want to protect their economic stakes despite rising military rivalry. In particular, lobbying efforts of diverse commercial groups that have different stakes in trade with China and the competition between those interest groups—especially, between groups that gain from trade with China and groups that lose—need to be observed in order to confirm whether this theory's causal mechanism works. Leaders' policy decisions on trade with China should reflect the competitive domestic political processes.

One major problem with regard to this alternative explanation is that the competition between the winners and losers of trade with China was difficult to observe during the Obama presidency.[84] Instead, there seemed to be bipartisan support when Washington criticized China's trade policy. In fact, China's "unfair" practices over trade with the United States were a very popular topic in Washington. In presidential debates and discussions in Congress, few leaders argued that the United States should take no steps on trade with China. While American workers were viewed as losers from increasing trade with China, a voice that proclaimed the need to utilize more Chinese economic inputs would have induced furor from both sides of the aisle.[85] Accordingly, the assumption of an explanation based on domestic politics—competition between domestic interests—was problematic in the first place.

An account of events based on domestic interests is also problematic because the role of lobbying—the hallmark of this theory's causal mechanism—in issues related with Sino-US trade was murky. Within the United States, an accurate description of major US firms' lobbying behavior regarding trade with China during the Obama administration would be that they lobbied neither for nor against China. Moreover, even if certain US industries lobbied the government in order to expand business opportunities in China, my theory can potentially subsume the domestic interest-based explanation. For instance, the US satellite industry exerted pressures on Washington to expand trade with China, but the logic this industry brought forth was that alternative trade partners were widely available for China in space technologies.[86] In this case, it can be argued that one of my theory's explanatory factors was the driving force behind the US industries' decision to pressure Washington.

Leaders' Belief

The other alternative theory suggests that the United States might have not imposed serious restrictions on trade with China to complement military containment measures because of leaders' convictions about the ability of economic engagement to shape the adversary's behavior. In this view, US leaders might uphold a liberal belief that suggests China's large gains from the US-led international trade system gives Washington significant leverage vis-à-vis Beijing, and the United States can utilize the prospects of continuing economic benefits to affect the trajectory of China's rise. More ambitiously, when economic engagement continues, China's fundamental preferences might eventually change and be in harmony with the United States.[87] If successful, China would become what Robert Zoellick called a "responsible stakeholder" in the US-led international order rather than a challenger.[88]

Many of these ideas were reinstated even when China actually became the world's second largest national economy and the United States indeed strengthened its military presence in the Asia-Pacific. For instance, Robert Zoellick argued that the United States should explore ways to establish "a new type of great power relationship" in large part based on extensive economic exchanges with China.[89] President Obama also stressed the need for cooperation between the two states for global economic growth and emphasized trade without protectionism, suggesting that active economic interactions had transformative effects.[90] Moreover, although economic recessions hit the United States and public antagonism about Chinese trade policy soared, many US leaders advocated the political and strategic contributions of continuing unimpeded trade with China.[91]

In the US-China case, this alternative explanation that focuses on US leaders' liberal convictions is unlikely to be subsumed by my argument. Moreover, it is difficult to determine whether my theory has a better ability than leaders' convictions in accounting for this particular case, given the limits to available evidence in examining a contemporary case.

Conclusion

This chapter examined whether the United States during the Obama administration was in a position to adopt compound containment against China. Although there are still severe limits in data, available evidence suggests that the United States was not in a position to counter the Chinese challenge using both military and commercial means. Several major US industries depended on Chinese economic inputs in order to ensure competitiveness, without effective alternative trade partners that could replace China.

In contrast, China could have found alternative trade partners in many important dimensions of its trade with the United States. Thus, it was unclear whether the United States could inflict significant relative losses on China by restricting bilateral trade. Accordingly, avoiding compound containment measures against China was a more prudent choice for Washington. Yet one alternative explanation that emphasizes the role of leaders' belief can also effectively account for this contemporary case, since the Obama administration repeatedly revealed its liberal convictions in the peace-creating effect of economic engagement.

CHAPTER 8

Conclusion

Containment has been an attractive option for a reigning great power that is determined to confront a challenging power. By stopping the challenging state from launching military aggression through internal and external balancing efforts, containment strategy aims to maintain international stability and protect the reigning state's relative power position. Yet, as long as military force and economic capacity are intertwined, the reigning power employing containment policy has strong incentives to reinforce military measures with economic restrictions. These economic measures upgrade military containment into compound containment, and help the reigning state to more effectively check the challenging state. In today's great power politics, if China grows more aggressive and the United States decides to strengthen military countermeasures against China, Washington will need to make a hard choice about whether to impose compound containment measures against Beijing.

In order to understand the decision to upgrade military containment to compound containment, a theory explaining the conditions under which a reigning power can effectively employ restrictive economic measures is needed. Most experts of grand strategy have focused on the reigning power's employment of military force in protecting its important national interests.[1] Moreover, many theoretical and empirical studies of the strategic uses of economic measures concentrate on identifying the independent role of economic instruments. Accordingly, economic restrictions that can be wielded by the reigning power to buttress military containment measures remain largely underexplored. While every military grand strategy should have its economic equivalent, this book focuses on the strategy of containment, and advances an argument on the use of economic complements to military force.

Below I summarize the theory and empirical analyses presented in this book. Then, I discuss the theoretical and policy contributions of the book. Finally, I introduce directions for future research.

Summary of the Argument and Case Studies

Compound containment is adopted when the reigning power implements policies that are designed to restrict the majority of important economic exchanges with the challenging power while there are ongoing military containment efforts implemented against the challenger. These economic restrictions try to inflict material losses on the challenging state, and thereby weaken that state's capacity to pose security concerns. Yet, imposing extensive restrictions on ongoing economic relations introduces losses for both the reigning and challenging power. Thus, the losses that are incurred by compound containment should be defined in relative terms. Compound containment, in short, becomes a viable option when the reigning power has an ability to inflict relative losses on the challenging power through economic restrictions.

Whether the reigning power has this ability—and, thus, whether compound containment is a viable option—is largely determined by a structural factor: the availability of alternative economic partners. Alternative economic partners refer to a state or group of states that can replace the majority of economic roles that are currently performed by the strategic competitor in case of serious disruptions in ongoing economic exchanges. The availability of these alternative partners determines the two competing powers' respective losses after the imposition of economic restrictions for the purpose of compound containment by the reigning power. In other words, the international elasticity of the two powers' economic roles constrains the reigning power's ability to inflict relative economic losses on the challenging power through compound containment. The availability of alternative economic partners represents international economic conditions, and is not necessarily determined by the reigning power's political influence.

Depending on the configuration of alternative economic partners for the two competing powers, the reigning state may or may not have an ability to inflict relative losses on the challenging state, and the presence or absence of this ability, in turn, affects the reigning power's decision on compound containment. The crux of my argument is that, when alternative economic partners are largely available for the reigning state but not for the challenging state, the reigning power can inflict relative losses on the challenger and, therefore, will adopt compound containment. In contrast, when alternative partners are available for the challenging power but not for the reigning power, the reigning state is not in a position to inflict relative losses on the challenging state through economic restrictions, and will eschew upgrading military containment into compound containment.

This book substantiates this argument through case studies of reigning powers' responses to challenging powers since the late nineteenth century. I attempted to examine all cases where a reigning state strengthened military countermeasures against a challenging state, and found a need and opportunity to reconsider extant commercial ties with the challenger. As listed in Figure 8.1, the cases that satisfied scope conditions of the theory are Britain's response to the German challenge during the years leading up to World War I, the United States' response to the Japanese challenge before the Pacific War, the United States' response to the Soviet Union during the early Cold War, and two US administrations' responses to the resurgent Soviet threat at the beginning of the "Second Cold War." In addition, the US response to a rising China during the Obama administration is also a case in point to examine the validity of my argument.

I find that historical evidence is largely consistent with the arguments of my theory, both in terms of the predicted behavior of the reigning power and proposed causal mechanisms. Britain did not restrict trade with a rising Germany because it was aware that compound containment would inflict greater harm on the British economy than on the German. While its leading industries could not effectively divert trade away from Germany, Germany could find alternative partners with which to trade, and Britain discovered that it would lose more if bilateral trade were restricted. In contrast, the United States abandoned trade with Japan in order to weaken that country's capacity to dominate East Asia. Its ability to divert the majority of trade away from Japan and the absence of alternative trade partners for Japan endowed Washington with an ability to inflict significant relative losses on the Japanese economy through compound containment. Similarly, the United States severed trade ties with the Soviet Union during the early Cold War in order to slow the USSR's industrial growth and military buildup. The absence of alternative trade partners for the Soviet Union in the immediate aftermath of World War II and the presence of alternative partners for the United States enabled Washington to inflict a relative loss

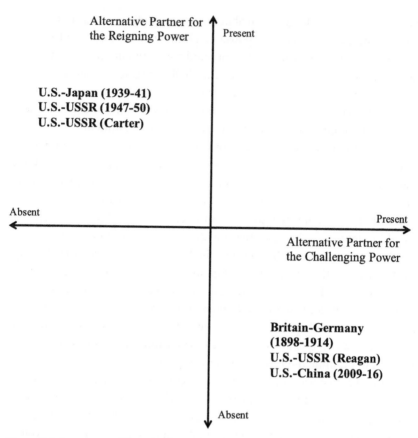

Figure 8.1. Summary of Case Studies

on the Soviet Union by restricting trade. Moreover, by comparing the Carter and Reagan administrations' responses to Soviet aggressions beginning in December 1979 and lasting until the mid-1980s, I tried to control for the effect of diverse confounding variables and examined how the variations in the explanatory factors during a short period of time affected the outcome. I found that the two administrations' diverging assessments of the availability of alternative trade partners for the United States and the USSR resulted in different decisions on compound containment. In addition to these historical cases, an examination of the US response to China during the Obama era suggests that my argument is potentially supported by this contemporary development as well.

In contrast to my argument, I find the two alternative explanations wanting. One alternative theory suggests that the reigning power will choose to maintain current economic ties with the challenging power in response to domestic interest groups that want to sustain economic exchanges with the challenging state. The hallmark of this approach is a bottom-up process whereby domestic groups mobilize themselves to protect commercial stakes and their interactions with other societal groups and national leaders, mainly through lobbying and activities related to elections. The other alternative explanation suggests that the reigning state continues economic exchanges with the challenger mainly because of its leaders' convictions about the ability of economic ties to pacify the challenging power. From this perspective, if the reigning state's leaders do not hold this belief, the reigning power adopts compound containment against the challenging power. Although logically consistent, these two alternative explanations are only partly corroborated historically or can be potentially subsumed by the structural argument offered in this book.

In sum, the reigning power's decisions to adopt or avoid compound containment against the challenging power can be best understood as a choice that reflects the constraints imposed by the international economic structure. This theory best describes the evidence for the reigning state's decisions in dealing with the challenging state since the late nineteenth century.

Theoretical Contributions

The argument and analyses presented in this book make several theoretical contributions. First, this book examines a topic that has been often overlooked by scholars of grand strategy. For many theorists of a reigning power's grand strategy, military balancing is the central way of responding to the challengers to the status quo. Nonetheless, manipulating economic exchanges should be taken more seriously because it is linked to the distribution of military capacities. Moreover, the international balance of power in important parts reflects the distribution of relative economic capacities. In addition, it is widely agreed that changes in the distribution of economic capacities herald the onset of intense geopolitical competition.[2] Therefore, simply focusing on military balancing or containment is often not enough in analyzing the grand strategy of a great power. Unless an adversary's economic capabilities are properly addressed, it might be difficult for a reigning state to protect important security interests and remove the root cause of its security concerns over the adversary. This book encourages grand strategy scholars to theoretically elaborate on the relationship between economic measures and military instruments, by showing how containment strategy can embrace the use of economic complements.

Second, this book addresses an information gap in the scholarship on the linkages between security and economy in international politics. Scholars of economic statecraft tend to focus on identifying the independent effect of economic tools in advancing strategic goals, often without taking seriously the complementary role of economic policies.[3] Moreover, a number of prominent scholars have explored the implications of economic exchanges for national security, but they have confined attention to strategic raw materials or dual-use technologies.[4] Meanwhile, many scholars have studied the relationship between military competition and economic exchanges.[5] In this research program, theories on the security externalities of trade suggest that an adversarial relationship generally leads to a decrease of trade.[6] Conversely, some theorists suggest that the magnitude of economic ties or the economic orientation of a country affect its military reaction against a security challenger.[7] Other scholars who emphasize economic side payments argue that some states might provide economic benefits to their allies in order to strengthen or constrain them, while still other scholars argue that positive economic inducements could be used to shape the behavior or even preferences of a security challenger.[8]

These theories, nonetheless, do not effectively address the inconsistency between the reigning state's military and economic strategies—that is, the coexistence of military containment policy and continuing extensive economic exchanges—in dealing with a challenging state. Scholars who subscribe to these theories commonly believe that a correlation exists between the severity of military competition and the magnitude of economic cooperation. It is often presumed that restrictive economic measures naturally follow if a state is determined to militarily confront another state. They also overlook the possibility that the reigning state will have incentives to use military and economic strategies simultaneously. This book accounts for these discrepancies in extant international relations literature.

Third, this book marries balance-of-power logic with insights from mainstream international economics. For balance-of-power theorists who take material capacities seriously, foreign economic exchanges are important because they can alter states' relative material power.[9] Missing in this approach is a sound understanding of how international economic exchanges—especially, international trade—actually contribute to material power. Modern economic theories of international trade provide useful insights to fill this loophole.[10] Trade theories commonly suggest that international trade increases overall national wealth not simply through profits obtained by selling goods in foreign markets, but more importantly by increasing the productive and allocative efficiency and overall performance of the economy. Indeed, this mechanism was clearly recognized by Joanne Gowa and Edward Mansfield in the early 1990s.[11] However, scholars of great power politics have strangely dismissed the main process through which trade affects national power.

By taking into account the efficiency-enhancing effect of trade, international relations theories would be able to present a more comprehensive and realistic assessment of the interaction between reigning and challenging powers. For instance, while many security studies scholars tend to focus implicitly on the simple wealth that is obtained by selling goods in foreign markets—and the surplus or deficit in the balance of payments—this perspective is not consistent with the prevalent economic approach to international trade. Expansion of processing trade and the large share of intrafirm trade in today's commerce between the great powers further necessitate an understanding of the efficiency-enhancing dimension of trade. In other words, this book "updates" security studies scholars' understanding of international trade and, thus, the implications of economic exchanges for the balance of power.

Policy Implications

Although this book in general attempts to develop an explanatory theory rather than a prescriptive theory, it nonetheless offers important policy lessons for today's reigning power.[12] Most prominently, this book presents policy prescriptions for the United States, which is increasingly under pressure to complement military containment policy against China with equivalent economic measures.

According to the analyses presented in this book, there is good reason to be pessimistic about the US ability to effectively implement compound containment measures against China, even if Washington showed its willingness to undermine the growth of the Chinese economic sphere or to organize an economic bloc that excludes Beijing. Many of the United States' major industries cannot effectively replace the role of China through inter-actions with others, while China would be able to find alternative partners in many important aspects of its economic relations with the United States. In this condition, although it might be difficult to argue that the United States would certainly lose more than China were it to impose compound containment, it can be cautiously suggested that the United States cannot be certain about its ability to impose more losses on China through economic restrictions. In the dangerous international realm where states need to pay careful attention to their relative power, avoiding compound containment would be the better, if not more viable, option for the United States.

Would the United States be able to take deliberate policy measures to divert its economic exchanges from China to minimize its own losses and strengthen cooperation among major economies to deny alternative part-ners to China? A powerful reigning state such as the United States can cer-tainly invest heavily in encouraging its major industries to "exit" China—or seek "decoupling" with China—and pressure other countries to replicate its restrictive economic policy against the adversary. Nonetheless, it is dubious whether such investment and pressure would prove effective in today's international system. There are multiple foreign economic actors compet-ing with and trying to outperform American firms that would readily capi-talize on US policies that decreased its own firms' market competitiveness. Thus, deliberately diminishing the use of Chinese economic inputs would involve large risk and potential loss for US companies. Moreover, although the United States might be the world's largest market as a single country, there is a larger integrated market, the EU, as well as several other large markets around the globe. It is unlikely that these big markets can be pres-sured by Washington to restrict trade with the Chinese market. Some might suggest that the United States can exercise pressure on other countries by utilizing its position as their security provider.[13] However, there is abundant historical evidence that shows such a method does not always work. During the Cold War—especially, from the late 1950s until the late 1980s—even when all major economies relied heavily on the United States to ensure their security, Washington's overt pressure on its allies to cut off economic exchanges with the Eastern bloc frequently failed or put the United States in an awkward situation.[14]

This does not mean that the United States would never be in a position to adopt compound containment against China. I do suggest, however, that a favorable situation in which to impose a security diseconomy for compound containment would not be created by the United States' deliberate domestic and international policy measures alone. Changes in market conditions—for instance, the introduction of innovative technologies by US firms, dramatic developments in preferential trade agreements among the world's major markets, and a universal decision among all the advanced economies to punish China's violation of intellectual property rights and currency policy—are prerequisites to effective economic countermeasures against China. Nonetheless, while the United States' political decisions do not necessarily determine international economic conditions and structure, deliberately creating the economic circumstances for a security diseconomy against China might be beyond Washington's capability. In this situation, rather than imposing self-defeating restrictions on trade with China, Washington would need to wait and see if China indeed continues its growth to become a "peer competitor" of the United States.

For some observers, the Trump administration's "trade war" with China intended to check the rising power through aggressive economic means.[15] One might also suggest that these US economic restrictions reflected an incipient form of compound containment strategy against China. Nonetheless, Trump's protectionist policies against China did not constitute economic measures for compound containment that were designed to weaken the targeted state's material capacity to launch military aggression. Instead, Trump's measures against China were close to a mixture of foreign economic policy and economic diplomacy. Foreign economic policies refer to policy measures or orientations that govern a state's economic transactions with foreign entities. They aim to advance national development and domestic economic prosperity, as well as to create desirable international economic conditions.[16] Economic diplomacy refers to the effort to create a favorable economic environment for a state's economic activities, actors, or policies through negotiations with foreign entities.[17] These measures commonly aim to achieve economic objectives, rather than strategic goals as in compound containment.

In trade wars, one state tries to change the economic policy of another state through the imposition of economic costs, and the targeted state replies by retaliating with economic countermeasures.[18] A trade war is a form of economic diplomacy and is an outcome of foreign economic policy. It has occurred in different political and geographical contexts, but is commonly aimed to advance economic interests. In the late nineteenth century, between 1891 and 1894, Wilhelmine Germany experienced a tariff war with Russia, which was resolved with the signing of a new tariff treaty in 1894. In the 1980s, the United States and Japan conducted a trade war that was motivated by large trade imbalances and what Washington considered unfair monetary policies in Tokyo. Similarly, the Trump administration's trade war against China intended to rectify Beijing's "unfair" commercial, monetary, and industrial policies. The main objective of this trade war was to address the targeted state's economic behavior and to establish a habit of "fair trade," not necessarily to induce certain strategic outcomes.

Therefore, it would be misleading to argue that Trump adopted compound containment against China. Whether an economic policy constitutes compound containment should not be determined by the magnitude of tensions or controversy between the reigning and challenging powers. Trade wars can entail fierce confrontations between states, but they are not usually conducted over military-strategic ends.

Directions for Future Research

This book sought to offer a parsimonious theory on a specific dimension of the competition between a reigning power and a challenging power. Therefore, this book can be considered a building block for a more sophisticated theorization of great powers' balancing strategy, and of the economic aspects of the competition between the great powers. The argument and analysis presented in this book leave three substantive topics for future research.

First, while this book focused on explaining the reigning power's strategy, future research can theorize the challenging power's strategy toward the reigning power, and examine the equilibrium outcomes from the interaction between the reigning and challenging states. The challenging power is in a different relative power position than the reigning state and has different concerns and interests in pursuing its security. For instance, while the reigning state may need to be concerned only about the challenging state, the challenger is worried about the competition with all other major states in its neighborhood. Moreover, the challenging state can be in a different stage of economic development than the reigning state and, thus, have different economic considerations. Therefore, the challenging state's calculations over economic exchanges with the reigning state can be driven by factors that are not considered in my theory. Once we have a good understanding of the challenging state's behavior concerning economic ties with the reigning power, the outcome of the interaction between the reigning and challenging powers can be better theorized.

Second, future studies can engage in theorizing the dynamic aspects of economic strategy in great power competition. For instance, both the reigning power and the challenging power may seek to develop new alternative trade partners as they engage in security competition. Nonetheless, as I discuss in the theory chapter, creating capable alternative economic partners or restricting the number of important economic actors might be beyond the ability of a great power. The presence or absence of alternative economic partners is a structural factor that represents the economic condition of a certain period. Nonetheless, my approach in this book did not take into account the continuing evolution of the international economy, or the intervention of critical events that dramatically change international economic landscape. Future research can focus on important international economic developments that alter the shape of international economic structure and, in turn, affect the trajectory of great power competition.[19]

Third, certain components of my theory—assumptions, causal mechanisms, and the explanatory factors—can be further elaborated to explain how all major states, not just the reigning state, economically deal with their security competitors. All states have incentives to utilize both military and economic means in countering challenges to their security interests. Thus, it would be both theoretically and practically reasonable to pursue a more general theory on a state's use of economic restrictions in dealing with a security competitor. This book can be a useful starting point for this future study.

NOTES

Chapter 1

1. For instance, see Dale C. Copeland, *The Origins of Major War* (Ithaca, NY: Cornell University Press, 2000); Robert Gilpin, *War and Change in World Politics* (New York: Cambridge University Press, 1981); Robert Gilpin, "The Theory of Hegemonic War," *Journal of Interdisciplinary History* 18, no. 4 (Spring 1988), pp. 591–613; Charles L. Glaser, "Will China's Rise Lead to War? Why Realism Does Not Mean Pessimism," *Foreign Affairs* 90, no. 2 (April 2011), pp. 80–91; Paul Kennedy, *The Rise and Fall of the Great Powers: Economic Change and Military Conflict from 1500 to 2000* (New York: Vintage Books, 1989); Jack S. Levy, "Declining Power and the Preventive Motivation for War," *World Politics* 40, no. 1 (October 1987), pp. 82–107; John J. Mearsheimer, *The Tragedy of Great Power Politics* (New York: Norton, 2001); A. F. K. Organski and Jacek Kugler, *The War Ledger* (Chicago: University of Chicago Press, 1980); Robert Powell, *In the Shadow of Power* (Princeton, NJ: Princeton University Press, 1999), pp. 115–48; John A. Vasquez, *The War Puzzle Revisited* (New York: Cambridge University Press, 2009), pp. 90–127; and Kenneth N. Waltz, "Structural Realism after the Cold War," *International Security* 25, no. 1 (Summer 2000), pp. 32–39.

2. For the definition of containment, see John Lewis Gaddis, *Strategies of Containment* (New York: Oxford University Press, 2005); Melvyn P. Leffler, *A Preponderance of Power* (Palo Alto, CA: Stanford University Press, 1993); and George F. Kennan, *American Diplomacy* (Chicago: University of Chicago Press, 2012). For the utility of containment strategy, see Graham Allison, *Destined for War: Can America and China Escape Thucydides's Trap?* (Boston: Houghton Mifflin Harcourt, 2017); Robert D. Blackwill and Ashley J. Tellis, *Revising U.S. Grand Strategy toward China* (New York: Council on Foreign Relations, 2015); Colin Dueck, *The Obama Doctrine: American Grand Strategy Today* (New York: Oxford University Press, 2015); John J. Mearsheimer, "Can China Rise Peacefully?," *National Interest*, October 25, 2014, https://nationalinterest.org/commentary/can-china-rise-peacefully-10204; Joseph S. Nye Jr., "The Case for Deep Engagement," *Foreign Affairs* 74, no. 4 (July–August 1995), pp. 90–102; Marc Trachtenberg, "Making Grand Strategy: The Early Cold War Experience in Retrospect," *SAIS Review* 19, no. 1 (Winter–Spring 1999),

pp. 33–40; and Stephen M. Walt, "The Case for Finite Containment: Analyzing U.S. Grand Strategy," *International Security* 14, no. 1 (Summer 1989), pp. 5–49.

3. For the relationship between military and economic capacities, see Edward Harllett Carr, *The Twenty Years' Crisis, 1919–1939* (New York: St. Martin's Press, 1966), p. 108; Robert Gilpin, *U.S. Power and the Multinational Corporation* (New York: Basic Books, 1975), p. 35; Mearsheimer, *Tragedy of Great Power Politics*, p. 46; and Kenneth N. Waltz, *Theory of International Politics* (New York: McGraw Hill, 1979), p. 131. For the need to link economic relations with security considerations, see Joanne Gowa and Edward D. Mansfield, "Alliances, Imperfect Markets, and Major-Power Trade," *International Organization* 58, no. 4 (Autumn 2004), pp. 775–805; Joseph M. Grieco, "Anarchy and the Limits of Cooperation: A Realist Critique of the Newest Liberal Institutionalism," *International Organization* 42, no. 3 (Summer 1988), pp. 485–507; Mearsheimer, *Tragedy of Great Power Politics*, pp. 51–53; and Waltz, *Theory of International Politics*, pp. 104–7.

4. Robert J. Art, *A Grand Strategy for America* (Ithaca, NY: Cornell University Press, 2003), pp. 113–20; David L. Asher, Victor D. Comras, and Patrick M. Cronin, *Pressure: Coercive Economic Statecraft and U.S. National Security* (Washington, DC: Center for New American Security, 2011); Alan P. Dobson, *U.S. Economic Statecraft for Survival, 1933–1991* (New York: Routledge, 2002); Richard N. Haass, ed., *Economic Sanctions and American Diplomacy* (New York: Council on Foreign Relations, 1998); Richard N. Haass and Meghan L. O'Sullivan, *Honey and Vinegar: Incentives, Sanctions, and Foreign Policy* (Washington, DC: Brookings Institute Press, 2000).

5. For instance, in addition to notes 1 and 2, see Stephen G. Brooks, G. John Ikenberry, and William C. Wohlforth, "Don't Come Home, America: The Case against Retrenchment," *International Security* 37, no. 3 (Winter 2012–13), pp. 7–51; Colin Dueck, *Reluctant Crusaders: Power, Culture, and Change in American Grand Strategy* (Princeton, NJ: Princeton University Press, 2006); Richard Fontaine and Kristin M. Lord, eds., *America's Path: Grand Strategy for the Next Administration* (Washington, DC: Center for New American Security, 2012); John J. Mearsheimer and Stephen M. Walt, "The Case for Offshore Balancing," *Foreign Affairs* 95, no. 4 (July–August 2016), pp. 70–83; and Barry R. Posen, *Restraint: A New Foundation for U.S. Grand Strategy* (Ithaca, NY: Cornell University Press, 2014).

6. Mearsheimer, *Tragedy of Great Power Politics*, p. 402; Gilpin, *War and Change*.

7. Asher, Comras, and Cronin, *Pressure*; David A. Baldwin, *Economic Statecraft* (Princeton, NJ: Princeton University Press, 1985); Jean-Marc F. Blanchard and Norrin M. Ripsman, *Economic Statecraft and Foreign Policy* (New York: Routledge, 2015); Daniel W. Drezner, "Sanctions Sometimes Smart: Targeted Sanctions in Theory and Practice," *International Studies Review* 13, no. 1 (March 2011), pp. 96–108; Bryan R. Early, *Busted Sanctions* (Stanford, CA: Stanford University Press, 2015); Haass and O'Sullivan, *Honey and Vinegar*; Gary Clyde Hufbauer, Jeffrey J. Schott, Kimberly Ann Elliott, and Barbara Oegg, *Economic Sanctions Reconsidered*, 3rd edition (Washington, DC: Peterson Institute for International Economics, 2007);

Jonathan Kirshner, *Currency and Coercion* (Princeton, NJ: Princeton University Press); Juan Zarate, *Treasury's War* (New York: Public Affairs, 2013).

8. Robert D. Blackwill and Jennifer M. Harris, *War by Other Means* (Cambridge, MA: Belknap, 2016), pp. 1–8.

9. Christina L. Davis, "Linkage Diplomacy: Economic and Security Bargaining in the Anglo-Japanese Alliance, 1902–23," *International Security* 33, no. 3 (Winter 2008-9), pp. 143–79; Steven E. Lobell, "Second Face of Security Strategies," *Security Studies* 17, no. 3 (2008), pp. 438–67; Lars S. Skålnes, "Grand Strategy and Foreign Economic Policy," *World Politics* 50, no. 4 (July 1998), pp. 582–616.

10. For instance, see Dale C. Copeland, *Economic Interdependence and War* (Princeton, NJ: Princeton University Press, 2015); Edward D. Mansfield and Brian M. Pollins, eds., *Economic Interdependence and International Conflict: New Perspectives on an Enduring Debate* (Ann Arbor: University of Michigan Press, 2003); Patrick J. McDonald, *The Invisible Hand of Peace: Capitalism, the War Machine, and International Relations Theory* (New York: Cambridge University Press, 2009); and Gerald Schneider and Nils Petter Gleditsch, eds., *Assessing the Capitalist Peace* (New York: Routledge, 2012).

11. Meanwhile, there are some theorists who show that military competitors or even warring states might continue trading with each other. However, they tend to focus on relations between great powers in balanced multipolarity. In an anarchic international structure where military power is evenly distributed among multiple states, it can be reasonably suggested that every state is the other's potential enemy. Therefore, each state has strong incentives to maintain trade ties even with its current adversary in order to avoid relative loss vis-à-vis other countries or out of fear of future conflict with them. However, the international structure in which the competition between the reigning and challenging powers takes place is often not multipolar. During the Cold War, the international structure was bipolar. Since the end of the Cold War, the structure has been unipolar. For instance, see Peter Liberman, "Trading with the Enemy: Security and Relative Economic Gains," *International Security* 21, no. 1 (Summer 1996), pp. 147–75; and Suzanne Werner, "In Search of Security: Relative Gains and Losses in Dyadic Relations," *Journal of Peace Research* 34, no. 3 (August 1997), pp. 289–302. Also see Jack S. Levy and Katherine Barbieri, "Trading with the Enemy during Wartime," *Security Studies* 13, no. 3 (Spring 2004), pp. 8–18.

12. For a notable exception, see Henry Farrell and Abraham L. Newman, "Weaponized Interdependence: How Global Economic Networks Shape State Coercion," *International Security* 44, no. 1 (Summer 2019), pp. 42–79. For new strategies in great power politics, see Kai He, "Undermining Adversaries: Unipolarity, Threat Perception, and Negative Balancing Strategies after the Cold War," *Security Studies* 21, no. 2 (2012), pp. 154–91; Robert A. Pape, "Soft Balancing against the United States," *International Security* 30, no. 1 (Summer 2005), pp. 7–45; T. V. Paul, *Restraining Great Powers* (New Haven: Yale University Press, 2018); and Brock F. Tessman, "System Structure and State Strategy," *Security Studies* 21, no. 2 (2012), pp. 192–231.

13. For this definition of economic sanctions, see Robert A. Pape, "Why Economic Sanctions Do Not Work," *International Security* 22, no. 2 (Fall 1997), pp. 90–136. Also see Drezner, "Sanctions Sometimes Smart."

14. This does not mean that economic measures cannot play important independent roles. On the contrary, I recognize that economic instruments can be useful substitutes for military force under certain circumstances. Yet there are numerous theoretical and empirical studies that examine the independent role of economic means. I focus on the complementary roles because the scholarship on this aspect of economic instruments is relatively underdeveloped.

15. For the role of alternative partners, see Albert O. Hirschman, *National Power and the Structure of Foreign Trade* (Berkeley: University of California Press, 1980 [1945]).

16. For the role of domestic commercial interests, see Scott L. Kastner, "When Do Conflicting Relations Affect International Trade?," *Journal of Conflict Resolution* 51, no. 4 (August 2007), pp. 664–88; Paul A. Papayoanou and Scott L. Kastner, "Sleeping with the (Potential) Enemy: Assessing the U.S. Policy of Engagement with China," *Security Studies* 9, no. 1 (1999), pp. 157–87. Also see Levy and Barbieri, "Trading with the Enemy"; and Steven E. Lobell, *The Challenge of Hegemony: Grand Strategy, Trade, and Domestic Politics* (Ann Arbor: University of Michigan Press, 2003).

17. For instance, see Henry M. Paulson, "A Strategic Engagement: Strengthening U.S.-Chinese Ties," *Foreign Affairs* 87, no. 5 (September–October 2008), pp. 59–77; and Condoleezza Rice, "Promoting the National Interest," *Foreign Affairs* 79, no. 1 (January–February 2000), pp. 45–62.

18. See Baldwin, *Economic Statecraft*; Hirschman, *National Power*; Kirshner, *Currency and Coercion*; Michael Mastanduno, *Economic Containment* (Ithaca, NY: Cornell University Press, 1992); and Michael Mastanduno, "Economic Statecraft, Interdependence, and National Security: Agendas for Research," *Security Studies* 9, no. 1 (1999), pp. 288–316.

19. See Copeland, *Economic Interdependence and War*; Joanne Gowa, *Allies, Adversaries, and International Trade* (Princeton, NJ: Princeton University Press, 1994); and Edward D. Mansfield, *Power, Trade, and War* (Princeton, NJ: Princeton University Press, 1995).

20. For realism's pessimism about international economic cooperation, see David A. Baldwin, ed., *Neorealism and Neoliberalism: The Contemporary Debate* (New York: Columbia University Press, 1993); James D. Fearon, "Bargaining, Enforcement, and International Cooperation," *International Organization* 52, no. 2 (Spring 1998), pp. 269–305; Robert Jervis, "Realism, Neoliberalism, and Cooperation: Understanding the Debate," *International Security* 24, no. 1 (Summer 1999), pp. 42–63; and John J. Mearsheimer, "The False Promise of International Institutions," *International Security* 19, no. 3 (Winter 1994–95), pp. 5–49.

21. For instance, see Michael J. Hiscox, "The Domestic Sources of Foreign Economic Policies," in John Ravenhill, ed., *Global Political Economy*, 3rd edition (Oxford: Oxford University Press, 2011), chap. 4; Robert Keohane and Helen Mil-

ner, eds., *Internationalization and Domestic Politics* (New York: Cambridge University Press, 1996); and Helen V. Milner, "The Political Economy of International Trade," *Annual Review of Political Science* 2 (1999), pp. 91–114.

22. Dong Jung Kim, "Choosing the Right Sidekick: Economic Complements to US Military Grand Strategies," *Journal of Strategic Studies* 39, nos. 5–6 (October 2016), pp. 899–921.

23. Aaron L. Friedberg, *A Contest for Supremacy* (New York: Norton, 2011).

Chapter 2

1. For this distinction, see Robert A. Pape, "Soft Balancing against the U.S.," *International Security* 30, no. 1 (Summer 2005), pp. 11–12.

2. For great power regions and regional hegemony, see John J. Mearsheimer, *Tragedy of Great Power Politics* (New York: Norton, 2001), pp. 40–42.

3. For instance, see Graham Allison, *Destined for War: Can America and China Escape Thucydides's Trap?* (Boston: Houghton Mifflin Harcourt, 2017); Dale C. Copeland, *The Origins of Major War* (Ithaca, NY: Cornell University Press, 2000); Robert Gilpin, *War and Change in World Politics* (New York: Cambridge University Press, 1981); Jack S. Levy, "Declining Power and the Preventive Motivation for War," *World Politics* 40, no. 1 (October 1987), pp. 82–107; and Mearsheimer, *Tragedy of Great Power Politics*, chap. 7.

4. John J. Mearsheimer, "The Gathering Storm: China's Challenge to U.S. Power in Asia," *Chinese Journal of International Politics* 3, no. 4 (Winter 2010), pp. 381–96.

5. Aaron L. Friedberg, "The Future of U.S.-China Relations: Is Conflict Inevitable?," *International Security* 30, no. 2 (Fall, 2005), pp. 7–45; Charles A. Kupchan, *How Enemies Become Friends: The Sources of Stable Peace* (Princeton, NJ: Princeton University Press, 2010).

6. Kelly M. Kadera, *The Power-Conflict Story: A Dynamic Model of Interstate Rivalry* (Ann Arbor: University of Michigan Press, 2001).

7. George F. Kennan, *American Diplomacy* (Chicago: University of Chicago Press, 2012).

8. For containment, see John Lewis Gaddis, *Strategies of Containment* (New York: Oxford University Press, 2005); and Melvyn P. Leffler, *A Preponderance of Power* (Palo Alto, CA: Stanford University Press, 1993).

9. For the concept of balancing, see Daniel H. Nexon, "The Balance of Power in the Balance," *World Politics* 61, no. 2 (April 2009), pp. 330–59; and Joseph M. Parent and Sebastian Rosato, "Balancing in Neorealism," *International Security* 40, no. 2 (Fall 2015), pp. 51–86.

10. For the concept of grand strategy, see Stephen G. Brooks, G. John Ikenberry, and William C. Wohlforth, "Don't Come Home, America: The Case against Retrenchment," *International Security* 37, no. 3 (Winter 2012–13), pp. 7–51.

11. Robert J. Art, *A Grand Strategy for America* (Ithaca, NY: Cornell University Press, 2003), p. 113.

12. For specific economic measures, see David A. Baldwin, *Economic Statecraft* (Princeton, NJ: Princeton University Press, 1985); Jonathan Kirshner, *Currency and Coercion* (Princeton, NJ: Princeton University Press); and Michael Mastanduno, *Economic Containment* (Ithaca, NY: Cornell University Press, 1992), pp. 39–63.

13. Michael Mastanduno, "Strategies of Economic Containment: U.S. Trade Relations with the Soviet Union," *World Politics* 37, no. 4 (July 1985), pp. 503–31.

14. Moreover, considering ongoing military confrontation with the challenging power, the boundaries between military-related and purely civilian economic exchanges are likely to be blurred.

15. See Lisa L. Martin, *Coercive Cooperation* (Princeton, NJ: Princeton University Press, 1992), p. 267; and Tor Egil Førland, "'Economic Warfare' and 'Strategic Goods,'" *Journal of Peace Research* 28, no. 2 (1991), p. 192.

16. For diverse aspects of the strategic employments of economic instruments, see Baldwin, *Economic Statecraft*.

17. For this definition of economic sanctions, see Robert A. Pape, "Why Economic Sanctions Do Not Work," *International Security* 22, no. 2 (Fall 1997), pp. 90–136. Also see Daniel W. Drezner, "Sanctions Sometimes Smart: Targeted Sanctions in Theory and Practice," *International Studies Review* 13, no. 1 (March 2011), pp. 96–108.

18. For the use of economic instruments in coercive diplomacy, see Jean-Marc F. Blanchard and Norrin M. Ripsman, *Economic Statecraft and Foreign Policy* (New York: Routledge, 2015).

19. Michael Mastanduno, "Strategies of Economic Containment," *World Politics* 37, no. 4 (1985), pp. 503–31; Michael Mastanduno, "Trade as a Strategic Weapon," *International Organization* 42, no. 1 (1988), pp. 121–50; Mastanduno, *Economic Containment*.

20. For hedging, see Evelyn Goh, *Meeting the China Challenge* (Washington, DC: East-West Center, 2005).

21. For soft balancing, see Robert A. Pape, "Soft Balancing against the United States," *International Security* 30, no. 1 (2005), pp. 7–45; and T. V. Paul, *Restraining Great Powers* (New Haven: Yale University Press, 2018).

22. This book considers that these assumptions are reasonable ones, and build on assumptions that are widely employed in the study of great power politics. For different perspectives about assumptions in social science theorization, see Mearsheimer, *Tragedy of Great Power Politics*, pp. 29–30.

23. Ibid., pp. 30–32; Sebastian Rosato, "The Inscrutable Intentions of Great Powers," *International Security* 39, no. 3 (Winter 2014–15), pp. 48–88.

24. James Fearon, "Rationalist Explanations for War," *International Organization* 49, no. 3 (1995), pp. 379–414; Stephen Kalberg, "Max Weber's Types of Rationality: Cornerstones for the Analysis of Rationalization Processes in History," *American Journal of Sociology* 85, no. 5 (March 1980), pp. 1145–79.

25. Charles A. Kupchan, *The Vulnerability of Empire* (Ithaca, NY: Cornell University Press, 1994); Jack Snyder, *Myths of Empire: Domestic Politics and International Ambition* (Ithaca, NY: Cornell University Press, 1991).

26. For the components of balancing behavior, see Parent and Rosato, "Balancing in Neorealism."

27. For accommodation, see T. V. Paul, ed., *Accommodating Rising Powers: Past, Present, and Future* (Cambridge: Cambridge University Press, 2016). For discussions on diverse responses to a rising power, see Bark R. Brawley, "The Political Economy of Balance of Power," in T. V. Paul, James J. Wirtz, and Michel Fortmann, eds., *Balance of Power* (Stanford, CA: Stanford University Press, 2004), chap. 3; and Randall L. Schweller, "Managing the Rise of Great Powers," in Alastair Ian Johnston and Robert S. Ross, eds., *Engaging China* (London: Routledge, 1999), chap. 1.

28. See James D. Morrow, "How Could Trade Affect Conflict?," *Journal of Peace Research* 36, no. 3 (July 1999), pp. 481–89.

29. Duncan Snidal, "Relative Gains and the Pattern of International Cooperation," *American Political Science Review* 85, no. 3 (September 1991), pp. 701–26.

30. Albert O. Hirschman, *National Power and the Structure of Foreign Trade* (Berkeley: University of California Press, 1980 [1945]), chap. 2.

31. For relative gains sensitivity, see Robert Powell, "Absolute and Relative Gains in International Relations Theory," *American Political Science Review* 85, no. 4 (December 1991), pp. 1303–20.

32. Joanne Gowa and Edward D. Mansfield, "Power Politics and International Trade," *American Political Science Review* 87, no. 2 (June 1993), pp. 408–20.

33. For different views on the implication of foreign economic exchanges to national power, see Robert Gilpin, *Global Political Economy: Understanding the International Economic Order* (Princeton, NJ: Princeton University Press, 2001).

34. For instance, see Cletus Coughlin, "The Controversy over Free Trade," *Federal Reserve Bank of St. Louis Review* 84, no. 1 (January–February 2002), pp. 1–22; Elhanan Helpman, "The Structure of Foreign Trade," *Journal of Economic Perspectives* 13, no. 2 (Spring 1999), pp. 121–44; and Paul R. Krugman, Maurice Obstfeld, and Marc J. Melitz, *International Economics*, 9th edition (New York: Addison-Wesley, 2012). For a similar view, see Klaus Knorr, *The War Potential of Nations* (Princeton, NJ: Princeton University Press, 1956), pp. 199–201.

35. Kenneth N. Waltz, "The Myth of Interdependence," in Charles P. Kindleberger, ed., *The International Corporation* (Cambridge, MA: MIT Press, 1970), pp. 205–23. Also see Robert O. Keohane and Joseph S. Nye, *Power and Interdependence*, 3rd edition (New York: Longman, 2001).

36. Hirschman, *National Power*. Also see Eugene Gholz and Daryl G. Press, "The Effects of Wars on Neutral Countries: Why It Doesn't Pay to Preserve the Peace," *Security Studies* 10, no. 4 (Summer 2001), pp. 1–57; and Nicholas J. Spykman, *America's Strategy in World Politics* (New York: Harcourt, 1942).

37. Several scholars have examined the role of multiple actors—or the presence of multipolarity—in making cooperation possible among relative gains maximizers. One of the main goals of this book is to supplement these arguments with an understanding of economic aspects of multiplayer interaction. In this context, the arguments on multipolarity should not be considered to offer an alternative explanation or introduce a confounding factor. Rather, they are building blocks of my

argument. I attempt to switch the notion of (multi)polarity with the availability of alternative economic partners, and thereby offer a more sophisticated argument on the role of the number of key actors. For instance, see Peter Liberman, "Trading with the Enemy: Security and Relative Economic Gains," *International Security* 21, no. 1 (Summer 1996), pp. 147–75; Snidal, "Relative Gains"; and Suzanne Werner, "In Search of Security: Relative Gains and Losses in Dyadic Relations," *Journal of Peace Research* 34, no. 3 (August 1997), pp. 289–302.

38. Bryan R. Early, *Busted Sanctions* (Stanford, CA: Stanford University Press, 2015); Martin, *Coercive Cooperation*.

39. Dale C. Copeland, *Economic Interdependence and War* (Princeton, NJ: Princeton University Press, 2015), pp. 43–46; Jack S. Levy and Katherine Barbieri, "Trading with the Enemy during Wartime," *Security Studies* 13, no. 3 (Spring 2004), pp. 1–47.

40. William Milberg and Deborah Winkler, *Outsourcing Economics* (New York: Cambridge University Press, 2013).

41. Gholz and Press, "Effects of Wars."

42. I do not argue that that the two competing great powers are incapable of making domestic economic adjustments to cope with changes in bilateral economic exchanges. According to mainstream international economics, nonetheless, all else being equal, a state's efficiency gains obtained from foreign economic exchanges are not fully replaceable with domestic activities.

43. For an overview of this approach, see Helen V. Milner, *Interests, Institutions, and Information: Domestic Politics and International Relations* (Princeton, NJ: Princeton University Press, 1997).

44. For instance, see Andrew Moravcsik, "Taking Preferences Seriously: A Liberal Theory of International Politics," *International Organization* 51, no. 4 (Autumn 1997), pp. 513–53.

45. For the role of domestic commercial interest groups in international political competition, see Scott L. Kastner, "When Do Conflicting Relations Affect International Trade?," *Journal of Conflict Resolution* 51, no. 4 (August 2007), pp. 664–88; and Paul A. Papayoanou and Scott L. Kastner, "Sleeping with the (Potential) Enemy: Assessing the U.S. Policy of Engagement with China," *Security Studies* 9, no. 1 (1999), pp. 157–87. Also see Steven E. Lobell, *The Challenge of Hegemony: Grand Strategy, Trade, and Domestic Politics* (Ann Arbor: University of Michigan Press, 2003); and Kevin Narizny, *The Political Economy of Grand Strategy* (Ithaca, NY: Cornell University Press, 2007).

46. Peter J. Katzenstein, ed., *The Culture of National Security* (New York: Columbia University Press, 1996); Alexander Wendt, *Social Theory of International Politics* (New York: Cambridge University Press, 1999).

47. Jonathan D. Caverley, *Democratic Militarism: Voting, Wealth, and War* (New York: Cambridge University Press, 2014); G. John Ikenberry, *Liberal Leviathan: The Origins, Crisis, and Transformation of the American World Order* (Princeton, NJ: Princeton University Press, 2012); John J. Mearsheimer, *The Great Delusion: Liberal Dreams and International Realities* (New Haven: Yale University Press, 2018); Ste-

phen M. Walt, *The Hell of Good Intentions: America's Foreign Policy Elite and the Decline of U.S. Primacy* (New York: Farrar, Straus and Giroux, 2018).

48. Colin Dueck, *Reluctant Crusaders: Power, Culture, and Change in American Grand Strategy* (Princeton, NJ: Princeton University Press, 2006).

49. William Harbutt Dawson, *Richard Cobden and Foreign Policy* (New York: Routledge, 2018 [1926]).

50. This logic has been repeatedly advanced in policy-relevant writings in the United States. For instance, see Richard N. Haass and Meghan L. O'Sullivan, *Honey and Vinegar: Incentives, Sanctions, and Foreign Policy* (Washington, DC: Brookings Institute Press, 2000); Henry M. Paulson, "A Strategic Engagement: Strengthening U.S.-Chinese Ties," *Foreign Affairs* 87, no. 5 (September–October 2008), pp. 59–77; and Condoleezza Rice, "Promoting the National Interest," *Foreign Affairs* 79, no. 1 (January–February 2000), pp. 45–62.

51. Moreover, these beliefs would be reinforced by leaders' concerns about unintended consequences of taking aggressive economic stance toward the challenging power. For instance, the reigning power's extensive economic restrictions can provoke the challenging power to become more aggressive, and in turn undermine the objective of containing that state's military adventures. Put differently, leaders might be concerned about overreaction, a spiral, or self-fulfilling prophecy.

52. For the testing of causal theories, see Jack Snyder, "Richness, Rigor, and Relevance in the Study of Soviet Foreign Policy," *International Security* 9, no. 3 (Winter 1984–85), pp. 89–108; and Arthur L. Stinchcombe, *Constructing Social Theories* (Chicago: University of Chicago Press, 1968).

53. For instance, see Henry E. Brady and David Collier, eds., *Rethinking Social Inquiry: Diverse Tools, Shared Standards* (New York: Rowman and Littlefield, 2004); Alexander L. George and Andrew Bennett, *Case Studies and Theory Development in the Social Sciences* (Cambridge, MA: MIT Press, 2005); and Stephen Van Evera, *Guide to Methods for Students of Political Science* (Ithaca, NY: Cornell University Press, 1997).

54. Angus Maddison, *The World Economy: A Millennial Perspective* (Paris: Organization for Economic Cooperation and Development, 2001); B. R. Mitchell, *International Historical Statistics* (London: Palgrave Macmillan, 1998); Arvind Subramanian, *Eclipse: Living in the Shadow of China's Economic Dominance* (Washington, DC: Peterson Institute for International Economics, 2011).

55. For instance, see Robert Art, "The U.S. and the Rise of China: Implications for the Long Haul," *Political Science Quarterly* 125, no. 3 (2010), pp. 359–91.

56. See Subramanian, *Eclipse*, chap. 2.

57. Paul W. Schroeder, *The Transformation of European Politics, 1763–1848* (Oxford: Clarendon Press, 1994).

58. Mearsheimer, *Tragedy of Great Power Politics*, p. 65.

59. Ibid., p. 63.

60. William C. Fuller, *Strategy and Power in Russia, 1600–1914* (New York: Free Press, 1992).

61. Thomas G. Paterson, *Meeting the Communist Threat: Truman to Reagan* (New York: Oxford University Press, 1988), p. 61.

62. See Mearsheimer, *Tragedy of Great Power Politics*, p. 382. Also see Peter J. Katzenstein, *A World of Regions: Asia and Europe in the American Imperium* (Ithaca, NY: Cornell University Press, 2005).

63. Sean M. Lynn-Jones, "Détente and Deterrence: Anglo-German Relations, 1911–1914," *International Security* 11, no. 2 (Fall 1986), pp. 121–50.

64. For British-US relations in the nineteenth century, see Kenneth Bourne, *Britain and the Balance of Power in North America, 1815–1908* (Berkeley: University of California Press, 1967); David L. Dykstra, *The Shifting Balance of Power: American-British Diplomacy in North America, 1842–1848* (Lanham, MD: University Press of America, 1999); and Dong Jung Kim, "A Prologue to Manifest Destiny: Why Britain Allowed the United States' Unchallenged Rise in North America, 1836–1848," *Political Science Quarterly* 134, no. 3 (2019), pp. 477–506.

Chapter 3

1. Portions of this chapter are adapted from Dong Jung Kim, "Realists as Free Traders: The Struggle for Power and the Case against Protectionism," *International Affairs* 94, no. 6 (2018), pp. 1269–86.

2. For the spiral dynamics in military competition between Britain and Germany, see Robert Jervis, *Perception and Misperception in International Politics* (Princeton, NJ: Princeton University Press, 1976), pp. 62–67; L. C. F. Turner, *Origins of the First World War* (New York: Norton, 1970); Jack L. Snyder, *The Ideology of the Offensive: Military Decision Making and the Disasters of 1914* (Ithaca, NY: Cornell University Press, 1984); and Stephen Van Evera, "The Cult of the Offensive and the Origins of the First World War," *International Security* 9, no. 1 (Summer 1984), pp. 58–107. This, however, does not mean that Britain did not attempt rapprochement with Germany before World War I. In 1906, when the Moroccan Crisis was being resolved, Britain and Germany took serious measures to recover their relationship. For instance, see Foreign Office General Correspondence 1906–1966, FO 371–75 and FO 371/79. Also see Sean M. Lynn-Jones, "Détente and Deterrence: Anglo-German Relations, 1911–1914," *International Security* 11, no. 2 (Fall 1986), pp. 121–50.

3. For Britain's military response to the German challenge, see David French, *British Economic and Strategic Planning, 1905–1915* (London: George Allen and Unwin, 1982); Michael Howard, *The Continental Commitment: The Dilemma of British Defence Policy in the Era of Two World Wars* (London: Maurice Temple Smith, 1972); Paul M. Kennedy, *The Rise and Fall of British Naval Mastery* (New York: Scribner, 1976), chap. 8; Nicholas A. Lambert, *Planning Armageddon: British Economic Warfare and the First World War* (Cambridge, MA: Harvard University Press, 2012); Paul M. Kennedy, *The Rise of the Anglo-German Antagonism, 1860–1914* (London: G. Allen and Unwin, 1980); C. J. Lowe and M. L. Dockrill, *The Mirage of Power, British Foreign Policy 1902–14*, vol. 1 (New York: Routledge, 2002), pp. 1–28; and Samuel R. Williamson, *The Politics of Grand Strategy: Britain and France Prepare for War, 1904–1914* (Cambridge, MA: Harvard University Press, 1969).

4. Francis Oppenheimer, *Stranger Within* (London: Faber and Faber, 1960), p. 158; Aaron L. Friedberg, *The Weary Titan: Britain and the Experience of Relative Decline, 1895–1905* (Princeton, NJ: Princeton University Press, 1988), pp. 24–26.

5. See G. R. Searle, *The Quest for National Efficiency: A Study in British Politics and Political Thought, 1899–1914* (Berkeley: University of California Press, 1971).

6. Quoted in ibid., p. 5.

7. James D. Startt, *Journalists for Empire* (New York: Greenwood Press, 1991), pp. 1–5.

8. Paul Readman, "The Liberal Party and Patriotism in Early Twentieth Century Britain," *Twentieth Century British History* 12, no. 3 (2001), p. 273; Paul Readman, *Land and Nation in England: Patriotism, National Identity, and the Politics of Land, 1880–1914* (Suffolk: Boydell Press, 2008).

9. Frans Coetzee, *For Party or Country: Nationalism and the Dilemmas of Popular Conservatism in Edwardian England* (New York: Oxford University Press, 1990), p. 42; Ross J. S. Hoffman, *Great Britain and the German Trade Rivalry, 1875–1914* (Philadelphia: University of Pennsylvania Press, 1933), chaps. 2 and 3.

10. Kenneth N. Waltz, *Theory of International Politics* (New York: McGraw Hill, 1979), p. 212. Also see Peter J. Katzenstein, "International Interdependence: Some Long-Term Trends and Recent Changes," *International Organization* 29, no. 4 (Autumn 1975), pp. 1021–34.

11. B. R. Mitchell, *International Historical Statistics: Europe 1750–2000* (New York: Palgrave Macmillan, 2003), pp. 662–63.

12. Arthur Balfour, "Insular Free Trade," August 1, 1903 (Cab. 37/65/47); Neville Chamberlin, *Mr. Chamberlain's Speeches*, ed. Charles W. Boyd, vol. 2 (London: Constable and Company, 1914), pp. 140–82. For the motivations behind Chamberlain's promotion of tariff reform, see Sydney H. Zebel, "Joseph Chamberlain and the Genesis of Tariff Reform," *Journal of British Studies* 7, no. 1 (November 1967), pp. 131–57.

13. A number of extant studies argue that European great powers before World War I eschewed restricting their economic exchanges with a current adversary out of fear of relative losses vis-à-vis a future enemy. In this chapter, I introduce a different perspective, which suggests that the prospects of encountering more relative losses than the adversary in a bilateral setup shaped Britain's decision to avoid compound containment. I take this approach because, as the 1900s progressed, Germany increasingly became the most threatening state for Britain. As Herbert Henry Asquith, prime minister beginning in 1908, stated, "The command of the sea, however important and however desirable it may be to other Powers, is, to us, a matter of life and death." Other states did not have the potential to pose a threat of such magnitude. For instance, see Peter Liberman, "Trading with the Enemy: Security and Relative Economic Gains," *International Security* 21, no. 1 (Summer 1996), pp. 147–75. For Asquith's statement, see *The Times*, ed., *Speeches by the Rt. Hon. H. H. Asquith from His First Appointment as a Minister of the Crown in 1892 to His Accession to the Office of Prime Minister April 1908* (London: Printing House Square, 1909), p. 309.

14. Chamberlin, *Mr. Chamberlain's Speeches*, pp. 140–82. The need for tariff reform emerged in the late nineteenth century. For earlier debate on tariff reform, see Benjamin H. Brown, *The Tariff Reform Movement in Great Britain 1881–1895* (New York: AMS Press, 1966). Also see Andrew J. Marrison, "The Development of a Tariff Reform Policy during Joseph Chamberlain's First Campaign, May 1903–February 1904," in W. H. Chaloner and Barrie M. Ratcliffe, eds., *Trade and Transport* (Manchester: Manchester University Press, 1977), pp. 214–41.

15. Quoted in Friedberg, *The Weary Titan*, p. 72.

16. Hoffman, *Great Britain*, p. 285.

17. Peter Cain, "Political Economy in Edwardian England: The Tariff Reform Controversy," in Alan O'Day, ed., *The Edwardian Age: Conflict and Stability* (Hamden, CT: Archon Books, 1979), pp. 41–42.

18. Arthur J. Balfour, "Insular Free Trade," August 1, 1903 (Cab. 37/65/47).

19. Cain, "Political Economy in Edwardian England," pp. 42–43; Coetzee, *For Party or Country*, p. 56.

20. For examples of the Unionist Party's continued focus on tariff reform throughout the 1900s, see the exchanges between Arthur Balfour and Austen Chamberlain in February 1907, in Balfour Papers, vol. 98 (Add MS 49780), pp. 236–54, Robert Cecil and Hugh Cecil, "Memorandum: The Taxes on Food," March 6, 1912, Tariff Reform, Including Papers on Canadian Tariffs, and Economic Arrangements between Canada and Germany (Add MS 88906/23/17), and Lord Lansdowne's memos and mails in Miscellaneous Foreign and Domestic Papers of Lord Lansdowne (Add MS 88906/23/22).

21. Andrew S. Thompson, "Tariff Reform: An Imperial Strategy, 1903–1913," *Historical Journal* 40, no. 4 (1997), pp. 1033–54.

22. For major commodities traded between Britain and Germany, see Treasury, "The Fiscal Problem," August 20, 1903 (Cab. 37/66/55), pp. 52, 56.

23. Peter Mathias, *The First Industrial Nation*, 2nd edition (London: Methuen, 1983), p. 225.

24. Sydney Pollard, "British and World Shipbuilding, 1890–1914," *Journal of Economic History* 17, no. 3 (September 1957), pp. 443–44.

25. Sidney Pollard and Paul Robertson, *The British Shipbuilding Industry, 1870–1914* (Cambridge, MA: Harvard University Press, 1979), pp. 37–48.

26. Cain, "Political Economy in Edwardian England," p. 45; Kennedy, *Anglo-German Antagonism*, p. 300. This, however, does not mean that the cost of materials and equipment was the only determinant of Britain's competitiveness in shipbuilding.

27. Treasury, "The Conditions and Effects of 'Dumping,'" July 7, 1903 (Cab. 37/65/42), p. 5.

28. The Tariff Commission, *Report of the Tariff Commission*, vol. 4, *The Engineering Industries* (London: P. S. King and Son, 1909), paragraphs 497–546.

29. Pollard, "British and World Shipbuilding," pp. 439–40.

30. Ibid. Being a major assembly industry, prosperity in shipbuilding had a large impact on the activities of its supplying industries such as machinery and

engineering, and iron and steel. See Pollard and Robertson, *British Shipbuilding Industry*, p. 6.

31. Mathias, *The First Industrial Nation*, p. 384.

32. Samuel B. Saul, *Studies in British Overseas Trade, 1870–1914* (Liverpool: Liverpool University Press, 1960), p. 31.

33. Ibid.; Pollard, "British and World Shipbuilding," p. 427.

34. Pollard and Robertson, *British Shipbuilding Industry*, p. 6.

35. Ibid., p. 92.

36. Mathias, *The First Industrial Nation*, p. 286; Pollard, "British and World Shipbuilding," p. 432.

37. Phyllis Deane and W. A. Cole, *British Economic Growth 1688–1959*, 2nd edition (Cambridge: Cambridge University Press, 1969), p. 234; Mathias, *The First Industrial Nation*, p. 282.

38. For the US challenge in the shipping industry, see Vivian Vale, *The American Peril: Challenge to Britain on North Atlantic, 1901–04* (Manchester: Manchester University Press, 1984).

39. Mathias, *The First Industrial Nation*, p. 287.

40. Roderick Floud, *The British Machine Tool Industry, 1850–1914* (Cambridge: Cambridge University Press, 1976), p. 4.

41. *Hansard's Parliamentary Debates*, 4th Series, vol. 130 (February 19, 1904, House of Lords) (London: Wyman and Sons), paragraph 361. For similar view, see Percy Ashley, "Foreign Competition in British Markets," Balfour Papers, vol. 98 (Add MS 49780), pp. 120–23. Also see Andrew Marrison, *British Business and Protection, 1903–1932* (Oxford: Clarendon Press, 1996), pp. 148–50; J. H. Clapham, *An Economic History of Modern Britain*, vol. 3 (Cambridge: Cambridge University Press, 1938), pp. 122–23.

42. For the British adoption of electricity for industrial and other purposes, see Clapham, *Economic History of Modern Britain*, pp. 128–42.

43. Quoted in Hoffman, *Great Britain*, p. 107.

44. For Britain's loss of market share in this industry, see Robert Allen, "International Competition in Iron and Steel, 1850–1913," *Journal of Economic History* 39, no. 4 (December 1979), pp. 911–37; Marrison, *British Business and Protection*, p. 139.

45. Mathias, *The First Industrial Nation*, pp. 378–81.

46. W. E. Minchinton, *The British Tinplate Industry* (Oxford: Clarendon Press, 1957), pp. 85–86; Geoffrey Tweedale, *Sheffield Steel and America: A Century of Commercial and Technological Interdependence, 1830–1930* (Cambridge: Cambridge University Press, 1987), pp. 180–81.

47. Clapham, *Economic History of Modern Britain*, pp. 152–53; Saul, *Studies in British Overseas Trade*, p. 32.

48. Charles T. Ritchie–Chancellor of Exchequer, "Preferential Tariffs," September 9, 1903 (Cab. 37/66/58), pp. 2–3.

49. For instance, see Tariff Commission, *Report of the Tariff Commission*, vol. 1, *The Iron and Steel Trades* (London: P. S. King and Son, 1904), paragraph 432.

50. P. F. Clarke, "The End of Laissez Faire and the Politics of Cotton," *Historical Journal* 15, no. 3 (September 1972), p. 493. For Britain's continuing price advantage, see John C. Brown, "Imperfect Competition and Anglo-German Trade Rivalry: Markets for Cotton Textiles before 1914," *Journal of Economic History* 55, no. 3 (September 1995), pp. 494–527.

51. Kennedy, *Anglo-German Antagonism*, p. 302.

52. Tariff Commission, *Report of the Tariff Commission*, vol. 2, *The Textile Trades*, Part I, *The Cotton Industry* (London: P. S. King and Son, 1905), paragraph 81.

53. From 1890–1894 to 1900–1904, the share of bleached, printed and dyed piece goods, and miscellaneous cotton in all cotton exports had risen from 50 percent to 66 percent (by value). See Marrison, *British Business and Protection*, p. 183.

54. Treasury, "The Fiscal Problem," August 20, 1903 (Cab. 37/66/55), p. 42; Mathias, *The First Industrial Nation*, p. 384.

55. Clapham, *Economic History of Modern Britain*, pp. 128–29; Saul, *Studies in British Overseas Trade*, p. 37.

56. *The Times*, ed., *Speeches by the Rt. Hon. H. H. Asquith from His First Appointment as a Minister of the Crown in 1892 to His Accession to the Office of Prime Minister April 1908* (London: Printing House Square, 1909), p. 190; H. H. Asquith, *Trade and the Empire* (London: Methuen, 1903), pp. 47, 57–58.

57. Treasury, "Will Our Purchasing Power Run Short?," September 25, 1903 (Cab. 37/66/62), pp. 5–6. Also see Balfour Papers, vol. 98 (Add MS 49780), p. 2; "Preferential Duties," May 9, 1899, Fiscalia (T 168/54); and Board of Trade, "The Export Policy of Trusts in Certain Foreign Countries," August 1903 (Cab. 37/66/57).

58. Cain, "Political Economy in Edwardian England," p. 50.

59. Campbell-Bannerman Papers, vol. 38 B (Add MS 41243 B), p. 69; Treasury, "The Conditions and Effects of 'Dumping,'" July 7, 1903 (Cab. 37/65/42).

60. "Price of Sugar," November 7, 1904, Miscellaneous Memoranda (T168/64).

61. Hoffman, *Great Britain*, pp. 114–38.

62. Thomas J. Misa, *A Nation of Steel: The Making of Modern America, 1865–1925* (Baltimore: John Hopkins University Press, 1995).

63. Treasury, "The Conditions and Effects of 'Dumping,'" July 7, 1903 (Cab. 37/65/42).

64. Percy Ashley, "Letter to Mr. Balfour," July 4, 1903, Balfour Papers, vol. 98 (Add MS 49780).

65. Alfred Marshall, "Memorandum on Fiscal Policy and International Trade (a Memorandum to Arthur Balfour)," August 31, 1903, Fiscalia (T 168/54), p. 39.

66. Treasury, "The Fiscal Problem," August 20, 1903 (Cab. 37/66/55), p. 56. The composition of Britain's exports to Germany remained largely unchanged until the war.

67. Lambert, *Planning Armageddon*, pp. 159–60.

68. Kennedy, *Anglo-German Antagonism*, pp. 294–95.

69. For an extensive study of this issue, see Lambert, *Planning Armageddon*, chap. 4. Also see Avner Offer, *The First World War: An Agrarian Interpretation* (New York: Oxford University Press, 1989).

70. Marshall, "Memorandum on Fiscal Policy," p. 39.

71. Balfour Papers, vol. 98 (Add MS 49780), p. 3.

72. Lambert, *Planning Armageddon*, p. 160.

73. According to Offer, Germany's major source of wheat shifted from Russia to Argentina before the war. Offer, *The First World War*, p. 289. For the influence of German businessmen in Latin America, see Philip Dehne, "From 'Business as Usual' to a More Global War: The British Decision to Attack Germans in South America during the First World War," *Journal of British Studies* 44, no. 3 (July 2005), pp. 516–35.

74. Quoted in Lambert, *Planning Armageddon*, p. 108.

75. Lambert, *Planning Armageddon*, pp. 164–66.

76. Quoted in Offer, *The First World War*, p. 289.

77. Hoffman, *Great Britain*, pp. 295–300.

78. As Edward Grey argued in 1915, "The blockade of Germany was essential to the victory of the Allies, but the ill-will of the United States meant their certain defeat." Lambert, *Planning Armageddon*, p. 373.

79. John McDermott, "A Needless Sacrifice: British Businessmen and Business as Usual in the First World War," *Albion* 21, no. 2 (Summer, 1989), pp. 263–82.

80. Dehne, "From 'Business as Usual,'" p. 523.

81. Between 1914 and 1916, American exports to the European states other than Britain, France, and Germany increased from $387 million to $1,063 million. See US Department of Commerce, *Historical Statistics of the United States, Colonial Times to 1970* (Washington, DC: Department of Commerce, 1975), p. 903.

82. Lambert, *Planning Armageddon*, p. 423.

83. David French, *British Strategy and War Aims* (London: George Allen and Unwin, 1986), p. 58.

84. Kennedy, *Anglo-German Antagonism*, p. 293.

85. For instance, see "Draft Despatch from the Marquess of Lansdowne to Sir F. Lascelles," May 1903, Fiscalia (T 168/59).

86. Cain, "Political Economy in Edwardian England," p. 36.

87. Hoffman, *Great Britain*, pp. 114–38. Also, Germany's exports to Eastern Europe rapidly expanded due to geographical proximity. See Marshall, "Memorandum on Fiscal Policy," p. 30.

88. Treasury, "The Conditions and Effects of 'Dumping,'" July 7, 1903 (Cab. 37/65/42).

89. *Hansard's Parliamentary Debates*, 4th Series, vol. 130 (February 19, 1904, House of Lords) (London: Wyman and Sons), paragraph 361. Also see paragraphs 348–50, 354–64.

90. Treasury, "The Conditions and Effects of 'Dumping,'" July 7, 1903 (Cab. 37/65/42), p. 9.

91. "Preference Tariffs within the Empire," May 26, 1903, Fiscalia (T 168/54).

92. Gerald W. Balfour, "The Central European Commercial Treaty Situation and Our Position in Relation Thereto," August 11, 1903 (Cab. 37/65/52). Also see Percy Ashley, "The German Tariff Controversy," Balfour Papers, vol. 98 (Add MS 49780), pp. 68–89.

93. For the British assessment of unfair foreign tariffs against British goods, see the Board of Trade, "Memorandum on the Comparative Incidence of Foreign and Colonial Import Tariffs on the Principal Classes of Manufactures Exported from the United Kingdom," Confidential Reports and Memoranda prepared by the Board of Trade, relative to Trade, Employment, Immigration, etc (Add MS 88906/23/14), pp. 9–17.

94. Hoffman, *Great Britain*, pp. 103–5.

95. Germany experienced a tariff war with Russia between 1891 and 1894. However, this controversy was resolved with the signing of a new tariff treaty in 1894. See "Commercial Diplomacy, 1860–1902," September 1903, Fiscalia (T. 168/54), pp. 35–39.

96. Sydney Buxton, "Commercial Negotiations with Portugal," March 17, 1911 (Cab. 37/105/29).

97. Erik Gartzke and Yonatan Lupu, "Trading on Preconceptions: Why World War I War Not a Failure of Economic Interdependence," *International Security* 36, no. 4 (Spring 2012), p. 131.

98. Lord Balfour of Burghleigh, "Fiscal Policy," August 19; September 1, 1903 (Cab. 37/65/54); Charles T. Ritchie, "Preferential Tariffs," September 9, 1903 (Cab. 37/66/58), pp. 8–9.

99. Lord George Hamilton, "Preferential Tariffs in Their Application to India," June 10, 1903 (Cab. 37/65/39). Also see Curzon of Kedleston, "Cotton Duties in India," *The Times*, June 2, 1908.

100. Asquith, *Trade and the Empire*, pp. 33–34.

101. A. K. Russell, *Liberal Landslide: The General Election of 1906* (Hamden: Archon Books, 1973), pp. 65–70.

102. "The Cabinet Crisis of 1903: Correspondence between the Prime Minister and the Duke of Devonshire," 1903 (Cab. 37/76/82); Political Papers (Add MS 88906/22/28). Also see E. H. H. Green, "The Political Economy of Empire, 1880–1914," in Andrew Porter, ed., *The Oxford History of the British Empire*, vol. 3 (Oxford: Oxford University Press, 1999), pp. 364–65.

103. Arthur J. Balfour, "The Cabinet Crisis of 1903: Correspondence between the Prime Minister and the Duke of Devonshire, No. 7," August 27, 1903 (Cab. 37/76/82).

104. Duke of Devonshire, "The Cabinet Crisis of 1903: Correspondence between the Prime Minister and the Duke of Devonshire, No. 8," August 27, 1903 (Cab. 37/76/82).

105. Charles T. Ritchie, "Preferential Tariffs," September 9, 1903 (Cab. 37/66/58).

106. *Hansard's Parliamentary Debates*, 4th series, vol. 130 (February 18, 1904, House of Lords) (London: Wyman and Sons), paragraph 162.

107. Percy Ashley, "Letter to Mr. Balfour," Balfour Papers, vol. 98 (Add MS 49780); Marshall, "Memorandum on Fiscal Policy."

108. *The Times, Speeches by Asquith*, pp. 167–68.

109. Ibid., pp. 185–86. Also see "A Dissection by Mr. Asquith," *Manchester Guardian*, May 22, 1903.

110. See Campbell-Bannerman Papers, vol. 38 B (Add MS 41243 B), pp. 44–45.

111. For the "free trade nationalism" of Edwardian Britain, see Frank Trentmann, "National Identity and Consumer Politics: Free Trade and Tariff Reform," in Donald Winch and Patrick K. O'Brien, eds., *The Political Economy of British Historical Experience, 1688–1914* (Oxford: Oxford University Press, 2002), pp. 215–42.

112. Cain, "Political Economy in Edwardian England," p. 44; Anthony Howe, *Free Trade and Liberal England, 1846–1946* (Oxford: Clarendon Press, 1997), pp. 247–49; Readman, "Liberal Party and Patriotism," pp. 281–88. For the focus on efficiency in Edwardian Britain, see Searle, *Quest for National Efficiency*. Also see Bernard Semmel, *The Rise of Free Trade Imperialism: Classical Political Economy, the Empire of Free Trade and Imperialism 1750–1850* (Cambridge: Cambridge University Press, 1970).

113. For instance, see Balfour Papers, vol. 98 (Add MS 49780), p. 3; *Hansard's Parliamentary Debates*, 4th Series, vol. 130 (February 19, 1904, House of Lords) (London: Wyman and Sons), paragraphs 348–50, 354–64; Marshall, "Memorandum on Fiscal Policy"; Treasury, "The Conditions and Effects of 'Dumping,'" July 7, 1903 (Cab. 37/65/42), p. 9.

114. Asquith, *Trade and the Empire*, p. 16; Balfour Papers, vol. 98 (Add MS 49780), p. 45; Robert Giffen, "Customs Duties and Free Trade," *The Times*, April 2, 1902; Robert Giffen, "The Dream of a British Zollverein," *Nineteenth Century*, no. 303 (May 1902), pp. 693–705.

115. Asquith, *Trade and the Empire*, p. 12; *Hansard's Parliamentary Debates*, vol. 126 (July 23, 1903, House of Lords) (London: Wyman and Sons), paragraph 145. Also see the statement of Winston Churchill, the President of the Board of Trade, in *Hansard's Parliamentary Debates*, vol. 3 (March 30, 1909), paragraph 292.

116. Balfour Papers, vol. 98 (Add MS 49780), p. 256.

117. Ibid., 258–59.

118. *Hansard's Parliamentary Debates*, 4th series, vol. 129 (February 8, 1904, House of Commons) (London: Wyman and Sons, 1904), cols. 634, 644.

119. Harold Cox, ed., *British Industries under Free Trade* (London: T. Fisher Unwin, 1903), pp. ix–xvi.

120. "Free Trade and the Position of Parties," *Edinburgh Review* 199, no. 408 (January–April 1904), pp. 547–55.

121. For a contemporary view of the Liberal cabinet's foreign policy leaders, see "Letters from Joseph Chamberlain to Lord Northcote," May 29, 1906, Henry Stafford, 1st Baron Northcote: Papers (PRO 30/56/1). For the composition and practice of the Liberal cabinet's foreign policy leaders, see Francis H. Hinsley, ed., *The Foreign Policy of Sir Edward Grey* (New York: Cambridge University Press, 1977); Kennedy, *Anglo-German Antagonism*, pp. 334–35; Thomas G. Otte, *The Foreign Office Mind: The Makings of British Foreign Policy, 1865–1914* (Cambridge: Cambridge University Press, 2011); Keith Robbins, *Sir Edward Grey* (London: Cassell, 1971); Zara S. Steiner, *The Foreign Office and Foreign Policy, 1898–1914* (Cambridge: Cambridge University Press, 1969); Zara S. Steiner, *Britain and the Origins of the First World War*, 2nd edition (Houndsmills, Basingstoke, Hampshire: Palgrave Macmil-

lan, 2003), pp. 171–90; and Keith M. Wilson, *The Policy of the Entente* (Cambridge: Cambridge University Press, 1985).

122. The Merchandise Marks Act of 1887 made it obligatory to print the country of origin on imported goods, while the Patent Law of 1907 made it mandatory for companies that used British patents to produce a certain portion of their goods on British soil.

123. Some might suggest that the fear of Russian aggression led Britain to eschew compound containment measures against Germany. This view, however, is not historically supported. Although there is good reason to believe that Britain was concerned about growing Russian power, this does not mean that the potential threat from Russia was salient enough to shape London's course of action with regard to Berlin. While the threat posed by Russia was mainly related to the defense of India, Germany threatened the safety of the British homeland and the balance of power on the European continent. In other words, the Russian threat and the German threat were different in kind and magnitude. Moreover, against the German challenge, Britain not only launched its own naval buildup, but also carefully prepared for economic warfare that would be adopted hand in hand with the deployment of military forces to aid the French if a war with Germany broke out. Britain never made similar military preparations against other great powers. These circumstances suggest that the Russian threat was not as salient as some scholars suggest, and that Britain's response to Germany was not closely related to the fear of Russian aggression in Central Asia. For instance, see Liberman, "Trading with the Enemy." For Britain's concerns about Russia's expansion in Central Asia, see Tanisha M. Fazal, *State Death: The Politics and Geography of Conquest, Occupation, and Annexation* (Princeton, NJ: Princeton University Press, 2007), pp. 123–28; Ira Klein, "The Anglo-Russian Convention and the Problem of Central Asia, 1907–1914," *Journal of British Studies* 11, no. 1 (1971), pp. 126–47; Wilson, *Policy of the Entente*, pp. 2–3, 15. For the reasoning underlying Britain's balancing policies against Germany, see Foreign Office, "Memorandum on the Present State of British Relations with France and Germany," January 1, 1907 (Cab. 37/86/1).

124. Russell, *Liberal Landslide*, pp. 65–67.

125. For instance, see Tariff Commission, *Report of the Tariff Commission*, vol. 1, paragraphs 425, 432, 438–70; and Tariff Commission, *Report of the Tariff Commission*, vol. 2, paragraph 92.

126. Edward J. Feuchtwanger, *Democracy and Empire: Britain, 1865–1914* (London: Arnold, 1989), pp. 276–77; Howe, *Free Trade and Liberal England*, pp. 256–66. Also see Roy Jenkins, *Asquith: Portrait of a Man and an Era* (New York: Chilmark Press, 1964), pp. 134–75.

127. Mark R. Brawley, *Power, Money, and Trade: Decisions That Shape Global Economic Relations* (Peterborough: Broadview Press, 2005), pp. 244–45.

128. Coetzee, *For Party or Country*, p. 71.

129. Ibid., pp. 117–26; Howe, *Free Trade and Liberal England*, pp. 278–79.

130. Quoted in Frank Trentmann, "The Transformation of Fiscal Reform: Reciprocity, Modernization, and the Fiscal Debate within the Business Community in

Early Twentieth-Century Britain," *Historical Journal* 39, no. 4 (December 1996), p. 1008.

131. Some might suggest that foreign economic relations were not within the realm of foreign policy leaders in the cabinet and Foreign Office. This is not true. The Foreign Office conducted commercial diplomacy and negotiations with other countries. British consuls in major commercial centers around the globe communicated with the Foreign Office. Moreover, the Foreign Office and the foreign secretary were continuously informed about international economic exchanges and economic developments in foreign countries. For an example of the Foreign Office's involvement in economic matters, see the correspondence on German economic affairs in FO 368/25.

132. See Andrew J. Marrison, "The Development of a Tariff Reform Policy during Joseph Chamberlain's First Campaign, May 1903–February 1904," in W. H. Chaloner and Barrie M. Ratcliffe, eds., *Trade and Transport* (Manchester: Manchester University Press, 1977), pp. 214–41.

133. Arthur J. Balfour, "Speeches on Fiscal Policy," October 13, 1903 (Cab. 37/66/64); "The Cabinet Crisis of 1903: Correspondence between the Prime Minister and the Duke of Devonshire," 1903 (Cab. 37/76/82); Charles T. Ritchie, "Preferential Tariffs," September 9, 1903 (Cab. 37/66/58).

134. See "Letters from Arthur Balfour to Lord Northcote" and "Letters from Joseph Chamberlain to Lord Northcote," in Henry Stafford, 1st Baron Northcote: Papers (PRO 30/56/1).

135. Howe, *Free Trade and Liberal England*, pp. 244–46, 256–66. Also see Herbert Henry Asquith, *Fifty Years of Parliament*, vol. 2 (London: Cassell, 1926), pp. 7–13.

136. Campbell-Bannerman Papers, vol. 5 (Add MS 41210), pp. 225–30; Spender Papers, vol. 3 (Add MS 46388), pp. 52, 55.

137. For anti-German sentiment among the British public, see Hoffman, *Great Britain*, pp. 224–72; Kennedy, *Anglo-German Antagonism*, pp. 361–85; David Silby, *The British Working Class and Enthusiasm for War, 1914–1916* (New York: Frank Cass, 2005).

138. For the importance of leaders in Britain's foreign relations, see Hinsley, *Foreign Policy of Grey*; Otte, *The Foreign Office Mind*; Robbins, *Sir Edward Grey*; Steiner, *Foreign Office and Foreign Policy*. Also see Herbert Henry Asquith, *Memories and Reflections, 1852–1927* (Boston: Little, Brown, 1928), pp. 264–85.

139. See David French, *British Economic and Strategic Planning, 1905–1915* (London: George Allen and Unwin, 1982); Howard, *The Continental Commitment*; Williamson, *The Politics of Grand Strategy*; and Lambert, *Planning Armageddon*.

140. Quoted in Wilson, *Policy of the Entente*, p. 60.

141. *The Times, Speeches by Asquith*, p. 309.

142. For a comprehensive study of this strategy, see Lambert, *Planning Armageddon*.

143. Searle, *Quest for National Efficiency*, pp. 171–72.

144. Maurice V. Brett, ed., *Journals and Letters of Reginald, Viscount Esher*, vol. 2 (London: I. Nicholson and Watson,1934), p. 370.

145. Steiner, *Britain and the Origins*, pp. 140–41.

146. For instance, Asquith, as chancellor of the exchequer (the cabinet position that pushed Asquith to side with the Radicals in military expenditure), wrote to Prime Minister Campbell-Bannerman that the navy was building its claims for a larger navy based on vague assumptions, while other powers' program and capability were not clear. See "Asquith to Campbell-Bannerman," October 30, 1906, Campbell-Bannerman Papers, vol. 5 (Add MS 41210), pp. 273–79. By the spring of 1909, nonetheless, most Liberals, including the Radicals, agreed that Britain needed to build more warships to counter Germany. See Feuchtwanger, *Democracy and Empire*, pp. 351–52.

147. Steiner, *Britain and the Origins*, pp. 144–54.

148. Edward Grey, "A Sense of the Waste of War," Manchester, February 3, 1914, in Duncan Brack and Tony Little, eds., *Great Liberal Speeches* (London: Politico's Publishing, 2001), p. 282.

Chapter 4

1. Kenneth Colegrove, "The New Order in East Asia," *Far Eastern Quarterly* 1, no. 1 (November 1941), pp. 5–24; Joyce Lebra-Chapman, ed., *Japan's Greater East Asia Co-prosperity Sphere in World War II: Selected Readings and Documents* (New York: Oxford University Press, 1975); Harold Sprout, "Changing Power Relations in the Pacific," *Annals of the American Academy of Political and Social Science*, no. 215 (May 1941), pp. 107–14. For the British and other countries' concern about the formation of a Japan-led political order, see "The Ambassador in Japan (Grew) to the Secretary of State, January 7, 1939, *Foreign Relations of the United States* (*FRUS* hereafter), 1939, vol. 3, p. 478.

2. "The Secretary of State to the Ambassador in Japan (Grew)," October 18, 1939, *FRUS*, 1939, vol. 3, p. 587.

3. Bruce Cumings, *Dominion from Sea to Sea: Pacific Ascendancy and American Power* (New Haven: Yale University Press, 2009); Russell F. Weigley, "The Role of the War Department and the Army," in Dorothy Borg and Shumpei Okamoto, eds., *Pearl Harbor as History: Japanese-American Relations 1931–1941* (New York: Columbia University Press, 1973), p. 202.

4. Quoted in Weigley, "Role of War Department," p. 182.

5. Herbert Feis, *The Road to Pearl Harbor: The Coming of War between the United States and Japan* (Princeton, NJ: Princeton University Press, 1950), p. 59; Jonathan G. Utley, *Going to War with Japan 1937–1941* (Knoxville: University of Tennessee Press, 1985), pp. 62, 83.

6. Moreover, the US military had long possessed war plans to defeat Japan and siege its homeland, known as "Plan Orange." This plan was first written before World War I, but continued to evolve throughout the 1930s until the outbreak of the Pacific War. See James H. Herzog, *Closing the Open Door: American-Japanese Diplomatic Negotiations, 1936–1941* (Annapolis: Naval Institute Press, 1973); Edward S. Miller, *War Plan Orange: The U.S. Strategy to Defeat Japan, 1897–1945* (Annapolis: Naval Institute Press, 1991).

7. Utley, *Going to War with Japan*, pp. 57–58.

8. Scott D. Sagan, "From Deterrence to Coercion to War: The Road to Pearl Harbor," in Alexander L. George and William E. Simons, eds., *The Limits of Coercive Diplomacy*, 2nd edition (Boulder, CO: Westview Press, 1994), pp. 59, 63.

9. Despite the opinion of Chief of Naval Operations Harold Stark, who wanted to send nearly a quarter of the Pacific Fleet to the Atlantic, Roosevelt decided to transfer only one carrier and one destroyer squadron, based on the advice of Cordell Hull, who told the president that it was not a good time to weaken the forces in the Pacific. Michael A. Barnhart, *Japan Prepares for Total War: The Search for Economic Security, 1919–1941* (Ithaca, NY: Cornell University Press, 1987), p. 221.

10. Weigley, "Role of War Department," pp. 180–84. Also see Scott D. Sagan, "The Origins of the Pacific War," *Journal of Interdisciplinary History* 18, no. 4 (Spring 1988), pp. 893–922.

11. Stephen E. Pelz, Race to Pearl Harbor: The Failure of the Second London Naval Conference and the Onset of World War II (Cambridge, MA: Harvard University Press, 1974), p. 217.

12. William Lockwood, "American-Japanese Trade: Its Structure and Significance," *Annals of the American Academy of Political and Social Science*, no. 215 (May 1941), p. 88.

13. James R. Herzberg, *A Broken Bond: American Economic Policies toward Japan, 1931–1941* (New York: Garland Publishing, 1988), p. v.

14. US Department of Commerce, *Foreign Commerce and Navigation of the United States*, calendar years 1938–1942 (Washington, DC: Government Printing Office, 1938, 1940, 1942). Also see Edward S. Miller, *Bankrupting the Enemy: The U.S. Financial Siege of Japan before Pearl Harbor* (Annapolis: Naval Institute Press, 2007), pp. 33–47.

15. See Mira Wilkins, "The Role of U.S. Business," in Dorothy Borg and Shumpei Okamoto, eds., *Pearl Harbor as History: Japanese-American Relations, 1931–1941* (New York: Columbia University Press, 1973), p. 372.

16. Miller, *Bankrupting the Enemy*, pp. 184–86, 247–48.

17. For instance, see William L. Langer and S. Everett Gleason, *The Undeclared War, 1940–1941* (New York: Harper, 1953); Albert L. Weeks, *Russia's Life Saver: Lend-Lease Aid to the USSR in World War II* (Lanham, MD: Lexington Books, 2004).

18. Japan's raw silk export to the United States was $99,572,976 (out of $195,086,088 of total exports to the United States) in 1937, $83,651,240 (out of $131,633,050) in 1938, $106,951,079 (out of $161,095,302) in 1939, $105,311,440 (out of $156,932,929) in 1940, and $51,807,250 (out of $82,476,927) in 1941. US Department of Commerce, *Foreign Commerce and Navigation of the United States*. Miller, *Bankrupting the Enemy*, p. 149.

19. "The Director of the War Plans Division of the Navy Department (Turner) to the Chief of Naval Operations (Stark)," July 19, 1941, *FRUS*, 1941, vol. 4, p. 840.

20. Lockwood, "American-Japanese Trade," pp. 89–90; Miller, *Bankrupting the Enemy*, pp. 149–50.

21. "The Director of the War Plans Division of the Navy Department (Turner) to the Chief of Naval Operations (Stark)," July 19, 1941, *FRUS*, 1941, vol. 4, p. 840.

22. Miller, *Bankrupting the Enemy*, pp. 152–55.

23. Between 1937 and 1940, the United States purchased gold worth about $693 million from Japan. See Lockwood, "American-Japanese Trade," p. 90.

24. "The Director of the War Plans Division of the Navy Department (Turner) to the Chief of Naval Operations (Stark)," July 19, 1941, *FRUS*, 1941, vol. 4, p. 840.

25. By 1939, US imports from East Asia were larger than imports from any other part of the world. British Malaya, the Netherlands East Indies, and the Philippines shipped more than half a billion dollars' worth of goods to the United States in 1940, accounting about a fifth of all US imports. See Jonathan Marshall, *To Have and Have Not: Southeast Asian Raw Materials and the Origins of the Pacific War* (Berkeley: University of California Press, 1995), pp. x, 7–14.

26. Miller, *Bankrupting the Enemy*, p. 148.

27. Wilkins, "Role of U.S. Business," p. 372.

28. Barnhart, *Japan Prepares for Total War*, p. 144.

29. Miller, *Bankrupting the Enemy*, pp. 81–82, 90.

30. Barnhart, *Japan Prepares for Total War*, p. 144.

31. Lockwood, "American-Japanese Trade," pp. 87–88; Miller, *Bankrupting the Enemy*, p. 33.

32. Barnhart, *Japan Prepares for Total War*, p. 146.

33. Kurt Bloch, "Japanese War Economy," *Annals of the American Academy of Political and Social Science*, no. 214 (May 1941), p. 17. Also, see E. E. Penrose, "Japan's Basic Economic Situation," *Annals of the American Academy of Political and Social Science*, no. 215 (May 1941), pp. 2–3.

34. For earlier assessments that Japan could find alternative trade partners, see "Memorandum by Mr. Roy Veatch, of the Office of the Adviser on International Economic Affairs," March 21, 1939, *FRUS*, 1939, vol. 3, pp. 521–23; and Herzberg, *A Broken Bond*, p. 69.

35. Miller, *Bankrupting the Enemy*, p. 32.

36. Ibid.

37. "The First Secretary of the British Embassy (Thorold) to Mr. T. K. Finletter, Special Assistant to the Secretary of State," August 21, 1941, *FRUS*, 1941, vol. 4, p. 862.

38. "Memorandum by the Assistant Secretary of State (Acheson) to the Secretary of State," September 22, 1941, *FRUS*, 1941, vol. 4, p. 883. Britain also controlled export of bauxite, manganese, cotton, foodstuffs, and iron ore. "The British Minister (Hall) to the Assistant Secretary of State (Acheson)," September 13, 1941, *FRUS*, 1941, vol. 4, pp. 873–75.

39. "The Consul General at Singapore (Patton) to the Secretary of State," February 27, 1941, *FRUS*, 1941, vol. 4, p. 788.

40. Barnhart, *Japan Prepares for Total War*, p. 179.

41. "Memorandum by the Assistant Secretary of State (Acheson) to the Secretary of State," September 22, 1941, *FRUS*, 1941, vol. 4, p. 884.

42. This, however, does not mean that Britain was always in harmony with the United States. Britain often considered making new commercial arrangements with

Japan. In such cases, the Roosevelt administration warned that it was against the interest of the United States. For instance, once Britain considered making some concessions to Japan in order to prevent Tokyo from selling raw materials to Germany through the Trans-Siberian Railways, the United States made it clear that "this Government would therefore naturally view with concern action by any other Government which would serve to tie the hands of that Government vis-à-vis Japan, or to assure the Japanese Government alternative supplies should supplies be cut off from the United States . . . the Government of the United States could not look with equanimity upon the conclusion of any arrangement between Great Britain and Japan which would operate arbitrarily to divert Japan's purchases from the markets of the United States to the markets of the British Commonwealth." See "The Department of State to British Embassy," May 21, 1940, *FRUS*, 1940, vol. 4, p. 571.

43. "The British Embassy to the Department of State," January 25, 1939, *FRUS*, 1939, vol. 3, pp. 490–93. Also see "The Ambassador in Japan (Grew) to the Secretary of State," January 30, 1939, *FRUS*, 1939, vol. 3, p. 495.

44. Irvine H. Anderson Jr., "The 1941 De Facto Embargo on Oil to Japan: A Bureaucratic Reflex," *Pacific Historical Review*, vol. 44, no. 2 (May 1975), p. 213.

45. Irvine H. Anderson Jr., *The Standard-Vacuum Oil Company and United States East Asian Policy, 1933–1941* (Princeton, NJ: Princeton University Press, 1975), pp. 155–56.

46. "Memorandum of Conversation, by the Secretary of State," March 3, 1941, *FRUS*, 1941, vol. 4, pp. 788–91.

47. "Memorandum by the Adviser on Political Relations (Hornbeck)," March 21, 1941, *FRUS*, 1941, vol. 4, p. 799.

48. Ibid., p. 798.

49. "Memorandum by the Consul General at Batavia (Dickover) of a Conversation with the Japanese Consul General (Saito)," February 2, 1940, *FRUS*, 1940, vol. 4, p. 2.

50. One long ton is equivalent to 2,240 lbs. See Anderson, *Standard-Vacuum Oil Company*, p. 154; Barnhart, *Japan Prepares for Total War*, pp. 166, 207; "Memorandum by the Advisor on Political Relations (Hornbeck)," January 11, 1941, *FRUS*, 1941, vol. 4, p. 778.

51. "Memorandum by the Advisor on Political Relations (Hornbeck)," July 19, 1940, *FRUS*, 1940, vol. 4, p. 587.

52. "Memorandum of Conversation, by the Chief of the Division of European Affairs (Moffat)," April 19, 1939, *FRUS*, 1939, vol. 3, pp. 529–30.

53. "Memorandum of Conversation, by the Chief of the Division of Far Eastern Affairs (Hamilton)," June 5, 1939, *FRUS*, 1939, vol. 3, pp. 538–40. Also see Cordell Hull, *The Memoirs of Cordell Hull* (New York: Macmillan, 1948), pp. 717–30.

54. Anderson, "1941 De Facto Embargo," pp. 218–19.

55. "Memorandum by the Adviser on Political Relations (Hornbeck) to the Under Secretary of State (Welles), January 16, 1941, *FRUS*, 1941, vol. 4, pp. 781–82. Also see Hull, *Memoirs of Cordell Hull*, pp. 688–700, 813–30.

56. Barnhart, *Japan Prepares for Total War*, p. 179.

57. "Memorandum by Mr. Joseph M. Jones of the Division of Far Eastern Affairs," April 20, 1939, *FRUS*, 1939, p. 532.

58. Feis, *Road to Pearl Harbor*, pp. 32–37.

59. "The Secretary of State to the Ambassador in Japan (Grew)," January 6, 1940, *FRUS*, 1940, vol. 1, pp. 635–36.

60. "The Ambassador in the Soviet Union (Steinhardt) to the Secretary of State," September 23, 1940, *FRUS*, 1940, vol. 1, p. 649. For the development of the rapprochement between Japan and the Soviet Union, see "The Ambassador in the Soviet Union (Steinhardt) to the Secretary of State," November 1, 1940, *FRUS*, 1940, vol. 1, p. 670; "The Secretary of State to the Ambassador in Japan," November 7, 1940, *FRUS*, 1940, vol. 1, p. 672.

61. For instance, in early 1941 it was reported that one hundred cars per day were moving westward vis the Trans-Siberian. "The Ambassador in the Soviet Union (Steinhardt) to the Secretary of State," April 24, 1941, *FRUS*, 1941, vol. 4, pp. 966–67.

62. "The Ambassador in the Soviet Union (Steinhardt) to the Secretary of State," May 27, 1941, *FRUS*, 1941, vol. 4, p. 972.

63. "The Ambassador in the Soviet Union (Steinhardt) to the Secretary of State," November 28, 1940," *FRUS*, 1940, vol. 1, pp. 676–77; "The Ambassador in the Soviet Union (Steinhardt) to the Secretary of State," December 27, 1940, *FRUS*, 1940, vol. 1, p. 679; "The Ambassador in the Soviet Union (Steinhardt) to the Secretary of State," May 27, 1941, *FRUS*, 1941, vol. 4, p. 972.

64. "Memorandum by the Assistant Secretary of State (Acheson) to the Secretary of State," September 22, 1941, *FRUS*, 1941, vol. 4, pp. 881–84.

65. Robinson Newcomb, "American Economic Action Affecting the Orient," *Annals of the American Academy of Political and Social Science*, no. 215 (May 1941), p. 133.

66. Miller, *Bankrupting the Enemy*, p. 155.

67. "Memorandum by Mr. Joseph M. Jones of the Division of Far Eastern Affairs," April 20, 1939, *FRUS*, 1939, p. 532.

68. This does not mean that interdepartmental disagreements did not exist in the United States. For instance, see Dean Acheson, *Present at the Creation: My Years in the State Department* (New York: Norton, 1969), pp. 9–47.

69. "Mr. John Carter Vincent of the Division of Far Eastern Affairs to the Adviser on Political Relations (Hornbeck)," January 20, 1939, *FRUS*, 1939, vol. 3, pp. 483–84; Marshall, *To Have and Have Not*, p. 26. Some claim that the United States imposed restrictions on exports to Japan to conserve resources domestically. This view, however, is not convincing. First, some countries were allowed to buy goods that the United States embargoed against Japan, implying that surplus products did exist in the United States. Second, conservation was not the primary cause of scrap embargo against Japan. The retained scrap was not vitally needed for the United States, although increasing demand for scrap certainly existed (see Feis, *Road to Pearl Harbor*, pp. 106–7). Roosevelt himself had publicly proclaimed that there was no shortage of scrap in the United States (see Barnhart, *Japan Prepares for*

Total War, p. 187). Third, the problem of an oil shortage was mostly fictitious. Japan mainly purchased oil from the US West Coast where oil was abundant, while the shortage occurred in East Coast (see Miller, *Bankrupting the Enemy*, pp. 181–90).

70. "Memorandum by the Adviser on Political Relations (Hornbeck) to the Under Secretary of State (Welles)," January 16, 1941, *FRUS*, 1941, vol. 4, p. 782.

71. The yen was not accepted in most countries from which Japan would purchase raw materials. "Memorandum by Mr. Joseph M. Jones of the Division of Far Eastern Affairs," April 20, 1939, *FRUS*, 1939, p. 531.

72. "The Chief of Arms and Munitions Control, Department of State (Green), to 148 Persons and Companies Manufacturing Airplane Parts," July 1, 1938, in *FRUS: Japan, 1931–1941* (*FRUS: Japan* hereafter), vol. 2, pp. 201–2.

73. "Memorandum by the Chief of the Division of Controls (Green)," *FRUS*, 1939, vol. 3, pp. 549–50.

74. "The Japanese Ambassador (Horinouchi) to the Secretary of State," January 6, 1940, in *FRUS: Japan*, vol. 2, pp. 206–7.

75. Ibid.

76. Utley, *Going to War with Japan*, p. 63.

77. "Memorandum prepared in the Department of State," December 29, 1939, *FRUS*, 1939, vol. 3, p. 551–52.

78. For the proclamations by the Roosevelt administration and controlled items, see Subcommittee on International Trade and Commerce of the Committee on International Relations, 94th Congress, 2nd Session, *Trading with the Enemy: Legislative and Executive Documents Concerning Regulation of International Transactions in Time of Declared National Emergency* (Washington, DC: Government Printing Office, 1976).

79. Pelz, *Race to Pearl Harbor*, p. 222.

80. For instance, see "Proclamation No. 2413, Signed by President Roosevelt, July 2, 1940," *FRUS: Japan*, vol. 2, pp. 211–13; "Proclamation No. 2417, Signed by President Roosevelt, July 26, 1940," *FRUS: Japan*, vol. 2, pp. 216–17; and "Regulations Governing the Exportation of Articles and Materials Designated in the President's Proclamation of July 2, 1940, Issued Pursuant to the Provision of Section 6 of the Act of Congress Approved July 2, 1940," *FRUS: Japan*, vol. 2, pp. 213–15; "Proclamation No. 2423, Signed by President Roosevelt, September 12, 1940," *FRUS: Japan*, vol. 2, pp. 220–21; and "Proclamation No. 2451, Signed by President Roosevelt, December 20, 1940," *FRUS: Japan*, vol. 2, p. 236.

81. Miller, *Bankrupting the Enemy*, pp. 118–20.

82. Utley, *Going to War with Japan*, p. 95.

83. "The Japanese Embassy to the Department of State," August 3, 1940, *FRUS: Japan*, vol. 2, pp. 219–20.

84. "The Director of the War Plans Division of the Navy Department (Turner) to the Chief of Naval Operations (Stark)," July 19, 1941, *FRUS*, 1941, vol. 4, pp. 836–40.

85. The Under Secretary of State (Welles) to President Roosevelt," July 31, 1941, *FRUS*, 1941, vol. 4, pp. 846–48.

86. "Memorandum by the Assistant Chief of the Division of Controls (Price) to

the Administrator of Export Control (Maxwell)," June 21, 1941, *FRUS*, 1941, vol. 4, p. 822.

87. "The Chief of the Division of Controls (Green) to the Administrator of Export Control (Maxwell)," January 1941, *FRUS*, 1941, vol. 4, pp. 783–84.

88. "Vice President Wallace to the Secretary of State," May 10, 1941, *FRUS*, 1941, vol. 4, pp. 815–16; "The Petroleum Coordinator for National Defense (Ickes) to the Administrator of Export Controls (Maxwell)," June 11, 1941, *FRUS*, 1941, vol. 4, p. 818.

89. Anderson, *Standard-Vacuum Oil Company*, pp. 155, 224, 230.

90. "The Acting Secretary of State to Collectors of Customs," August 1, 1941, *FRUS*, 1941, vol. 4, p. 850.

91. Miller, *Bankrupting the Enemy*, p. 205.

92. Ibid., pp. 191–204.

93. Herzberg, *A Broken Bond*, pp. 211–12; Peter C. Hoffer, "American Businessmen and the Japan Trade, 1931–1941: A Case Study of Attitude Formation," *Pacific Historical Review* 41, no. 2 (May 1972), pp. 189–205; Marshall, *To Have and Have Not*, pp. 58–59; John W. Masland, "Commercial Influence upon American Far Eastern Policy, 1937–1941," *Pacific Historical Review* 11, no. 3 (September 1942), pp. 281–99; Roland N. Stromberg, "American Business and the Approach of War 1935–1941," *Journal of Economic History* 13, no. 1 (Winter 1953), pp. 58–78; Wilkins, "Role of U.S. Business," pp. 341–76.

94. Hoffer, "American Businessmen," p. 202.

95. "Memorandum of Conversation, by the Adviser on Political Relations (Hornbeck)," January 13, 1939, *FRUS*, 1939, vol. 3, pp. 482–83.

96. "Memorandum of Conversation, by the Assistant Chief of the Division of Far Eastern Affairs (Ballantine)," January 24, 1939, *FRUS*, 1939, vol. 3, pp. 488–89.

97. "Mr. John Carter Vincent of the Division of Far Eastern Affairs to the Adviser on Political Relations (Hornbeck)," January 20, 1939, *FRUS*, 1939, vol. 3, pp. 483–84.

98. "The Ambassador in Japan (Grew) to the Secretary of State," January 7, 1939, *FRUS*, 1939, vol. 3, pp. 478–81.

99. Marshall, *To Have and Have Not*, p. 128.

100. Feis, *Road to Pearl Harbor*, p. 94.

101. "The Japanese Embassy to the Department of State," October 7, 1940, *FRUS: Japan*, pp. 223–24.

102. "The Department of State to the Japanese Embassy," October 23, 1940, *FRUS: Japan*, p. 229.

103. "Memorandum by the Secretary of State," October 8, 1940, *FRUS: Japan*, p. 226.

104. "Memorandum by the Assistant Secretary of State (Berle)," November 30, 1940, *FRUS: Japan*, p. 230.

105. "Memorandum by the Chief of the Division of Far Eastern Affairs (Hamilton)," July 22, 1941, *FRUS*, 1941, vol. 4, p. 834.

Chapter 5

1. Portions of this chapter are adapted from Dong Jung Kim, "Economic Containment as a Strategy of Great Power Competition," *International Affairs* 95, no. 6 (2019), pp. 1423–41.

2. The US strategic position toward the USSR during the formative stage of the Cold War is clearly summarized in an NSC-approved telegraph to the US ambassador in Moscow, which contained a message to be delivered to Stalin. In this communication, Ambassador Walter Bedell Smith was instructed to inform Stalin "1. That any further encroachment by the Soviet Union, by countries under its control, or by Communist parties dominated by it, beyond the present limits of Communist power, would be regarded by this country as an act of Soviet aggression. 2. That it is definitely not true that this Government is aiming in any way, shape or form at an imperialistic expansion of its own power or at the preparation of military aggression against the Soviet Union or any other country in Eastern Europe or elsewhere." See "Lovett to Smith," April 24, 1948, *FRUS*, 1948, vol. 4, p. 835. Also see "The Ambassador in the Soviet Union to the Secretary of State," April 5, 1946, *FRUS*, 1946, vol. 6, pp. 732–36; "Report by the National Security Council to President Truman (NSC 5/2)," February 12, 1948, *FRUS*, 1948, vol. 4, p. 50; Melvyn P. Leffler, "The American Conception of National Security and the Beginning of the Cold War, 1945–48," *American Historical Review* 89, no. 2 (April 1984), pp. 346–81; Thomas G. Paterson, *On Every Front: The Making and Unmaking of the Cold War* (New York: Norton, 1992), p. 65.

3. "The Ambassador in the Soviet Union to the Secretary of State," June 1, 1946, *FRUS*, 1946, vol. 6, p. 758.

4. For the US containment of the USSR, see John Lewis Gaddis, *Strategies of Containment* (New York: Oxford University Press, 2005).

5. Secretary of Defense, September 27, 1947, Records of the Secretary of Defense, RG 330, National Archives and Records Agency (quoted in Frank Cain, *Economic Statecraft during the Cold War* [London: Routledge, 2007], pp. 1–2). Still, during 1947, the United States wanted to be careful about the deployment of its forces on the European continent and to the Mediterranean because doing so would require significant mobilization of the country. See "Memorandum by the Joint Chief of Staff to the Secretary of Defense," January 8, 1948, *FRUS*, 1948, vol. 4, p. 8.

6. See Alexander Baykov, *Soviet Foreign Trade* (Princeton, NJ: Princeton University Press, 1946), p. 77; "Memorandum by the Under Secretary of State for Economic Affairs to the Secretary of State," December 3, 1946, *FRUS*, 1946, vol. 6, p. 859; "Memorandum by Mr. Emilio G. Collado, Deputy on Financial Affairs to the Assistant Secretary of State for Economic Affairs," February 4, 1946, *FRUS*, 1946, vol. 6, pp. 823–25; and Philip Hanson, *The Rise and Fall of the Soviet Economy* (London: Longman, 2003), p. 45.

7. Baykov, *Soviet Foreign Trade*, pp. 80–82. Also see Nikolai Mikhailov, "The Soviet Peacetime Economy," *Foreign Affairs* 24, no. 4 (July 1946), pp. 633–37.

8. Hanson, *Rise and Fall*, p. 30.

9. Michael Mastanduno, *Economic Containment: CoCom and the Politics of East-West Trade* (Ithaca, NY: Cornell University Press, 1992), p. 72.

10. "The Chargé in the Soviet Union to the Secretary of State," January 16, 1946, *FRUS*, 1946, vol. 1, p. 1274.

11. Legislative Reference Service of the Library of Congress, *A Background Study on East-West Trade*, 89th Congress, 1st Session (Washington, DC: Government Printing Office, 1965), p. 4.

12. Philip J. Funigiello, *American-Soviet Trade in the Cold War* (Chapel Hill: University of North Carolina Press, 1988), p. 34; Mastanduno, *Economic Containment*, p. 71.

13. For instance, see Benn Steil, *The Marshall Plan: Dawn of the Cold War* (New York: Simon and Schuster, 2018).

14. Department of Commerce, *Export Control*, Thirteenth Quarterly Report (Washington, DC: Government Printing Office, 1950), pp. 25–27; "Report by the Ad Hoc Subcommittee of the Advisory Committee of the Secretary of Commerce," May 4, 1948, *FRUS*, 1948, vol. 4, pp. 537–38.

15. "United States Policy on Trade with the Soviet Union and Eastern Europe," November 26, 1947, *FRUS*, 1948, vol. 4, p. 490.

16. "Report by the Ad Hoc Subcommittee of the Advisory Committee of the Secretary of Commerce," May 4, 1948, *FRUS*, 1948, vol. 4, p. 537.

17. Thomas G. Paterson, *Soviet-American Confrontation* (Baltimore: Johns Hopkins University Press, 1973), p. 69.

18. "Manganese Supply Position Continues to Be Serious," April 25, 1949, *FRUS*, 1949, vol. 5, pp. 105–6.

19. Paterson, *Soviet-American Confrontation*, p. 73.

20. "United States Policy on Trade with the Soviet Union and Eastern Europe," November 26, 1947, *FRUS*, 1948, vol. 4, p. 490.

21. "Report by the Ad Hoc Subcommittee of the Advisory Committee of the Secretary of Commerce," May 4, 1948, *FRUS*, 1948, vol. 4, p. 538.

22. Ibid., pp. 541–42.

23. Alec Nove, *An Economic History of the USSR, 1917–1991*, 3rd edition (New York: Penguin Books, 1992), p. 323.

24. Robert A. Pollard, *Economic Security and the Origins of the Cold War, 1945–1950* (New York: Columbia University Press, 1985), p. 137.

25. Herbert Feis, "The Conflict over Trade Ideologies," *Foreign Affairs* 25, no. 2 (January 1947), p. 223.

26. Paterson, *Soviet-American Confrontation*, pp. 118–19.

27. See James K. Libby, "CoCom, Comecon, and the Economic Cold War," *Russian History* 37 (2010), pp. 135–42; and Robert Mark Spaulding, "Trade, Aid, and Economic Warfare," in Richard H. Immerman and Petra Goedde, eds., *The Oxford Handbook of the Cold War* (New York: Oxford University Press, 2013), p. 396. For trade within the Soviet bloc, see Edward Ames, "International Trade without Markets: The Soviet Bloc Case," *American Economic Review* 44, no. 5 (December 1954), pp. 791–807.

28. Thomas J. McCormick, *America's Half-Century: United States Foreign Policy in the Cold War* (Baltimore: Johns Hopkins University Press, 1989), p. 68.

29. Paterson, *Soviet-American Confrontation*, pp. 59–60. Until 1946, the Soviet Union had been a major benefactor of US loans and aid. See "Memorandum by the Under Secretary of State for Economic Affairs to the Secretary of State," December 3, 1946, *FRUS*, 1946, vol. 6, p. 859; "Memorandum by Mr. Emilio G. Collado, Deputy on Financial Affairs to the Assistant Secretary of State for Economic Affairs," February 4, 1946, *FRUS*, 1946, vol. 6, pp. 823–25.

30. Charles S. Maier, "The World Economy and the Cold War in the Middle of the Twentieth Century," in Melvyn P. Leffler and Odd Arne Westad, eds., *The Cambridge History of the Cold War* (Cambridge: Cambridge University Press, 2010), p. 50.

31. Paterson, *Soviet-American Confrontation*, p. 60.

32. Ibid., p. 67.

33. "Export Controls to Eastern Europe," March 9, 1948, *FRUS*, 1948, vol. 4, pp. 523–24; "The United States High Commissioner for Germany (McCloy) to the Secretary of State," October 17, 1949, *FRUS*, 1949, vol. 5, p.155; "The Secretary of State to Certain Diplomatic Offices," January 12, 1950, *FRUS*, 1950, vol. 4, p. 66. Also see US Congress, Senate, Committee on Interstate and Foreign Commerce, *Export Controls and Policies in East-West Trade*, 82nd Congress, 1st Session (Washington, DC: Government Printing Office, 1951), pp. 2–6.

34. "United States Policy on Trade with the Soviet Union and Eastern Europe," November 26, 1947, *FRUS*, 1948, vol. 4, p. 493.

35. "Marshall to Harriman," August 27, 1948, *FRUS*, 1948, vol. 4, p. 567.

36. Alan P. Dobson, *U.S. Economic Statecraft for Survival, 1933–1991* (New York: Routledge, 2002), p. 106.

37. Ian Jackson, *The Economic Cold War: America, Britain and East-West Trade, 1948–63* (New York: Palgrave, 2001), p. 33; Mastanduno, *Economic Containment*, p. 75.

38. Jackson, *The Economic Cold War*, pp. 41, 57, 62.

39. "George W. Perkins to Secretary of State," November 7, 1949, *FRUS*, 1949, vol. 5, pp. 37–38; Ian Jackson, "Economics and the Cold War," in Richard H. Immerman and Petra Goedde, eds., *The Oxford Handbook of the Cold War* (New York: Oxford University Press, 2013), p. 57.

40. Jackson, *The Economic Cold War*, p. 31.

41. Mastanduno, *Economic Containment*, pp. 89–90; Roberts Osgood, *NATO: The Entangling Alliance* (Chicago: University of Chicago Press, 1962), p. 69; Vibeke Sørensen, "Economic Recovery versus Containment: The Anglo-American Controversy over East-West Trade, 1947–51," *Cooperation and Conflict* 24 (1989), p. 70.

42. Dobson, *U.S. Economic Statecraft*, p. 112. For US avoidance of using overt pressure toward the Europeans, see the exchanges in "The Secretary of Commerce to the Executive Secretary of the National Security Council," *FRUS*, 1950, vol. 4, p. 83; and "Memorandum by the Acting Secretary of State for European Affairs (Thompson) to the Secretary of State," May 2, 1950, *FRUS*, 1950, vol. 4, p. 101.

43. Cain, *Economic Statecraft*, p. 30.

44. Frank M. Cain, "Exporting the Cold War: British Response to the USA's Establishment of COCOM, 1947–51," *Journal of Contemporary History* 29, no. 3 (July 1994), p. 509.

45. "Ambassador in France (Caffery) to the Acting Secretary of State," January 19, 1949, *FRUS*, 1949, vol. 5, p. 69; Sørensen, "Economic Recovery versus Containment," pp. 75–76.

46. "The Chancellor of the Federal Republic of Germany to the Chairman of the Allied High Commission for Germany," February 2, 1950, *FRUS*, 1950, vol. 4, pp. 73–74.

47. For the view emphasizing the impact of US pressure, see Gunnar Adler-Karlsson, *Western Economic Warfare, 1947–1967* (Stockholm: Almqvist and Wiksell, 1968), pp. 22–28; and Richard J. Ellings, *Embargoes and World Power* (Boulder, CO: Westview Press, 1985), p. 80.

48. Adler-Karlsson, *Western Economic Warfare*, pp. 22–28, 45–49. Also see US Congress, Senate, Committee on Interstate and Foreign Commerce, *Export Controls and Policies in East-West Trade*, 82nd Congress, 1st Session (Washington, DC: Government Printing Office, 1951); and Ian Jackson, "Economics," in Saki R. Dockrill and Geraint Hughes, eds., *Palgrave Advances in Cold War History* (New York: Palgrave Macmillan, 2006), pp. 170–71.

49. Cain, "Exporting the Cold War," pp. 512–19; Cain, *Economic Statecraft*, 33–39; Jackson, *The Economic Cold War*, pp. 90–110.

50. US Congress, Senate, Committee on Foreign Relations, *East-West Trade, Hearing before the Committee on Foreign Relations*, 83rd Congress, 2nd Session, April 9, 1954 (Washington, DC: Government Printing Office, 1954), p. 5.

51. See Adler-Karlsson, *Western Economic Warfare*, p. 5; Ellings, *Embargoes and World Power*, pp. 72–73; and Jackson, *The Economic Cold War*, p. 18.

52. "United States Policy on Trade with the Soviet Union and Eastern Europe," November 26, 1947, *FRUS*, 1948, vol. 4, p. 491.

53. See *FRUS*, 1948, vol. 4, p. 552 n. 3.

54. "United States Policy on Trade with the Soviet Union and Eastern Europe," November 26, 1947, *FRUS*, 1948, vol. 4, p. 494.

55. "The Ambassador in the Soviet Union to the Secretary of State," January 19, 1946, *FRUS*, 1946, vol. 6, p. 820. Also see "Memorandum by the Chief of the Division of Eastern European Affairs to the Under Secretary of State," January 21, 1946, *FRUS*, 1946, vol. 6, pp. 820–21.

56. Moscow's unwillingness to return the equipment provided by Washington under Lend-Lease was at the center of this decision. See "Memorandum by the Under Secretary of State for Economic Affairs to the Secretary of State," December 3, 1946, *FRUS*, 1946, vol. 6, pp. 858–59; "The Secretary of State to the Ambassador in the Soviet Union," December 23, 1946, *FRUS*, 1946, vol. 6, pp. 860–62; "Outline of Main Points of Settlement Proposed by the United States Side," June 25, 1947, *FRUS*, 1947, pp. 696–702.

57. Funigiello, *American-Soviet Trade*, p. 33.

58. Secretary of Commerce, *First Quarterly Report under the Second Decontrol Act of 1947* (Washington, DC: Government Printing Office, 1947), p. iii.

59. "United States Policy on Trade with the Soviet Union and Eastern Europe," November 26, 1947, *FRUS*, 1948, vol. 4, p. 491.

60. Jackson, *The Economic Cold War*, pp. 18–19.

61. Many believed that the Cominform was created to sabotage the Marshall Plan and Europe's recovery. See "Control of Exports to the USSR and Eastern Europe," November 14, 1947, *FRUS*, 1948, vol. 4, p. 506; "Immediate U.S. Economic Policy toward Soviet Sphere (EWP D-9/i)," November 19, 1947, *FRUS*, 1948, vol. 4, p. 499.

62. "United States Policy on Trade with the Soviet Union and Eastern Europe," November 26, 1947, *FRUS*, 1948, vol. 4, pp. 491, 495, 496.

63. "Control of Exports to the USSR and Eastern Europe," November 14, 1947, *FRUS*, 1948, vol. 4, p. 506.

64. "United States Policy on Trade with the Soviet Union and Eastern Europe," November 26, 1947, *FRUS*, 1948, vol. 4, p. 492.

65. "Control of Exports to the USSR and Eastern Europe," December 17, 1947, *FRUS*, 1948, vol. 4, p. 512.

66. "The 'R' Procedure for Export Control," undated, *FRUS*, 1948, vol. 4, pp. 512–13; "Department of Commerce Press Release," January 15, 1948, *FRUS*, 1948, vol. 4, p. 514.

67. Pollard, *Economic Security*, p. 162.

68. Funigiello, *American-Soviet Trade*, p. 36; Paterson, *Soviet-American Confrontation*, p. 71.

69. "Export Controls to Eastern Europe," March 9, 1948, *FRUS*, 1948, vol. 4, p. 523.

70. "Conclusions and Recommendations of the London Conference of October 24–26 of United States Chiefs of Mission to the Satellite States," *FRUS*, 1949, vol. 5, p. 31.

71. "Memorandum by the Assistant Secretary of State for Economic Affairs (Thorp) to the Secretary of State (Marshall)," May 6, 1948, *FRUS*, 1948, vol. 4, p. 543; "East-West Trade Developments," June 14, 1948 (Bureau of Economic Affairs Files: Lot 54D361), *FRUS*, 1948, vol. 4, p. 548.

72. "Report by the Ad Hoc Subcommittee of the Advisory Committee of the Secretary of Commerce," May 4, 1948, *FRUS*, 1948, vol. 4, p. 539.

73. Cain, "Exporting the Cold War," p. 504.

74. Ibid., p. 505. This committee presented a list comprised of two categories of goods: 1A (items with direct and indirect military application) and 1B (the remainder, to be controlled case by case, and items that have military implications when sold in large quantities).

75. Legislative Reference Service of the Library of Congress, *A Background Study on East-West Trade*, 89th Congress, 1st Session (Washington, DC: Government Printing Office, 1965), p. 38.

76. "The Secretary of State to Certain Diplomatic Offices," April 26, 1950, *FRUS*, 1950, vol. 4, pp. 87–93.

77. "Memorandum of Conversation by the Acting Advisor to the Division of Occupied Areas Economic Affairs," *FRUS*, 1948, vol. 4, p, 525.

78. Ibid. Also see Dobson, *U.S. Economic Statecraft*, p. 89; William J. Long, *U.S. Export Control Policy: Executive Autonomy vs. Congressional Reform* (New York: Columbia University Press, 1989), p. 15.

79. Mastanduno, *Economic Containment*, p. 71. Also see "The Secretary of State (Acheson) to the Embassy in the United Kingdom," *FRUS*, 1950, vol. 4, pp. 174–76; Adler-Karlsson, *Western Economic Warfare*, p. 5.

80. For different interpretations of US economic strategy, see Jackson, *The Economic Cold War*, pp. 4–7; and Tor Egil Førland, "'Economic Warfare' and 'Strategic Goods': A Conceptual Framework for Analyzing COCOM," *Journal of Peace Research* 28, no. 2 (1991), pp. 191–204.

81. Funigiello, *American-Soviet Trade*, pp. 9–10.

82. Paterson, *Soviet-American Confrontation*, pp. 57–58, 63.

83. Long, *U.S. Export Control Policy*, p. 24.

84. US Congress, Senate, Committee on Banking and Currency, *Extension of Export Controls Hearings*, 81st Congress, 1st Session, 1949, p. 186.

85. Mastanduno, *Economic Containment*, p. 74. Also see Cain, *Economic Statecraft*, pp. 33–39.

86. Paterson, *Soviet-American Confrontation*, p. 67.

87. Jackson, *The Economic Cold War*, p. 15; Paterson, *Soviet-American Confrontation*, p. 264.

88. Republican senator Arthur Vandenberg played a crucial role in deriving bipartisan support for President Truman. See Dean Acheson, *Present at the Creation* (New York: Norton, 1969), pp. 221–25.

89. Funigiello, *American-Soviet Trade*, pp. 10–11; Paterson, *Soviet-American Confrontation*, pp. 3–8.

90. Alexander Gerschenkron, *Economic Relations with the USSR* (New York: Committee on International Economic Policy, 1945).

91. Pollard, *Economic Security*, p. 161.

92. "Summary of Discussion on Problems of Relief, Rehabilitation and Reconstruction of Europe," May 29, 1947, *FRUS*, 1947, vol. 3, p. 235. Also see "The Director of the Policy Planning Staff to the Under Secretary of State," March 23, 1947, *FRUS*, 1947, vol. 3, p. 228.

93. "The Ambassador in the Soviet Union to the Secretary of State," June 23, 1947, *FRUS*, 1947, vol. 3, p. 266.

94. Acheson, *Present at the Creation*, p. 232; Hadley Arkes, *Bureaucracy, the Marshall Plan, and the National Interest* (Princeton, NJ: Princeton University Press, 1972), p. 53; Diane B. Kunz, *Butter and Guns: America's Cold War Economic Diplomacy* (New York: Free Press, 1997), p. 34.

95. Funigiello, *American-Soviet Trade*, pp. 30–31.

96. Førland, "'Economic Warfare' and 'Strategic Goods,'" p. 192.

97. "Comments on Moscow's Despatch No. 558," October 1, 1949, *FRUS*, 1950, vol. 4, pp. 107–8.

98. Ibid., 108.

Chapter 6

1. By 1979, total US exports to the Soviet Union amounted to $3.4 billion, grains accounting for $2.6 billion, manufactured goods for $600 million, and high-technology products for around $200 million. US Congress, Senate, Committee on Banking, Housing, and Urban Affairs, Subcommittee on International Finance, *U.S. Embargo of Food and Technology to the Soviet Union*, Hearings, 96th Congress, 2nd Session, January 22 and March 24, 1980, p. 21.

2. Peggy L. Falkenheim, "Post-Afghanistan Sanctions," in David Leyton-Brown, ed., *The Utility of International Economic Sanctions* (New York: St. Martin's Press, 1987), p. 111; Robert L. Paarlberg, "Lessons of the Grain Embargo," *Foreign Affairs* 59, no. 1 (Fall 1980), pp. 157–58.

3. US Congress, *U.S. Embargo*, p. 89.

4. Abraham S. Becker, *U.S.-Soviet Trade in the 1980s* (Santa Monica, CA: Rand, 1987).

5. For instance, see Stephen G. Brooks and William C. Wohlforth, "Economic Constraints and the End of the Cold War," in William C. Wohlforth, ed., *Cold War Endgames: Oral History, Analysis, Debates* (University Park: Penn State University Press, 2002), pp. 273–309.

6. John Lewis Gaddis, *Strategies of Containment* (New York: Oxford University Press, 2005), pp. 348–49; Robert G. Kaiser, "U.S.-Soviet Relations: Goodbye to Détente," *Foreign Affairs* 59, no. 3 (1980), pp. 500–521.

7. See Presidential Directive/NSC-62, https://www.jimmycarterlibrary.gov/assets/documents/directives/pd62.pdf; and Jimmy Carter, "State of the Union Address Delivered before a Joint Session of the Congress," January 23, 1980, https://www.presidency.ucsb.edu/documents/the-state-the-union-address-delivered-before-joint-session-the-congress. Also see Zbigniew Brzezinski, *Power and Principle: Memoirs of the National Security Advisor, 1977–1981* (New York: Farrar, Strauss and Giroux, 1983), p. 454.

8. Franklin D. Holzman, "U.S.-Soviet Economic Relations," *Final Report to National Council for Soviet and East European Research*, April 1980, pp. 25–33.

9. US Congress, *U.S. Embargo*, p. 45 n. 1.

10. Ibid., p. 45.

11. US Congress, Senate, Subcommittee on International Economic Policy of the Committee on Foreign Relations, *East-West Economic Relations*, Hearings, 97th Congress, 1st Session, September 16, 1981, p. 5.

12. US Congress, *U.S. Embargo*, pp. 2, 10.

13. Ibid., pp. 10, 24–25.

14. Animesh Ghoshal, "Going against the Grain: Lessons of the 1980 Embargo," *World Economy* 6, no. 2 (June 1983), pp. 183–84.

15. Brzezinski, *Power and Principle*, p. 431.

16. US Congress, *U.S. Embargo*, p. 28.

17. Ibid., p. 63. Also see Homer E. Moyer and Linda A. Mabry, "Export Controls as Instruments of Foreign Policy: The History, Legal Issues, and Policy Lessons of Three Recent Cases," *Law and Policy in International Business* 15, no. 1 (1983), pp. 43–44.

18. US Congress, *U.S. Embargo*, p. 118.

19. Ibid., p. 54.

20. Cyrus R. Vance, *Hard Choices: Critical Years in America's Foreign Policy* (New York: Simon and Schuster, 1983), p. 389.

21. Falkenheim, "Post-Afghanistan Sanctions," p. 120; Michael Howard, "Return to the Cold War?," *Foreign Affairs* 59, no. 3 (1980), pp. 465–66; Lisa L. Martin, *Coercive Cooperation: Explaining Multilateral Economic Sanctions* (Princeton, NJ: Princeton University Press, 1992), p. 193.

22. Moyer and Mabry, "Export Controls," pp. 45–46; US Congress, *U.S. Embargo*, p. 119.

23. See Kazimierz Grzybowski, "United States–Soviet Union Trade Agreement of 1972," *Law and Contemporary Problems* 37, no. 3 (Summer 1972), pp. 395–428; and Daniel Yergin, "Politics and Soviet-American Trade: The Three Questions," *Foreign Affairs* 55, no. 3 (April 1977), pp. 517–38. For US domestic constraints related with human rights issues, see Bruce W. Jentleson, "The Western Alliance and East-West Energy Trade," in Gary K. Bertsch, ed., *Controlling East-West Trade and Technology Transfer* (Durham, NC: Duke University Press, 1988), p. 328; and Michael Mastanduno, *Economic Containment* (Ithaca, NY: Cornell University Press, 1992), pp. 146–47.

24. Ghoshal, "Going against the Grain," pp. 183–84.

25. Falkenheim, "Post-Afghanistan Sanctions," p. 111; Paarlberg, "Lessons of the Grain Embargo," pp. 157–58.

26. Falkenheim, "Post-Afghanistan Sanctions," p. 118; Mastanduno, *Economic Containment*, pp. 224–26.

27. International Monetary Fund, "Directions of Trade Statistics," http://elibrary-data.imf.org/.

28. Moyer and Mabry, "Export Controls," p. 33.

29. Mastanduno, *Economic Containment*, p. 224.

30. For the Reagan administration's security strategy, see White House, NSDD-32, https://www.reaganlibrary.gov/sites/default/files/archives/reference/scanned-nsdds/nsdd32.pdf. Also see Caspar W. Weinberger, "U.S. Defense Strategy," *Foreign Affairs* 64, no. 4 (Spring 1986), pp. 675–97.

31. Quoted in Gaddis, *Strategies of Containment*, p. 351.

32. See White House, NSDD-32.

33. Ibid.; Louis J. Walinsky, "Coherent Defense Strategy: The Case for Economic Denial," *Foreign Affairs* 61, no. 2 (Winter 1982), p. 272.

34. US Congress, *East-West Technology Transfer: A Congressional Dialog with the Reagan Administration* (Washington, DC: Government Printing Office, 1984), p. 21. In 1981, the United States accounted for 3.3 percent of legal exports of Western high technology to the USSR. See Bruce W. Jentleson, *Pipeline Politics: The Complex Political Economy of East-West Energy Trade* (Ithaca, NY: Cornell University Press, 1986), p. 179.

35. Portions of this section are adapted from Dong Jung Kim, "Economic Containment as a Strategy of Great Power Competition," *International Affairs* 95, no. 6 (2019), pp. 1423–41.

36. Ronald Reagan, "Statement on an Extension of the United States–Soviet Union Grain Sales Agreement," http://www.presidency.ucsb.edu/ws/index.php?pid=42801#ixzz1r2tLQZQ8

37. Alexander M. Haig, *Caveat: Realism, Reagan, and Foreign Policy* (New York: Macmillan, 1984), p. 251.

38. US Congress, Senate, Subcommittee on International Economic Policy of the Committee on Foreign Relations, *East-West Economic Relations*, Hearings, 97th Congress, 1st Session, September 16, 1981, p. 11.

39. Congressional Research Service, *An Assessment of the Afghanistan Sanction: Implications for Trade and Diplomacy in the 1980s* (Washington, DC: Government Printing Office, 1981), pp. 47–49.

40. Falkenheim, "Post-Afghanistan Sanctions," pp. 113–15; Moyer and Mabry, "Export Controls," pp. 44–45, 49–52; Paarlberg, "Lessons of the Grain Embargo," pp. 151–53.

41. Paarlberg, "Lessons of the Grain Embargo," p. 155; Moyer and Mabry, "Export Controls," p. 50.

42. Falkenheim, "Post-Afghanistan Sanctions," pp. 115–16.

43. American Presidency Project, "Ronald Reagan: Statement on an Extension of the United States–Soviet Union Grain Sales Agreement," http://www.presidency.ucsb.edu/ws/index.php?pid=42801#ixzz1r2tLQZQ8

44. Haig, *Caveat*, p. 245; George P. Schultz, *Turmoil and Triumph: Diplomacy, Power, and the Victory of the American Ideal* (New York: Scribner, 1995), pp. 135, 138, 140; Vance, *Hard Choices*, p. 393.

45. Jentleson, *Pipeline Politics*, p. 175; Jentleson, "Western Alliance," p. 315.

46. Philip J. Funigiello, *American-Soviet Trade in the Cold War* (Chapel Hill: The University of North Carolina Press, 1988), p. 198.

47. US Congress, Senate, Subcommittee on International Economic Policy of the Committee on Foreign Relations, *East-West Economic Relations*, Hearings, 97th Congress, 1st Session, September 16, 1981, p. 11.

48. US Congress, House, the Subcommittee on Europe and the Middle East of the Committee on Foreign Affairs, *United States–West European Relations in 1980*, Hearings, 96th Congress, 2nd Session, June 25, July 22, September 9, 15, and 22, 1980, pp. iv–vii. Also see Congressional Research Service, *An Assessment of the Afghanistan Sanction*, p. 98; Haig, *Caveat*, p. 245; Angela E. Stent, "East-West Economic Relations and the Western Alliance," in Bruce Parrott, ed., *Trade, Technology, and Soviet-American Relations* (Bloomington: Indiana University Press, 1985), 283–323.

49. Quoted in Jentleson, "Western Alliance," p. 315.

50. Jentleson, *Pipeline Politics*, p. 195.

51. Abraham S. Becker, "Main Features of United States–Soviet Trade," *Proceedings of the Academy of Political Science* 36, no. 4 (1987), pp. 67–77.

52. As I discuss in Chapter 2, I do not argue compound containment measures seamlessly cover all economic exchanges. Instead, I focus on the decision on major economic exchanges with the challenger. Even when compound containment is adopted, there could be ongoing, less important economic exchanges. Similarly,

even when compound containment is avoided, minor economic exchanges can be restricted.

53. Moyer and Mabry, "Export Controls," p. 76; Michel Tatu, "U.S.-Soviet Relations: A Turning Point?," *Foreign Affairs* 61, no. 3 (1982), pp. 600–601; US Congress, *East-West Technology Transfer*, p. 14.

54. David A. Baldwin, *Economic Statecraft* (Princeton, NJ: Princeton University Press, 1985), p. 280; Martin, *Coercive Cooperation*, p. 222.

55. Quoted in Funigiello, *American-Soviet Trade*, p. 207.

56. Mastanduno, *Economic Containment*, p. 264.

57. Paarlberg, "Lessons of the Grain Embargo," p. 146.

58. US Congress, *U.S. Embargo*, pp. 24–25.

59. Ibid., p. 10.

60. American Presidency Project, "Ronald Reagan: Statement on an Extension of the United States-Soviet Union Grain Sales Agreement," http://www.presidency.ucsb.edu/ws/index.php?pid=42801#ixzz1r2tLQZQ8

61. Funigiello, *American-Soviet Trade*, pp. 194–95.

62. Brzezinski, *Power and Principle*, p. 430.

Chapter 7

1. Portions of this chapter are adapted from Dong Jung Kim, "Trading with the Enemy? The Futility of US Commercial Countermeasures against the Chinese Challenge," *Pacific Review* 30, no. 3 (2017), pp. 289–308.

2. For instance, see Department of Defense, *Sustaining U.S. Global Leadership: Priorities for 21st Century Defense*, January 2012, http://www.defense.gov/news/defense_strategic_guidance.pdf; Department of Defense, *Quadrennial Defense Review 2014*, http://www.defense.gov/pubs/2014_Quadrennial_Defense_Review.pdf; Ministry of Defense, *Defense of Japan*, 2011–2014, http://www.mod.go.jp/e/publ/w_paper/; Raymond T. Odierno, "The U.S. Army in a Time of Transition," *Foreign Affairs* 91, no. 3 (2012), pp. 7–11; and Kirk Spitzer, "U.S. Army to Asia: 'We're Back,'" *Time*, December 7, 2012. Also see Carnes Lord and Andrew S. Erickson, eds., *Rebalancing U.S. Forces: Basing and Forward Presence in the Asia-Pacific* (Annapolis: Naval Institute Press, 2014).

3. US Department of State, "U.S.-Vietnam Comprehensive Partnership," December 16, 2013, http://www.state.gov/r/pa/prs/ps/2013/218734.htm; "A Deepening Partnership with Vietnam," *New York Times*, October 24, 2014; "Philippines Offers U.S. Forces Access to Military Bases," *Reuters*, March 14, 2014. Also see Committee on Foreign Relations, 113th Congress, *Re-balancing the Rebalance: Resourcing U.S. Diplomatic Strategy in the Asia-Pacific Region* (Washington, DC: Government Printing Office, 2014).

4. Aaron L. Friedberg, *A Contest for Supremacy* (New York: Norton, 2011). Moreover, since the US military was undergoing a reduction in overall size and experienced severe budgetary constraints, an increase of US forces in Asia, although not massive, suggested that Washington was taking the Chinese military challenge very seriously.

5. US Census, "Trade in Goods with China," http://www.census.gov/foreign-trade/balance/c5700.html

6. World Trade Organization (WTO), *Trade Profiles 2013* (Geneva: WTO, 2013), p. 43.

7. WTO, *Trade Profiles 2016* (Geneva: WTO, 2013), p. 78.

8. Depending on the model used for estimation, the exact size of the effect of trade on China's GDP growth diverges. However, few doubt that international trade has contributed to China's economic growth. For instance, see Yilmaz Akyüz, "Export Dependence and Sustainability of Growth in China," *China and World Economy* 19, no. 1 (2011), pp. 1–23; "How Fit Is the Panda?," *The Economist*, September 27, 2007; John Knight and Sai Ding, *China's Remarkable Economic Growth* (Oxford: Oxford University Press, 2012); Justin Yifu Lin, *Demystifying the Chinese Economy* (New York: Cambridge University Press, 2012); Xiaohui Liu, Peter Burridge, and P. J. N. Sinclair, "Relationship between Economic Growth, Foreign Direct Investment, and Trade: Evidence from China," *Applied Economics* 34, no. 11 (2002), pp. 1433–40; and Dani Rodrick, "What's So Special about China's Exports?," *China and World Economy* 14, no. 5 (September 2006), pp. 1–19.

9. For instance, the Department of Commerce gathers information on how much each US firm trades with foreign entities, and the Internal Revenue Service compiles reports from US companies on their specific business activities around the world for tax purposes. These firm-level data, however, are not released for public view.

10. An economic simulation for this purpose would require extensive firm-specific data, but those data are confidential information. A different way of calculating the United States' expected losses would be using simulation models currently being used by US governmental agencies that report to the White House and Congress (for instance, the United States International Trade Commission (USITC)'s USAGE model). However, even such models build on strong assumptions that might not correctly represent the Sino-US relationship. Moreover, focusing on examining the aggregate impact of certain policy decisions, they would not be able to predict outcomes in one specific bilateral relationship. For an application of the simulation models, see USITC, *China's Agricultural Trade: Competitive Conditions and Effects on U.S. Exports* (Washington, DC: USITC, 2011), Appendix F.

11. Of course, there are official statements from US leaders and writings by current and former officials who discuss relations with China in their private capacities. Still, these are not undisputable primary sources showing the underlying thinking and processes through which US decisions regarding China are made.

12. See Donald R. Davis, "Intra-industry Trade: A Heckscher-Ohlin-Ricardo Approach," *Journal of International Economics* 39, no. 3 (November 1995), pp. 201–26; Ronald R. Davis and David E. Weinstein, "An Account of Global Factor Trade," *American Economic Review* 91, no. 5 (December 2001), pp. 1423–53; Paul R. Krugman, Maurice Obstfeld, and Marc J. Melitz, *International Economics: Theory and Policy*, 9th edition (New York: Addison-Wesley, 2012); and John Romalis, "Factor Proportions and the Structure of Commodity Trade," *American Economic Review* 94, no. 1 (March 2004), pp. 67–97.

13. These economic transactions are often called offshoring or outsourcing. Still, they can be taken into account within the framework of foreign trade through the concept of "trade in tasks." See William Milberg and Deborah Winkler, *Outsourcing Economics: Global Value Chains in Capitalist Development* (New York: Cambridge University Press, 2013). Also see Gene M. Grossman and Esteban Rossi-Hansberg, "Trading Tasks: A Simple Theory of Offshoring," *American Economic Review* 98, no. 5 (December 2008), pp. 1978–97. As Gregory Mankiw points out, "Outsourcing is just a new way of doing international trade." See "Why 'Outsourcing' May Lose Its Power as a Scare Word," *New York Times*, August 13, 2006.

14. Many consumer goods entail the cost of labor. In this case, US retailers/ wholesalers purchase from China rather than from American firms because Chinese goods entail lower labor costs. In effect, purchasing from China involves paying for Chinese labor, which is cheaper than US labor. See Cletus Coughlin, "The Controversy over Free Trade," *Federal Reserve Bank of St. Louis Review* 84, no. 1 (January–February 2002), pp. 1–22; Elhanan Helpman, "The Structure of Foreign Trade," *Journal of Economic Perspectives* 13, no. 2 (Spring 1999), pp. 121–44; and Krugman, Obstfeld, and Melitz, *International Economics*.

15. Wayne M. Morrison, "China-U.S. Trade Issues," *CRS Report to Congress*, May 21, 2012, p. 10.

16. See USITC, *Journal of International Commerce and Economics* 3, no. 1 (May 2011). Also see Wayne M. Morrison, "China-U.S. Trade Issues," *CRS Report to Congress*, September 30, 2011, p. 9.

17. Judith M. Dean, "Testimony before the U.S.-China Economic and Security Review Commission," Hearing on the Evolving U.S.-China Trade and Investment Relationship, June 14, 2012, http://www.uscc.gov/hearings/2012hearings/written_testimonies/12_6_14/Dean.pdf; Theresa M. Greaney and Mary E. Lovely, "China, Japan, and the United States: Deeper Economic Integration," *Journal of Asian Economics* 20, no. 6 (November 2009), pp. 593–95; USITC, *The Economic Effect of Significant U.S. Import Restraints*, 7th update (Washington, DC: USITC, 2011).

18. Items that comprise 1 percent or more of US imports from China are listed in this table (five-digit end-use code).

19. Author's calculation based on data from US Census (NAICS six digit), http://sasweb.ssd.census.gov/relatedparty/

20. For more specific discussions, see USITC, *The Year in Trade 2013* (Washington, DC: USITC, 2014).

21. Gregory N. Mankiw and Phillip Swagel, "The Politics and Economics of Offshore Outsourcing," AEI Working Paper Series, July 2006, https://dash.harvard.edu/bitstream/handle/1/2770517/Mankiw_PoliticsEconomics.pdf

22. Andrew B. Bernard, J. Bradford Jensen, Stephen J. Redding, and Peter K. Schott, "Firms in International Trade," *Journal of Economic Perspectives* 21, no. 3 (Summer 2007), pp. 105–30; Stephen D. Cohen, *Multilateral Corporations and Foreign Direct Investment* (New York: Oxford University Press, 2007); Robert Feenstra, "Integration of Trade and Disintegration of Production in the Global Economy," *Journal of Economic Perspectives* 12, no. 4 (Fall 1998), pp. 31–50; Geoffrey Jones,

Multinationals and Global Capitalism (New York: Oxford University Press, 2005); James R. Markusen, "The Boundaries of Multinational Enterprises and the Theory of International Trade," *Journal of Economic Perspectives* 9, no. 2 (Spring 1995), pp. 169–89; Milberg and Winkler, *Outsourcing Economics*.

23. For instance, see Bernard et al., "Firms in International Trade"; Markusen, "Boundaries of Multinational Enterprises"; and Milberg and Winkler, *Outsourcing Economics*.

24. For the importance of maintaining a stable global supply chain, see Deloitte Development LLC, "The Ripple Effect: How Manufacturing and Retail Executives View the Growing Challenge of Supply Chain Risk," http://www.deloitte.com/assets/Dcom-UnitedStates/Local%20Assets/Documents/Consulting/us_consulting_therippleeffect_041213.pdf

25. Milberg and Winkler, *Outsourcing Economics*; Grossman and Rossi-Hansberg, "Trading Tasks."

26. For instance, see Anita Chan, ed., *Walmart in China* (Ithaca, NY: Cornell University Press, 2011); and Robert E. Scott, "The Wal-Mart Effect: Its Chinese Imports Have Displaced Nearly 200,000 U.S. Jobs," Economic Policy Institute Issue Brief, no. 235, June 26, 2007.

27. Jingjing Jiang, "Wal-Mart's China Inventory to Hit U.S.$18b This Year," *China Daily*, November 29, 2004, http://www.chinadaily.com.cn/english/doc/2004–11/29/content_395728.htm

28. Scott, "The Wal-Mart Effect."

29. Kevin Brown, "Rising Chinese Wages Pose Relocation Risk," *Financial Times*, February 15, 2011.

30. Accenture, "Wage Increase in China: Should Multinationals Rethink Their Manufacturing and Sourcing Strategies?," 2011, http://www.accenture.com/sitecollectiondocuments/pdf/accenture_wage_increases_in_china.pdf; Deloitte, "2013 Global Manufacturing Competitiveness Index," 2012, http://www.deloitte.com/assets/Dcom-UnitedStates/Local%20Assets/Documents/us_pip_GMCI_11292012.pdf

31. For instance, many expected that Vietnam could easily absorb low-value-added activities from China. See "Plus One Economy," *The Economist*, September 2, 2010.

32. Li and Fung Research Centre, "Industrial Cluster Series," No. 6, June 2010, http://www.funggroup.com/eng/knowledge/research/LFIndustrial6.pdf. Also see Douglas Zhihua Zeng, ed., *Building Engines for Growth and Competitiveness in China: Experience with Special Economic Zones and Industrial Clusters* (Washington, DC: World Bank, 2010).

33. For instance, see US Government Accountability Office, "Offshoring: U.S. Semiconductor and Software Industries Increasingly Produce in China and India," *Report to the Committee on Foreign Affairs*, GAO-06-423, September 2006, pp. 13–20.

34. Milberg and Winkler, *Outsourcing Economics*, pp. 123–28. For evidence that the Southeast Asian states are unlikely to be able to replace China, see USITC,

ASEAN: Regional Trends in Economic Integration, Export Competitiveness, and Inbound Investment for Selected Industries (Washington, DC: USITC, 2010).

35. Keith Bradsher, "Even as Wages Rise, China Exports Grow," *New York Times*, January 9, 2014; Tom Orlik, "Rising Wages Pose Dilemma for China," *Wall Street Journal*, May 17, 2012.

36. An industry's decision to use foreign economic inputs is determined by the prospects of profit, not calculation of cost—including the cost of labor—per se. In this context, the dependence on Chinese economic inputs is eventually determined by whether countries other than China can allow major US industries to attain their current level of profit. Unless other countries could provide labor and tasks at levels comparable to current Chinese quality and reliability—not simply at current cost—major US industries' profits would diminish. If China plays a unique role with regard to US industries' profit, other countries are unable to replace China's role.

37. "The Boomerang Effect: As Chinese Wages Rise, Some Production Is Moving Back to the Rich World," *The Economist*, April 21, 2012; "The End of Cheap China: What Do Soaring Chinese Wages Mean for Global Manufacturing?," *The Economist*, March 10, 2012.

38. Ralph E. Gomory, "Testimony," in US-China Economic and Security Review Commission, *Hearing on China's Industrial Policy and its Impact on U.S. Companies, Workers, and the American Economy*, March 24, 2009. Ironically, low wages, unfair labor standards, and lax enforcement of environmental protection laws also make China attractive for US manufacturers. See US-China Economic and Security Review Commission, *2009 Report to Congress*, 111th Congress, 1st Session (Washington, DC: Government Printing Office, 2009), pp. 67–69.

39. "In Shift of Jobs, Apple Will Make Some Macs in U.S.," *New York Times*, December 6, 2012.

40. For similar views, see Martin N. Bailey, "Adjusting to China: A Challenge to the U.S. Manufacturing Sector," Brookings Policy Brief, no. 179, January 2011; Robert Lawrence and Lawrence Edwards, *Rising Tide: Is Growth in Emerging Economies Good for the United States?* (Washington, DC: Peterson Institute, 2011).

41. USITC, *China: Effects of Intellectual Property Infringement and Indigenous Innovation Policies on the U.S. Economy* (Washington, DC: USITC, 2011); US-China Economic and Security Review Commission, *Assessing China's Efforts to Become an "Innovation Society"—a Progress Report* (Washington, DC: US-China Economic and Security Review Commission, 2012).

42. See Bureau of Industry and Security, *U.S. Dual-Use Export Controls for China Need to Be Strengthened, Final Report*, no. IPE-17500, March 2006; Ian F. Fergusson, "The Export Administration Act: Evolution, Provisions, and Debate," *CRS Report to Congress* (RL31832), July 2009; Ian F. Fergusson and Paul K. Kerr, "The U.S. Export Control System and the President's Reform Initiative," *CRS Report to Congress* (R41916), July 2011; and Susan V. Lawrence and David MacDonald, "U.S.-China Relations: Policy Issues," *CRS Report for Congress* (R41108), August 2012. Indeed, the United States' advanced technology product (ATP) exports to China have outpaced US ATP exports to other parts of the world. See Alexander

Hammer, Robert Koopman, and Andrew Martinez, "Overview of U.S.-China Trade in Advanced Technology Products," *United States International Trade Commission Journal of International Commerce and Economics* 3, no. 1 (May 2011), pp. 5–12.

43. Of course, other advanced economies are concerned about the economic impact of technology transfer and weak intellectual property rights protection in China, as well as the problem of the undervalued yuan. Still, all else being equal, they would be inclined to expand their sales to China if the United States restricted its exports. For the EU's concerns about trade with China, see http://ec.europa.eu/trade/policy/countries-and-regions/countries/china/

44. Oliver Bräuner, "China's Rise as a Global S&T Power and China-EU Cooperation," USITC Policy Brief, no. 29, September 2011, p. 90.

45. Nicola Casarini, *Remaking Global Order: The Evolution of Europe-China Relations and Its Implication for East Asia and the United States* (New York: Oxford University Press, 2009), pp. 44–45, 81–139; May-Britt Stumbaum, "Risky Business? The EU, China and Dual-Use Technology," Occasional Paper no. 80, European Union Institute for Security Studies, October 2009, pp. 14–15.

46. Mitchel B. Wallerstein, "Losing Controls," *Foreign Affairs* 88, no. 6 (November–December 2009), pp. 17–18.

47. Committee on Science and Technology, House of Representatives, *Impact of U.S. Export Control Policies on Science and Technology Activities and Competitiveness*, Hearings, 111th Congress, First Session, 2009, p. 30. Also see Committee on Science, Security, and Prosperity, Committee on Scientific Communication and National Security, and National Research Council, *Beyond "Fortress America": National Security Controls on Science and Technology in a Globalized World* (Washington, DC: National Academies Press, 2009); Committee on Science, Engineering, and Public Policy, *Rising Above the Gathering Storm: Energizing and Employing America for a Brighter Economic Future* (Washington, DC: National Academies Press, 2007); May-Britt Stumbaum, *The Security and Technology Relationship between Europe and China* (La Jolla, CA: June 24, 2010); May-Brit U. Stumbaum, "Testimony before the U.S.-China Economic and Security Review Commission," in US-China Economic and Security Review Commission, *Hearings on China-Europe Relationship and Transatlantic Implications*, 112th Congress, 2nd Session, April 19, 2012, pp. 81–91; Øystein Tunsjø, "Testimony before the U.S.-China Economic and Security Review Commission," in US-China Economic and Security Review Commission, *Hearings on China-Europe Relationship*; and Gundran Wacker, "Testimony before the U.S.-China Economic and Security Review Commission," in US-China Economic and Security Review Commission, *Hearings on China-Europe Relationship*.

48. Foreign Agricultural Service, "People's Republic of China-Oilseeds and Products Annual," March 2014, http://gain.fas.usda.gov/Recent%20GAIN%20Publications/Oilseeds%20and%20Products%20Annual_Beijing_China%20-%20Peoples%20Republic%20of_2-28-2014.pdf; US-China Economic and Security Review Commission, *2013 Report to Congress*, 113th Congress, 1st Session (Washington, DC: Government Printing Office, 2013), pp. 5–6.

49. For data on China's agricultural trade, USITC, *China's Agricultural Trade: Competitive Conditions and Effects on U.S. Exports* (Washington, DC: USITC, 2011). Also see US Department of Agriculture, "World Agricultural Supply and Demand Estimate Report," at http://www.usda.gov/oce/commodity/wasde/

50. China also buys a large quantity of US scraps, smelting and refining them into pure forms of nonferrous metals (mainly aluminum and copper) to sell on domestic and international markets. Still, using scraps is only one method of China's nonferrous metal production. Also, other suppliers of scraps are available to China on the market. For instance, see Alexander Hammer and Lin Jones, "China's Dominance as a Global Consumer and Producer of Copper," *USITC Executive Briefings on Trade*, August 2012.

51. See UNComtrade, http://comtrade.un.org/data/

52. Furthermore, China could find alternative providers of business services as well. International business services, including entrepreneurial skills, IT solutions, logistics, financial skills, and other sales know-how, are very important for organizing, maintaining, and upgrading diverse production activities. While China strives to advance its economic organization and structure, these services can be provided not only by the United States, but also by firms from other advanced economies around the world, including Europe. For the role of international business services and discussions on the competitors of U.S. service providers, see USITC, *Economic Effect of Restraints*, chap. 3.

53. See UNComtrade.

54. See Kemal Derviş, Joshua Meltzer, and Karim Foda, "Value-Added Trade and Its Implications for International Trade Policy," *Brookings Opinion*, April 2, 2013, http://www.brookings.edu/research/opinions/2013/04/02-implications-international-trade-policy-dervis-meltzer; and John B. Benedetto, "Implications and Interpretations of Value-Added Trade Balances," *Journal of International Commerce and Economics* 4, no. 2 (November 2012), pp. 39–61.

55. This estimate builds on the data provided by China Customs Statistics and Chinese Ministry of Commerce. See Judith M. Dean, Mary E. Lovely, and Jesse Mora, "Decomposing China-Japan-U.S. Trade: Vertical Specialization, Ownership, and Organizational Form," *Journal of Asian Economics* 20, no. 6 (November 2009), pp. 596–610. Also see Robert Koopman, Zhi Wang, and Shang-jin Wei, "How Much of Chinese Exports Is Really Made in China? Assessing Foreign and Domestic Value-Added in Gross Exports," Office of Economics Working Paper, no. 2008–03-B, USITC, March 2008.

56. See USITC, *Economic Effect of Restraints*, pp. 3–20. Also see Dean, "Testimony."

57. UN Comtrade Data.

58. For instance, in 2007 approximately 51.9 percent of China's exports to the EU consisted of processing exports. Dean, Lovely, and Mora, "Decomposing China-Japan-U.S. Trade," p. 606.

59. These top ten export destinations include the EU, the United States, Hong Kong, Japan, South Korea, Russia, India, Malaysia, Singapore, and Australia.

60. Indeed, Chinese leaders have been aware of the problem of export concentration in certain markets and have tried to diversify China's export destinations. For instance, see "China Issues First White Paper on Foreign Trade, Explaining Surplus," *Xinhua*, December 2011, http://mt.china-embassy.org/eng/zyxwdt/t885476.htm

61. Keith Bradsher and Diane Cardwell, "U.S. Slaps High Tariffs on Chinese Solar Panels," *New York Times*, May 17, 2012.

62. Michael D. Swaine, *America's Challenge: Engaging a Rising China in the Twenty-First Century* (Washington, DC: Carnegie Endowment for International Peace, 2011), p. 186.

63. David Shambaugh, "The New Strategic Triangle: U.S. and European Reactions to China's Rise," *Washington Quarterly* 28, no. 3 (Summer 2005), pp. 7–25.

64. Kristin Archick, Richard F. Grimmett, and Shirley Kan, "European Union's Arms Embargo on China: Implications and Options for U.S. Policy," *CRS Report for Congress*, May 27, 2005.

65. For instance, see David D. Hale and Lyric Hale, "Reconsidering Revaluation," *Foreign Affairs* 87, no. 1 (January–February 2008), pp. 57–66. For a summary of different positions in US trade policy, see Daniel W. Drezner, *U.S. Trade Strategy: Free versus Fair* (New York: Council on Foreign Relations, 2006).

66. Richard N. Cooper, "Is Economic Power a Useful and Operational Concept?," Discussion draft, September 2003; Richard N. Cooper, "Living with Global Imbalances: A Contrarian View," Policy Briefs, PB05-3, November 2005, Peterson Institute for International Economics; Aaditya Mattoo and Avrind Subramanian, "Leave China Out of a Trade Pact at Your Peril," *Financial Times*, December 8, 2011.

67. For instance, see Charles E. Schumer and Lindsey O. Graham, "Will It Take a Tariff to Free the Yuan?," *New York Times*, June 8, 2005; and C. Fred Bergsten, "Correcting the Chinese Exchange Rate," Testimony before the Hearing on China's Exchange Rate Policy, Committee on Ways and Means, U.S. House of Representatives, September 15, 2010. For Mitt Romney's emphasis on designating China as currency manipulator, see "Transcript and Audio: Second Presidential Debate," *NPR*, October 16, 2012, http://www.npr.org/2012/10/16/163050988/transcript-obama-romney-2nd-presidential-debate

68. For instance, see Arvind Subramanian, "Preserving the Open Global Economic System: A Strategic Blueprint for China and the United States," Policy Brief, PB13-16, June 2013, Peterson Institute for International Economics.

69. Nick Carey and James B. Kelleher, "Special Report: Does Corporate America Kowtow to China?," *Reuters*, April 27, 2011.

70. For discussions of these US laws and legal procedures, see USITC, *Year in Trade 2013*, chap. 2.

71. White House, "State of the Union Address," January 2010, http://www.whitehouse.gov/the-press-office/remarks-president-state-union-address; White House, "Remarks by the President at the Export-Import Bank's Annual Conference," March 11, 2010, http://www.whitehouse.gov/the-press-office/remarks-president-export-import-banks-annual-conference

72. See *The President's Trade Policy Agenda*, 2009–2011, http://www.ustr.gov/2010-trade-policy-agenda

73. Gary Clyde Hufbauer and Sean Lowry, "U.S. Tire Tariffs: Saving Few Jobs at High Cost," Policy Brief, PB12-9, April 2012, Pearson Institute for International Economics. Also see John Bussey, "Get Tough Policy on Chinese Tires Falls Flat," *Wall Street Journal*, January 20, 2012; "U.S. Adds Tariffs on Chinese Tires," *New York Times*, September 11, 2009; "Solar Tariff Upheld, but May Not Help in U.S.," *New York Times*, November 7, 2012.

74. For examples of widely cited counterevidence, see Michael J. Ferrantino, Robert B. Koopman, Zhi Wang, and Falan Yinug, "The Nature of U.S.-China Trade in Advanced Technology Products," *Comparative Economic Studies* 52, no. 2 (2010), pp. 207–24; and USITC, *Economic Effect of Restraints*. Also see Neil C. Hughes, "A Trade War with China?," *Foreign Affairs* 84, no. 4 (July–August 2005), pp. 94–106; and Henry M. Paulson, "A Strategic Economic Engagement," *Foreign Affairs* 87, no. 5 (September–October 2008), pp. 59–77.

75. Many have argued that the United States should strengthen and return home the R&D, and stop further outsourcing of important technological products (which require the outflow of US technology). For instance, see Gary P. Pisano and Willy C. Shih, "Restoring American Competitiveness," *Harvard Business Review*, July–August 2009.

76. In particular, controlling inflow of high and dual-use technology to China was deemed critical given the likely scenario of military confrontation between the two powers. US-China Economic and Security Review Commission, *2011 Report to Congress* (Washington, DC: Government Printing Office, 2011), pp. 7–8; Bureau of Industry and Security, *U.S. Dual-Use Export Controls for China Need to Be Strengthened.*

77. Jim Garamone, "Gates Proposes Revamp of Export System," *American Forces Press Service*, April 20, 2010, http://www.defense.gov/news/newsarticle.aspx?id=58830

78. Wallerstein, "Losing Controls." Also see Center for Strategic and International Studies, *Briefing of the Working Group on the Health of the U.S. Space Industrial Base and the Impact of Export Controls*, February 2008, http://csis.org/files/media/csis/pubs/021908_csis_spaceindustryitar_final.pdf; Committee on Science, Security, and Prosperity, *Beyond "Fortress America"*; Committee on Science, Engineering, and Public Policy, *Rising Above the Gathering Storm*; and Committee on Science and Technology, House of the Representatives, 111th Congress, 1st Session, *Impacts of U.S. Export Control Policies on Science and Technology Activities and Competitiveness* (Washington, DC: Government Printing Office, 2009).

79. U.S. Government Accountability Office, "Export Controls: Challenges with Commerce's Validated End-User Program May Limit Its Ability to Ensure that Semiconductor Equipment Exported to China Is Used as Intended," *Report to the Committee on Foreign Affairs*, GAO-08-1095, September 2008; Committee on Science and Technology, *Impacts of U.S. Export Control Policies*, p. 30.

80. The Validated End User (VEU) program, introduced by the Department of Commerce in June 2007, aimed to make it easier for American firms to export dual-use items to China. Also, the president's reform initiative has not started to expand the list of controlled items. Christopher F. Corr and Jason T. Hungerford, "The Struggles of Shipping Dual-Use Goods to China," *China Business Review*, January–February 2010; Fergusson and Kerr, "U.S. Export Control System."

81. For a general overview of the TPP, see Ian F. Fergusson, William H. Cooper, Remy Jurenas, and Brock R. Williams, "The Trans-Pacific Partnership (TPP) Negotiations and Issues for Congress," *CRS Report* (R42694), December 2013.

82. Shao Binhong, ed., *China and the World: Balance, Imbalance, and Rebalance* (Leiden: Koninklijke Brill NV, 2013); Jay Newton-Small, "Why Trying to Hurt China in the Trade Game Could Backfire," *Time*, January 14, 2014; Amitendu Palit, *The Trans-Pacific Partnership, China and India: Economic and Political Implications* (New York: Routledge, 2014); David Pilling, "It Won't Be Easy to Build an 'Anyone but China' Club," *Financial Times*, May 22, 2013.

83. Mattoo and Subramanian, "Leave China Out"; Arvind Subramanian, "Preserving the Open Global Economic System: A Strategic Blueprint for China and the United States," Policy Brief, PB13-16, June 2013, Peterson Institute for International Economics.

84. Arvind Subramanian, "The Curious Case of the Protectionist Dog That Has Not Barked," *Financial Times*, July 10, 2013.

85. Daniel W. Drezner, "The Outsourcing Bogeyman," *Foreign Affairs* 83, no. 3 (May–June 2004), pp. 22–34; Linda Levine, "Offshoring (of Offshore Outsourcing) and Job Loss among U.S. Workers," *CRS Report for Congress* (RL32292), December 2012; Michael Spence, "The Impact of Globalization on Income and Employment," *Foreign Affairs* 90, no. 4 (July–August 2011), pp. 28–41.

86. For instance, see Bureau of Industry and Security, *U.S. Space Industry "Deep Dive" Assessment: Impact of U.S. Export Controls on the Space Industrial Base* (Washington, DC: BIS, 2014).

87. See Paulson, "A Strategic Engagement."

88. Robert B. Zoellick, "Whither China: From Membership to Responsibility?," Remarks to National Committee on U.S.-China Relations, September 21, 2005, https://2001-2009.state.gov/s/d/former/zoellick/rem/53682.htm

89. Robert B. Zoellick, "The Great Powers' Relationship Hinges on the Pacific," *Financial Times*, June 4, 2013; Robert B. Zoellick, "U.S., China, and Thucydides," *National Interest*, July–August 2013. Also see Amitai Etzioni, "Is China a Responsible Stakeholder?," *International Affairs* 87, no. 3 (2011), pp. 539–53.

90. See *The President's Trade Policy Agenda*, 2009–2011, http://www.ustr.gov/2010-trade-policy-agenda; "America, China, and Protectionism: Wearing Thin," *The Economist*, September 14, 2009.

91. Gary Clyde Hufbauer, Jacob Funk Kirkegaard, Woan Foong Wong, and Jared Woollacott, *U.S. Protectionist Impulses in the Wake of the Great Recession* (Washington, DC: Peterson Institute for International Economics, 2010); Wayne M. Morrison, "China-U.S. Trade Issues," *CRS Report* (RL33536), July 2014.

Chapter 8

1. For instance, see Robert J. Art, *A Grand Strategy for America* (Ithaca, NY: Cornell University Press, 2003); Richard K. Betts, *American Force* (New York: Columbia University Press, 2012); John J. Mearsheimer and Stephen M. Walt, "The Case for Offshore Balancing," *Foreign Affairs* 95, no. 4 (July–August 2016), pp. 70–83; Barry R. Posen, *Restraint: A New Foundation for U.S. Grand Strategy* (Ithaca, NY: Cornell University Press, 2014); John J. Mearsheimer, "Imperial by Design," *National Interest*, no. 111 (January–February 2010), pp. 16–34. Even the scholars who view that grand strategy is about using diverse military and nonmilitary resources have indeed focused on explaining appropriate ways to employ US military force. For instance, see Stephen G. Brooks, G. John Ikenberry, and William C. Wohlforth, "Don't Come Home America: The Case against Retrenchment," *International Security* 37, no. 3 (Winter 2012–13), pp. 7–51; Colin Dueck, *Reluctant Crusaders: Power, Culture, and Change in American Grand Strategy* (Princeton, NJ: Princeton University Press, 2006); and Joseph S. Nye Jr., "The Case for Deep Engagement," *Foreign Affairs* 74, no. 4 (July–August 1995), pp. 90–102.

2. Robert Gilpin, "The Theory of Hegemonic War," *Journal of Interdisciplinary History* 18, no. 4 (Spring 1988), pp. 591–613; John J. Mearsheimer, *The Tragedy of Great Power Politics* (New York: Norton, 2001); Kenneth N. Waltz, "Structural Realism after the Cold War," *International Security* 25, no. 1 (Summer 2000), pp. 32–39.

3. David A. Baldwin, *Economic Statecraft* (Princeton, NJ: Princeton University Press, 1985); Gary Clyde Hufbauer, Jeffrey J. Schott, Kimberly Ann Elliott, and Barbara Oegg, *Economic Sanctions Reconsidered*, 3rd edition (Washington, DC: Peterson Institute for International Economics, 2007); Richard Rosecrance, *The Rise of the Trading State* (New York: Basic Books, 1986). Also see Daniel W. Drezner, *The Sanctions Paradox: Economic Statecraft and International Relations* (New York: Cambridge University Press, 1999); and Robert A. Pape, "Why Economic Sanctions Do Not Work," *International Security* 22, no. 2 (Fall 1997), pp. 90–136. A notable exception is Michael Mastanduno, *Economic Containment* (Ithaca, NY: Cornell University Press, 1992), which focuses on the complementary role of economic manipulation within the context of military containment. Meanwhile, some scholars address the economic benefits of military engagement. Still, they do not discuss how economic policies could complement military strategy. For instance, see Daniel W. Drezner, "Military Primacy Doesn't Pay (Nearly as Much as You Think)," *International Security* 38, no. 1 (Summer 2013), pp. 52–79; Eugene Gholz and Daryl G. Press, "The Effects of Wars on Neutral Countries: Why It Doesn't Pay to Preserve the Peace," *Security Studies* 10, no. 4 (2001), pp. 1–57; and Richard W. Maass, Carla Norrlof, and Daniel W. Drezner, "Correspondence: The Profitability of Primacy," *International Security* 38, no. 4 (Spring 2014), pp. 188–205.

4. Stephen D. Krasner, *Defending the National Interest: Raw Materials Investments and U.S. Foreign Policy* (Princeton, NJ: Princeton University Press, 1978); Gordon H. McCormick and Richard E. Bissell, eds., *Strategic Dimensions of Eco-*

nomic Behavior (New York: Praeger, 1984); Nicholas J. Spykman, *America's Strategy in World Politics: The United States and the Balance of Power* (Hamden, CT: Archon Books, 1970), p. 273. Also see Dick K. Nanto, "Economics and National Security: Issues and Implications for U.S. Policy," *CRS Report* (R41589), January 2011.

5. For a recent study of the pacifying effect of commerce, see Dale C. Copeland, *Economic Interdependence and War* (Princeton, NJ: Princeton University Press, 2015); and Gerald Schneider and Nils Petter Gleditsch, eds., *Assessing the Capitalist Peace* (New York: Routledge, 2012). Also see Edward D. Mansfield and Brian M. Pollins, eds., *Economic Interdependence and International Conflict: New Perspectives on an Enduring Debate* (Ann Arbor: University of Michigan Press, 2003); and Patrick J. McDonald, *The Invisible Hand of Peace: Capitalism, the War Machine, and International Relations Theory* (New York: Cambridge University Press, 2009).

6. Joanne Gowa, *Allies, Adversaries, and International Trade* (Princeton, NJ: Princeton University Press, 1994); Joanne Gowa and Edward D. Mansfield, "Alliances, Imperfect Markets, and Major-Power Trade," *International Organization* 58, no. 4 (Autumn 2004), pp. 775–805; Edward D. Mansfield, *Power, Trade, and War* (Princeton, NJ: University Press, 1994).

7. Steven E. Lobell, *The Challenge of Hegemony: Grand Strategy, Trade, and Domestic Politics* (Ann Arbor: University of Michigan Press, 2003); Paul A. Papayoanou, "Interdependence, Institutions, and the Balance of Power: Britain, Germany, and World War I," *International Security* 20, no. 4 (Spring, 1996), pp. 42–76; David M. Rowe, "World Economic Expansion and National Security in Pre–World War I Europe," *International Organization* 53, no. 2 (Spring 1999), pp. 195–231. Also see Kevin Narizny, *The Political Economy of Grand Strategy* (Ithaca, NY: Cornell University Press, 2007).

8. Christina L. Davis, "Linkage Diplomacy: Economic and Security Bargaining in the Anglo-Japanese Alliance, 1902–23," *International Security* 33, no. 3 (Winter 2008–9), pp. 143–79; Steven E. Lobell, "Second Face of Security Strategies: Anglo-German and Anglo-Japanese Trade Concessions during the 1930s," *Security Studies* 17, no. 3 (2008), pp. 438–67; Lars S. Skålnes, "Grand Strategy and Foreign Economic Policy: British Grand Strategy in the 1930s," *World Politics* 50, no. 4 (July 1998), pp. 582–616.

9. For a treatment of this issue, see Klaus Knorr, *The War Potential of Nations* (Princeton, NJ: Princeton University Press, 1956).

10. For useful overview of the trade theories, see Cletus Coughlin, "The Controversy over Free Trade," *Federal Reserve Bank of St. Louis Review* 84, no. 1 (January–February 2002), pp. 1–22; and Paul R. Krugman, Maurice Obstfeld, and Marc J. Melitz, *International Economics: Theory and Policy*, 9th edition (New York: Addison-Wesley, 2012).

11. Joanne Gowa and Edward D. Mansfield, "Power Politics and International Trade," *American Political Science Review* 87, no. 2 (June 1993), pp. 408–20.

12. For prescriptive theory, see Charles L. Glaser, *Rational Theory of International Politics: The Logic of Competition and Cooperation* (Princeton, NJ: Princeton

University Press, 2010), chap. 1; and John J. Mearsheimer, "Realists as Idealists," *Security Studies* 20, no. 3 (July–September 2011), pp. 424–30.

13. Brooks, Ikenberry, and Wohlforth, "Don't Come Home America."

14. For instance, see Gunnar Adler-Karlsson, *Western Economic Warfare, 1947–1967* (Stockholm: Almqvist and Wiksell, 1968); Philip J. Funigiello, *American-Soviet Trade in the Cold War* (Chapel Hill: University of North Carolina Press, 1988); Ian Jackson, *The Economic Cold War: America, Britain and East-West Trade, 1948–63* (New York: Palgrave, 2001); Bruce W. Jentleson, *Pipeline Politics: The Complex Political Economy of East-West Energy Trade* (Ithaca, NY: Cornell University Press, 1986); Mastanduno, *Economic Containment*. It is also dubious if the United States would be able to exert such pressures on the West European states in order to control their economic activities with China. For potential protest from Europe, see Nicola Casarini, *Remaking Global Order: The Evolution of Europe-China Relations and Its Implication for East Asia and the United States* (New York: Oxford University Press, 2009); May-Britt Stumbaum, "Testimony before the U.S.-China Economic and Security Review Commission," in US-China Economic and Security Review Commission, *Hearings on China-Europe Relationship and Transatlantic Implications*, 112th Congress, 2nd Session, April 19, 2012, pp. 81–91; Øystein Tunsjø, "Testimony before the U.S.-China Economic and Security Review Commission," in US-China Economic and Security Review Commission, *Hearings on China-Europe*.

15. "Beijing Warns U.S. against Trying to Contain China's Rise," *Financial Times*, October 31, 2017; "The U.S. Sees the Trade War as a Tactic to Contain China. So Does Beijing," *South China Morning Post*, July 4, 2018. Also see Peter Navarro, *The Coming China Wars* (Upper Saddle River, NJ: FT Press, 2008); and Peter Navarro and Greg Autry, *Death by China* (Upper Saddle River. NJ: FT Press, 2011).

16. Krugman, Obstfeld, and Melitz, *International Economics*.

17. Nicholas Bayne and Stephen Woolcock eds., *The New Economic Diplomacy* (New York: Routledge, 2017).

18. *New York Times, Trade Wars: Tariffs in the 21st Century* (New York: New York Times Educational Publishing, 2018).

19. Moreover, while the empirical analyses of this book focus on the reigning state's decision on trade with the challenging state, this does not mean that trade is the only economic exchange that matters in great power competition. On the contrary, other economic interactions, including finance and investment, can affect the reigning state's relative power position vis-à-vis the challenging state. Future research can focus on the reigning power's decisions on these and other economic issue areas.

INDEX

Printed and bound by CPI Group (UK) Ltd, Croydon, CR0 4YY

09/06/2025

14686096-0002